Leslie Marmon Silko's *Ceremony*

A CASEBOOK

CASEBOOKS IN CRITICISM

General Editor, William L. Andrews

LESLIE MARMON SILKO'S
Ceremony

◆ ◆ ◆

A CASEBOOK

Edited by
Allan Chavkin

OXFORD
UNIVERSITY PRESS

2002

OXFORD
UNIVERSITY PRESS

Oxford   New York

Athens   Auckland   Bangkok   Bogotá   Buenos Aires   Cape Town
Chennai   Dar es Salaam   Delhi   Florence   Hong Kong   Istanbul   Karachi
Kolkata   Kuala Lumpur   Madrid   Melbourne   Mexico City   Mumbai   Nairobi
Paris   São Paulo   Shanghai   Singapore   Taipei   Tokyo   Toronto   Warsaw

and associated companies in
Berlin   Ibadan

Copyright © 2002 by Oxford University Press, Inc.

Published by Oxford University Press, Inc.
198 Madison Avenue, New York, New York 10016

Library of Congress Cataloging-in-Publication Data
Leslie Marmon Silko's Ceremony : a casebook / edited by Allan Chavkin.
p. cm. — (Casebooks in criticism)
Includes bibliographical references.
ISBN 0-19-514283-7; ISBN 0-19-514284-5 (pbk.)
1. Silko, Leslie, 1948– Ceremony. 2. Indians in literature.
I. Chavkin, Allan Richard, 1950– II. Series.
PS3569.I44 C45   2002
813'.54—dc21   2001033835

1 3 5 7 9 8 6 4 2

Printed in the United States of America
on acid-free paper

For Nancy
my soul mate

Acknowledgments

I am especially obliged to these individuals who provided help of various kinds: John Blair, Lydia Blanchard, Mark Busby, Nancy Chavkin, Robin Cohen, Angela Ingram, and Leslie Marmon Silko. I also appreciate the financial support of the Office of Sponsored Projects of Southwest Texas State University for a Research Enhancement Grant. I owe thanks to the library staff of the university, who provided assistance numerous times. I am indebted to William L. Andrews, General Editor of *Casebooks in Criticism*; Elissa Morris, Acquiring Editor at Oxford University Press; Stacey Hamilton, Production Editor at Oxford University Press; and Jeremy Lewis, Editorial Assistant at Oxford University Press for their excellent advice. I am also grateful to the two anonymous reviewers of the casebook proposal for their helpful suggestions and comments.

Credits

Allen, Paula Gunn. "Special Problems in Teaching Leslie Marmon Silko's *Ceremony*." *American Indian Quarterly* 14 (1990): 379–86. Reprinted from the *American Indian Quarterly* by permission of the University of Nebraska Press. Copyright © 1979 by the University of Nebraska Press.

Beidler, Peter G. "Animals and Theme in *Ceremony*." *American Indian Quarterly* 5 (1979): 13–18. Reprinted from the *American Indian Quarterly* by permission of the University of Nebraska Press. Copyright © 1979 by the University of Nebraska Press.

Bell, Robert C. "Circular Design in *Ceremony*." *American Indian Quarterly* 5 (1979): 47–62. Reprinted from the *American Indian Quarterly* by permission of the University of Nebraska Press. Copyright © 1979 by the University of Nebraska Press.

Carr, Denny. Photograph of Leslie Marmon Silko originally appeared in *Sun Tracks* 3.1 (Fall 1976). Permission to reprint granted by the *Sun Tracks* Series Editor.

Cohen, Robin. "Of Apricots, Orchids, and Wovoka: An Interview with Leslie Marmon Silko." *Southwestern American Literature* 24.2 (Spring 1999): 63–65, 68–71. Reprinted by permission.

Coltelli, Laura. "Leslie Marmon Silko." *Winged Words: American Indian Writers Speak*. Lincoln: University of Nebraska Press, 1990. 137–53. Reprinted by

can *Women Writers' Revisions of Nature, Gender, and Race.* Charlottesville: University Press of Virginia, 1997. 114–44. Reprinted with the permission of University Press of Virginia.

Weaver, Jace. "Leslie Marmon Silko." *That the People Might Live: Native American Literatures and Native American Community.* New York: Oxford University Press, 1997. Copyright © 1997 by Jace Weaver. Reprinted by permission.

Contents

Leslie Marmon Silko's *Ceremony*

A   CASEBOOK

Introduction

ALLAN CHAVKIN

❖ ❖ ❖

IN THE TURBULENT 1960S, empowerment movements, Native cultural awakening, and a strong interest in American Indians helped provide the impetus for what Kenneth Lincoln has called the Native American Renaissance, the flowering of a dynamic new literature written by American Indians.[1] The beginning of this Renaissance is usually associated with the publication of N. Scott Momaday's *House Made of Dawn* (1968), which won the Pulitzer Prize. Momaday's novel and other works, including the highly regarded novel by James Welch, *Winter in the Blood* (1974), reached a large reading public. But of the numerous works of the Native American Renaissance published between 1968 and the present, it is Leslie Marmon Silko's *Ceremony* that has received the greatest critical acclaim.

In an influential article in the *New York Times Book Review*, Frank Mac-Shane praised the novel for its unique blending of the European narrative tradition with American Indian storytelling. He suggested that Silko was able to bridge the boundaries of gender and culture to convey the reality of American Indian experience to non-Indian readers. "Her novel is one of the most realized works of fiction devoted to Indian life that has been written in this country, and it is a splendid achievement" (15). Impressed with Silko's cross-cultural abilities and her "dual sensibility" that enabled her to interweave American Indian and European narrative forms into a master-

piece, he proclaimed Silko "without question . . . the most accomplished Indian writer of her generation" (15).

Leslie Marmon Silko was born on March 5, 1948, to Mary Virginia Leslie
and Lee Howard Marmon and grew up in Old Laguna, a pueblo near Albuquerque, New Mexico. Like the protagonist of *Ceremony*, she is of mixed ancestry. Her great grandmother, a Laguna who had been educated at the Indian boarding school in Carlisle, Pennsylvania, lived next door and taught
her about Laguna culture. Silko began her education at Laguna Bureau of
Indian Affairs School, then attended Catholic schools in Albuquerque, and
later received a B.A. from the University of New Mexico. After attending
law school at the University of New Mexico for three semesters, she became disenchanted with the possibility of attaining social justice through
law and turned to writing.[2]

The first major event in her writing career was the publication of seven
stories in Kenneth Rosen's anthology of short fiction by American Indians,
The Man To Send Rain Clouds (1974). In addition to the often reprinted title
story, the volume also included "Yellow Woman," which was reprinted in
Frank MacShane's *Two Hundred Years of Great American Short Stories* (1976).
Rosen's anthology was the first collection of contemporary American Indian fiction to be published by a major commercial press (Viking Press).
Thus, some influential people such as MacShane became aware of the
work of Silko, whose short stories dominated Rosen's book. No doubt the
most important reader alerted to Silko's talent in Rosen's anthology was
Richard Seaver, a senior editor at Viking Press known for his interest in
publishing experimental contemporary literature. When Silko submitted
the manuscript of her nontraditional novel *Ceremony*, he accepted it as one
of the Richard Seaver Books of Viking Press. A difficult novel that inter-
weaves sections in poetry of Laguna mythology with the tale of Tayo's
struggles, *Ceremony* quickly became one of the best known works by an
American Indian. Since its publication in 1977, more than a half million
copies of the book have been sold, and it is now one of the most frequently
taught contemporary novels in higher education.[3]

For a major work that so quickly became part of the canon, its genesis
now seems strange and fortuitous. Silko's original intention was modest;
she desired to write a light-hearted story about a mother's constant struggle to thwart the attempts of her veteran-son to obtain alcohol. Silko had
heard such amusing stories, and she had observed first-hand the incredible
lengths some veterans, including some of her own cousins, would go to
for a cold beer on a reservation that prohibited alcohol. Some of these
veterans were decorated war heroes, who in the postwar period never

could function effectively again because of their alcoholism and associated problems.

As Silko began to write her "funny" story, the humor seemed to drain out, and instead the sense of loss and pain inherent in the situation came to the foreground. In an unpublished manuscript of this "funny story," housed at the Beinecke Rare Book and Manuscript Library of Yale University, the protagonist (named Louie) has been badly wounded in the war. Because liquor on the reservation is illegal and one must travel at least ten miles to purchase it in bars at Budville and Cubero, Louie, desperate for alcohol, drinks Aqua Velva, straining it first through pieces of bread. He even tries Sterno once. On occasion he is so drunk that he does not know where he is and finds himself waking up under a junked automobile or behind the post office, all his money and possessions stolen. In brief, the story that was supposed to be "funny" metamorphoses quickly into a sad and pathetic tale.

Believing that Silko reinforced negative stereotypes in *Ceremony*, some Native Americans have criticized her for her portrayal of alcoholic Indians in the novel. Actually one of Silko's aims in *Ceremony* was to subvert the stereotype of the drunken Indian by showing the causes of alcoholism and by making readers sympathize with the alcoholic Indian's plight. Silko knew that most returning veterans, such as her father who had served in the Aleutian Islands, did not become alcoholic, and she wondered why some veterans could return from the war to the community and function again within it, while others could not. The humiliation and shame she felt when observing a veteran unconscious from excessive drinking prompted her to explore the sources of such self-destructive behavior and to ponder this question: Why did some veterans become misfits, while others could return to the community to lead stable and productive lives? The novel attempts to answer this question and to explore the vitality and hardiness of the American Indian community in the latter part of the twentieth century.

Certainly, the problem of Tayo's alienation has complex roots. The novel implies that if one is to understand properly Tayo's problem, one must see it in its historical context; that is, one must see it against the background of the tragic story of Native Americans after the arrival of the Europeans. Whole tribes became extinct without any natural resistance to the diseases of the whites, and millions of American Indians perished. But *Ceremony* implies that no matter how terrible the deaths from disease and other causes associated with the European colonization were, the most destructive disease the Native Americans suffered as a consequence of European arrival on American shores was despair.

As Silko pondered this disease of despair and the source of the veterans' alcoholism, she recalled that after World War II ended, frequently the Pueblo and the Navajo performed traditional purification rituals for returning veterans. Unfortunately, the effectiveness of these rituals for some of the soldiers was inadequate, which some people interpreted as evidence of the inadequacy of American Indian beliefs. Silko suggests, however, that because these rituals were not devised with modern warfare in mind, they must be modified if they are to be effective. That is why Tayo must seek healing from Betonie after the ceremony of Ku'oosh, a traditional Laguna medicine man, fails. The curing rituals or "ceremonies" were based on the re-enactments of mythic stories through chant, song, and ritual. An unorthodox healer whose outlook is shaped by both white and American Indian cultures, Betonie combines parts of a traditional curing ritual based on the traditional Navajo Red Antway ceremony with professional counseling techniques. He sends Tayo on a quest that culminates in the veteran's healing and reconnection to the community.

Written primarily in 1973 and 1974 while the depressed Silko resided in Ketchikan Alaska, *Ceremony* has an autobiographical basis. In fact, the writing of the novel became a ceremony for its author, who, suffering the headaches and nausea that plagued Tayo, wrote the novel to triumph over the despair that nearly destroys her protagonist. Before she decided to tell the story of her World War II veteran who survives the Bataan Death March, she attempted to write a work with a female character in some of the same sad circumstances as the depressed Tayo. But after writing a number of pages, she abandoned the work because the female protagonist seemed excessively autobiographical; she felt that this autobiographical protagonist would limit her creativity. Despite the switch from the female protagonist to Tayo, the novel still is somewhat autobiographical. Silko has related that as Tayo began to recover, she also did, and she emphasized that "I wrote this novel to save my life."

But that statement might lead some to conclude that she wrote the novel after careful planning. Actually, *Ceremony* was a product of the author's unconscious, not careful planning. In fact, Silko was about a third of the way through the novel when she began to realize that the story should focus on Tayo. She had previously lived for two years with the Navajos, whose ceremonies arose out of stories, and she suddenly realized at this point in the writing of the novel that her story of the troubled World War II veteran Tayo could be a new kind of ceremony. As a result, she revised the novel to account for her new concept and added the first pages with mythic poems. Later she would end the novel in similar fashion. By beginning and ending the novel with mythic poems, Silko underscores her assumption that traditional tribal solutions are relevant to the problems of Tayo and the other despairing veterans. Throughout the book American Indian myth is linked to present-day events. The importance of the circular structure and the concept of the novel as a new kind of healing ceremony becomes evident if one examines the manuscript drafts and the author's notes in her papers at the Beinecke Rare Book and Manuscript Library of Yale University. Apparently, Silko's editor Richard Seaver misunderstood her intentions and planned to publish the book without the poem at the end. He left intact Silko's original ending and abandoned his plan to publish the novel with a revised ending only after she vehemently protested. Silko believed Seaver wanted to conclude *Ceremony* as if it were "only a novel," but she wanted the ending to reinforce the notion that the novel itself was a healing ceremony.

From the vast scholarship published on *Ceremony*, I have selected for this casebook a variety of essays from different theoretical and critical approaches, including formalist, historical, cultural, genre-based, semiotic, ecofeminist, ethical, and reader response approaches, to name some of them. The selections are published in full here with only a few exceptions. Rachel Stein's chapter from her book is slightly condensed with the material on *Almanac of the Dead* omitted. Kenneth Lincoln's "Blue Medicine" is a self-contained section from his chapter on Silko in *Native American Renaissance*. Kenneth Roemer condensed and updated for this casebook his article, originally published in *Modern Fiction Studies*. Although I have included Laura Coltelli's entire conversation with Silko, I omitted the brief biographical profile that introduces the interview. I include a substantial excerpt from Robin Cohen's long interview with the author, which reveals the autobiographical basis of the novel and contains other important insights. In any case, this collection, which ranges from the earliest important critical responses to the novel (e.g., Beidler's and Bell's) to the most recent (e.g., Roemer's), presents a history of the critical reception of the work. The main purpose of this casebook, though, is to make *Ceremony* more accessible. Silko has suggested that when this novel was published in 1977, it was often regarded as too difficult for university students. With the opening up of the canon and with the interest in multiculturalism in recent years, the novel is not only frequently assigned as required reading for university students but also for some advanced high school students. Yet many readers still find *Ceremony* difficult, and therefore it is my hope that this collection will remove obstacles to understanding and appreciating this challenging work.

Although the essays range widely in critical approach and content, they do assume the centrality of Silko's American Indian heritage in *Ceremony*. For non-Indian readers both the source of greatest difficulty and the source of greatest originality is Silko's heavy reliance on Pueblo and Navajo cultures, traditions, and mythologies. It is appropriate, then, that most of the essays in this volume help readers become familiar with this material, thereby enhancing their enjoyment and appreciation of the novel.[4]

In the first essay in this collection, one of the earliest critical responses to the book, the fundamentally different attitudes of American Indians and whites toward animals provide a key to understanding the novel. In "Animals and Theme in *Ceremony*," Peter G. Beidler argues that it is imperative to understand the symbolic role of animals in the novel if one is to understand the meaning of the work. Understanding Silko's use of animals enables the reader to understand Tayo's growth. Silko reveals that the white man's attitude toward animals is destructive, and initially under the influence of white culture, Tayo comes to "grow away from plants and animals." In losing reverence for animal life, he also loses his self-respect and views himself as "useless and inanimate," according to Beidler. *Ceremony* is the tale of Tayo's process of recovery, and the "best measure of that recovery . . . is Tayo's changed attitude toward animal life." Beidler explains how this change in attitude is most apparent in three different areas. His discussion of the symbolism of the crossbreed cattle underscores its importance in understanding the nature of Tayo's recovery.

In "Circular Design in *Ceremony*," Robert C. Bell observes that the traditional American Indian myth pattern employs for its framework the hero-quest "to establish prototype ceremonial procedures for curing rituals called chantways." Typically, the ceremonial myth presents a courageous protagonist who becomes involved in a difficult situation "that requires supernatural aid." Bell offers compelling evidence that the curing ritual of the Red Antway of the Navajo is an important influence on *Ceremony*, and he includes at the end of his article the text of the Coyote Transformation Prototype Ceremony from this curing ritual. Silko's hoop transformation ceremony parallels this Coyote Transformation rite, which was recorded and translated by Father Berard Haile in 1933–1934. Bell's examination of Silko's sources and his explanation of the novel's symbolic circular design and its tripartite structure help clarify the author's intentions.

In "An Act of Attention: Event Structure in *Ceremony*," Elaine Jahner emphasizes the importance in the narrative of "events," a complex phenomenon characterized by "boundary experiences marking stages of life for the protagonist." She suggests that there are two types of narratives that shape the events—the contemporary narrative of Tayo's struggles (presented in prose) and the myth narrative (presented in poetry). The two are inextricably connected and influence each other, and the reader and Tayo, as they move from event to event, must attempt to understand the relationship between the contemporary action and the mythic prototype. Gradually, Tayo and the reader learn how myth relates to action in the present. Employing "the mythic way of knowing as the basic structural element," *Ceremony* is fundamentally different from seemingly similar works that use myth as a deliberate literary device. In fact, with emphasis "less on what is known than on how one comes to know certain things," *Ceremony* is an example of "an emerging type of American Indian novel," different from other types of American novels.

In the selection entitled "Blue Medicine" from the last chapter of his book *Native American Renaissance*. Kenneth Lincoln illuminates *Ceremony* by explaining how Silko incorporates mythology in the novel. The cohering theme of the work is the need of all for "a safe return." With aid of Betonie and his assistant Shush, Tayo goes on a healing quest and experiences the traditional Scalp Ceremony for warriors who have returned from war. Tayo's pilgrimage is to the north to the mythic origin of Ts'eh, where she resides with the hunter on the sacred mountain. Particularly helpful to the reader are Lincoln's discussions of the naming ceremony, mythic storytelling, witchery, the ceremonial directions according to Pueblo mythology (accompanied by a diagram), color symbolism, the mythological overtones, and the seasonal symbolism.

John Purdy in "The Transformation: Tayo's Genealogy in *Ceremony*" sees Silko in the long-standing literary tradition of Laguna storytellers who explain how their world has changed and who dramatize how one can modify old ways to accommodate the new situation in which individuals find themselves. The process of the protagonist of the novel is one in which he becomes increasingly aware of how his personal experiences relate to those that are told in the mythic stories of the Laguna. By the end of the novel, Tayo has metamorphosed from a sick individual to a powerful representative of his people. Purdy suggests that *Ceremony* is a story that should be regarded as a rewriting or adaptation and transformation of traditional Laguna stories, especially that of the Sun Man's battle with Kaup'a'ta, the Evil Gambler. With the advice of Spider Woman, who informs him what the Evil Gambler will do, Sun Man ascends a mountain to rescue rain clouds from Kaup'a'ta. Silko's story parallels this myth, for Tayo climbs the mountain and with the help of Ts'eh and the hunter brings the rains, defeats evil, and becomes the Laguna hero. Earlier Tayo was a spiritually dispossessed individual, lost and wandering, but now he can see the meaning of events. This new knowledge empowers him to triumph over his nemesis Emo.

In his genre-based critical approach, Reed Way Dasenbrock poses this question: Can *Ceremony* most usefully be examined in the tradition of Native American literature or American literature or another category? Some see such categories as neutral or utilitarian, but Dasenbrock argues that the categories are culturally grounded and "help shape the phenomena we perceive." He suggests that both the broad category of American literature and the narrower one of Native American literature are "misleading" for Silko, and he offers "the more useful" category of "Southwestern literature" to interpret not only Silko's work but also that of Rudolfo Anaya. Dasenbrock explains that Southwestern literature has less *a* single tradition than a heritage of contact and conflict and thus is a useful lens through which to view *Ceremony* with its half-Laguna, half-white protagonist, who at the beginning of the novel feels alienated from both Laguna and white cultures, two cultures in contact and conflict. It is important that readers recognize "the otherness" of texts such as *Ceremony* and *Bless Me, Ultima* and not approach them with expectations founded only on Anglo-American cultural and narrative forms. Silko is a product of two cultures, and because her work embodies the tension between the two, she is "Southwestern in the sense of representing through that very conflict the meeting and battleground that is the Southwest."

In "Special Problems in Teaching Leslie Marmon Silko's *Ceremony*," Paula Gunn Allen explains the ethical issues involved in teaching about the "sacred," that is, "any material that is drawn from ritual and myth." Her ethical dilemma is that her obligation as a professor to present students with essential information to understand Native American literature containing substantial content drawn from sacred material is at loggerheads with her obligation as a mixed-blood Laguna Pueblo with traditions requiring her to remain silent about such material. To violate this unwritten ethical code and reveal sacred material to outsiders is to risk tragic consequences. However, white civilization values the accessibility of knowledge, and students who enroll in courses in Native American Studies often do so because they are "voraciously interested in the exotic aspects of Indian ways," including traditional spiritual practices and beliefs. *Ceremony* is an especially problematical novel to teach because it relies heavily on Laguna rituals and mythology. Critical of Silko for recounting stories in *Ceremony* that are not to be told to outsiders, Allen describes odd happenings at Laguna Pueblo related to *Ceremony* and explores the implications of an ethical dilemma that has developed because of the conflicting values of two different cultures.

In "'The Very Essence of Our Lives': Leslie Silko's Webs of Identity," Louis Owens's knowledge of Pueblo Indian culture and contemporary theory (especially the ideas of Bakhtin and Foucault) enables him to provide a provocative reading of the novel. His analysis of how key myths function in the novel—such as those of Corn Woman and Ts'eh—is particularly helpful and he argues that mythology is not used as a metaphorical framework, as it often is in modernist texts, but as an intrinsic part of reality which Tayo experiences. He emphasizes that a key theme is the need for change and adaptation. "The central lesson of this novel is that through the dynamism, adaptability, and syncretism inherent in Native American cultures, both individuals and the cultures within which individuals find significance and identity are able to survive, grow, and evade the deadly traps of stasis and sterility." While the mixed-blood character has been viewed almost universally as a tragic figure, Silko suggests this character's potential for "authenticity and a coherent identity."

Catherine Rainwater employs a sophisticated semiotic approach in a detailed analysis of the novel. In "The Semiotics of Dwelling in Leslie Marmon Silko's *Ceremony*," she argues that the novel reveals that reality is the direct result of the versions of the real we construct. Two ideas are at the heart of American Indian epistemology as Silko represents it in *Ceremony*: "reality" is partly a result of semiosis, for many elements of "reality" yield "to human thought and imagination expressed through art and language"; and there are important, inseparable connections "among self, community, and the physical and metaphysical dimensions of the land." The narrative of a self emerges from the land in which the narrative of one's people has arisen. Dispossession of "home" is a key aspect of all American Indian experience. The majority of contemporary American Indian stories semiotically encode a crisis preoccupied with dwelling in a place that to some extent no longer survives. Silko inscribes in *Ceremony* what she perceives as a "uniquely Indian variety of such a crisis over a "home' that *once* existed." She tries "to resolve in textual space what cannot be resolved in geographical space." Although American Indians can never regain the American continent as it existed before the colonization by Europeans, "they can appropriate the textual space of the novel; and if 'story' precedes reality perhaps American Indian writers may begin through semiosis to reconstruct and reinhabit their home." Readers are exhorted to recognize the crisis portrayed in the novel and to change their way of living. Instability is at the core of the work and defines the crisis of dwelling. Such instability is aptly symbolized in the novel by the destructive energy of the atom bomb. Tayo comes to realize that it is his responsibility to offer a new story of reality and avoid the story of complete annihilation that humanity is currently considering. Rainwater concludes: "In *Ceremony*, Silko encodes a crisis of dwelling designed to assist the reader in creating a new map through a new, alternative story."

In "The Function of the Landscape of *Ceremony*," Robert M. Nelson views the landscape as a character in the novel, and he argues that the pattern or "interior landscape of Tayo's mind is not only tuned" to the pattern of the culture he needs to return to, but it is also in accord with the actual landscape. Nelson presents a detailed analysis of the specific places that are part of Tayo's healing pilgrimage. While Tayo's salvation depends on retelling and adapting the important stories of his heritage, the meanings of the stories are inextricably connected to the land. "The world Tayo has probed in all directions relative to the Pueblo is a world of places, places that offer up and confirm their power to revitalize the human spirit and the life of the People."

Using the theories of Mikhail Bakhtin, Wolfgang Iser, and Tzvetan Todorov, James Ruppert argues that Silko's intentions in *Ceremony* are "mediational," as she attempts to translate the languages of the Other and enable Native and non-Native readers to better understand each other's "cultural codes." Mediation as defined by Ruppert is "an artistic and conceptual standpoint, constantly flexible, which uses the epistemological frameworks of Native American and Western cultural traditions to illuminate and enrich each other." Ruppert analyzes how the form of *Ceremony* enables Silko to achieve one of her primary aims—to blend reality and myth. Moreover, "as the reality-based stories are raised to myth, Silko emphasizes how myths grow, compliment, and structure reality—how mythic discourse and practical discourse are built out of the same components." By the end of the novel, Tayo and the reader achieve a new kind of perception, a mythic knowing.

In a slightly revised and condensed version of her chapter on Silko from *Shifting the Ground: American Women Writers' Revisions of Nature, Gender, and Race*, Rachel Stein examines the novel from the perspective of a feminist ecocritic. She reveals how Silko employs the storytelling and spiritual heritage of the Laguna Pueblo "to reframe the history of the European conquest of America" as an opposition predicated on "irreconcilable notions of land use and land tenure" and as "a struggle between different cultural orientations toward the natural world" rather than as an irresolvable racial hostility. In Silko's novel, the Indians' nonexploitative, reciprocal relationship with nature is confronted by the whites' domination of the natural world and of the Native peoples whom they deem closer to nature. Thus, in *Ceremony*, nature becomes the contested ground between these two opposing cultures. In order to redress this conflict, Silko's mixed-blood protagonist re-creates traditional Laguna stories and ceremonies that counter the destructive ideology of the whites.

In the section on Silko from his book *That the People Might Live: Native American Literatures and Native American Community*, Jace Weaver presents a useful overview of her career and the importance of *Ceremony* within it. He argues that her writing is subversive as it explores injustice, racism, and related issues in such a way as to attract the attention of the dominant culture even as it addresses a Native audience. He reveals in *Ceremony* and some of Silko's other works the centrality of the power of the story to combat evil and heal the Native people. And crucial to Silko's work is the importance of the community. Completely uprooted from the community, Rocky is doomed; in contrast, Tayo is saved because he is able to reconnect to the community. Appalled at the history of exploitation of American Indians, Silko employs her subversive writing "to defend Native peoples and community," for the battle "for Native lands and sovereignty has never ended."

Kenneth Roemer's "Silko's Arroyos as Mainstream" uses the approach of canon formation study to present a new perspective on *Ceremony*. He suggests that *Ceremony* is the single most widely taught Native American novel and that it is more securely part of the canon of American Literature than any other American Indian novel. Therefore, he intends to investigate how the canonization of *Ceremony* occurred and what forces contributed to its being so widely recognized by scholars of American Indian literature and other literature and nonliterature instructors in universities and secondary schools. In the first part of his article he analyzes the cultural, historical, institutional, publication, marketing, and reception contexts that shaped the reputation of *Ceremony*, while in the second part he focuses on the compelling literary qualities that were instrumental in helping the novel to become part of the canon. Roemer also considers some of the important literary, cultural, and social implications of the canonization of *Ceremony*. He points out that the popularity of this novel has some negative ramifications: for example, the privileging of novels as the most influential genre of written expression by Native Americans, the difficulty of new masterpieces to attract serious attention and become part of the canon, and the unfortunate assumptions of readers with limited knowledge that *Ceremony* presents the crucial paradigm of Indian experience. Roemer concludes his article with intriguing proposals to cope with the problems associated with the canonization of *Ceremony*.

This casebook concludes with two interviews. In her conversation with Laura Coltelli, Silko comments on a number of issues that help the reader to understand *Ceremony*, including the role of Helen-Jean, the importance of oral tradition and storytelling, the different concepts of time, the role of women in Pueblo society, and the purpose of the Gallup section of the novel. In the excerpt from Robin Cohen's interview, Silko poignantly explains how she wrote *Ceremony* to save her life. She also comments on a number of other subjects, including her preference for experimental forms and her "forgetting" to organize *Ceremony* by chapters.

This book will complement three others on Silko's work: Helen Jaskoski's *Leslie Marmon Silko: A Study of the Short Fiction*, Gregory Salyer's *Leslie Marmon Silko*, and Louise K. Barnett and James L. Thorson's *Leslie Marmon Silko: A Collection of Critical Essays*, a collection that does not include any essays devoted to *Ceremony* but focuses on Silko's other work, especially *Almanac of the Dead*. The essays and interviews in this casebook on *Ceremony* provide readers with crucial information, especially on Native American beliefs, that will enhance their understanding and appreciation of this complex novel.

Notes

1. As Hertha D. Sweet Wong has pointed out, there has been much controversy and no agreement about the appropriate term to use for American Indians (9), and therefore the reader will not find in this volume any consistency in the use of the terms. I use Native American, Indian, and American Indian interchangeably for variety, as do many critics.

2. In this Introduction, my views of Silko's career and the genesis of *Ceremony* are based on my examination of Silko's papers at the Beinecke Rare Book and Manuscript Library of Yale University. Among the papers are drafts of an untitled essay in which Silko explains the origins of *Ceremony* and her intentions in the novel. I also found helpful Silko's recollections of her career and the genesis of *Ceremony* in formal presentations and informal interviews when she was my colleague and the Mitte Endowed Chair in Creative Writing at Southwest Texas State University during the 2000–2001 academic year.

3. Unless an author of an essay in this casebook indicates otherwise, the reader can assume that all page references to quotations from *Ceremony* included in the texts of the essays in this collection are from the original 1977 publication of the

novel or the Penguin Books paperback reprint in 1986. Pagination of the Penguin Books reprint is the same as the original Viking Press edition.

4. What I express here in this paragraph about Silko's American Indian heritage being both the source of her greatest originality and the greatest obstacle to understanding her work also applies to the fiction of Louise Erdrich; in fact, the language here is similar to a paragraph on page 2 of my Introduction to *The Chippewa Landscape of Louise Erdrich*.

Works Cited

Barnett, Louise K., and James L. Thorson, eds. *Leslie Marmon Silko: A Collection of Critical Essays*. Albuquerque: University of New Mexico Press, 1999.

Chavkin, Allan, ed. *The Chippewa Landscape of Louise Erdrich*. Tuscaloosa: University of Alabama Press, 1999.

Jaskoski, Helen. *Leslie Marmon Silko: A Study of the Short Fiction*. New York: Twayne, 1998.

Lincoln, Kenneth. *Native American Renaissance*. Berkeley: University of California Press, 1983.

MacShane, Frank. "American Indians, Peruvian Jews." Rev. of *Ceremony*, by Leslie Marmon Silko. *New York Times Book Review* 12 June 1977: 15.

Salyer, Gregory. *Leslie Marmon Silko*. New York: Twayne, 1997.

Silko, Leslie Marmon. *Ceremony*. New York: Viking, 1977.

Wong, Hertha D. Sweet. *Louise Erdrich's "Love Medicine": A Casebook*. New York: Oxford University Press, 2000.

Animals and Theme in *Ceremony*

PETER G. BEIDLER

◆   ◆   ◆

Thought-Woman, the spider,
named things and
as she named them
they appeared.

She is sitting in her room
thinking of a story now

I'm telling you the story
she is thinking.

—From the epigraph to *Ceremony*

L ESLIE MARMON SILKO'S *Ceremony* is a novel about people. It is
impossible, however, to understand the people, their problems, or the
solutions to those problems without becoming aware of the role animals
play in the novel. Certainly, it is impossible to understand the scope and
meaning of Tayo's growth without giving careful attention to Silko's use of
animals to define that growth.

To understand the nature of Tayo's development it is necessary that we
recognize Silko's representation of the white man's attitude toward animal
life. As ranchers, for example, white men raise stupid Herefords that are ill-
adapted to desert terrain and available food supplies, then fence and corral
them so that they cannot run free. The white ranchers do not know, as
Tayo's uncle Josiah does, that "cattle are like any living thing. If you separate them from the land for too long, keep them in barns and corrals, they
lose something" (p. 74). The white ranchers' initial response to the hardier
and more adaptable Mexican cattle is to make sport of destroying them:
"They rode massive powerful roping horses that were capable of jerking
down a steer running full speed, knocking the animal unconscious and
frequently injuring or killing it" (p. 212).

As hunters the white men are even more destructive. In addition to
robbing the mountains of trees, the white loggers took "ten or fifteen deer

each week and fifty wild turkeys in one month," and then "shot the bears and mountain lions for sport" (p. 186). The attitude of white men toward nature and animals is summarized in the story told by the witch who had predicted the arrival of "*white skin people*" on Indian land:

> *Then they grow away from the earth*
> *then they grow away from the sun*
> *then they grow away from the plants and animals.*
> *They see no life*
> *When they look*
> *they see only objects.*
> *The world is a dead thing for them*
> *the trees and rivers are not alive.*
> *The deer and bear are objects*
> *They see no life.*
> (p. 135)

The white man's attitude that game animals are merely objects made for him to destroy carries over also into his attitude toward smaller animals and insects. The science teacher in the white school had brought in "a tubful of dead frogs, bloated with formaldehyde" (p. 194) for dissection, then laughed when a Jemez girl said that she had been taught never to kill frogs because if she did terrible floods would come. Another teacher had taught Tayo to kill flies because "they are bad and carry sickness" (p. 101). In response to this training, and because he found it "fun to chase them" (p. 101), Tayo as a boy had one day proudly killed and collected piles of flies on the kitchen floor for Josiah to see. Josiah had then informed Tayo that it was a fly who a long time before had asked forgiveness for the people and so saved them from death: "Since that time the people have been grateful for what the fly did for us" (p. 101).

As a soldier in the white man's World War II, Tayo has, like the "*white skin people*" of the witch's prediction, come to "*grow away from the plants and animals*" (p. 135). In following his brother Rocky away from the ways of his people and toward the ways of the white man, Tayo has lost perspective on the importance of animals. He has become almost as bad as his friend Harley, who proclaims that animals are not "worth anything anyway" (p. 23). Nothing is more expressive of the distance he has been driven from Josiah"s principles than the fact that in the war flies have for him come to be those "bad" things his white teacher told him they were. His response to jungle flies is a white man's response in that it is both destructive and mechanical: "Tayo . . . slapped at the insects mechanically" (p. 8). And when his brother is killed, Tayo takes his grief and frustration out on the flies: "He had not been able to endure the flies that had crawled over Rocky; the had enraged him. He had cursed their sticky feet and wet mouths, and when he could reach them he had smashed them between his hands" (p. 102). The white man's war has driven Tayo's reverence for the creatures of nature to an unprecedented low.

Tayo's lack of respect for animal life carries over into his lack of respect for his own. As a result of his experience in the war, he has come to think of himself as useless and inanimate. At the Los Angeles Veterans' Administration hospital where he is recovering from what the white doctors call battle fatigue, he thinks of himself as invisible and dead. Reaching into his mouth he finds a tongue which is "dry and dead, the carcass of a tiny rodent" (p. 15). Like the white men of the witch's story he sees no life about him. He has no desire to return home where "they are dead and everything is dying" (p. 16). He thinks of himself as an inanimate object. While waiting for the train home after being released from the hospital, he thinks of himself as dying "the way smoke dies, drifting away in currents of air, twisting in thin swirls, fading until it exists no more" (p. 17). Later, at home, waiting for Harley to ready a mule for him to ride, Tayo thinks of himself as being "like a fence post" (p. 25). Once on the mule he wishes Josiah were alive so he could tell his uncle that he is almost convinced that he is "brittle red clay, slipping away with the wind, a little more each day" (p. 27). His desire to destroy the flies is little more than a misdirected desire to destroy himself: "He didn't care any more if he died" (p. 39).

Ceremony is the story of Tayo's return from death to life, the story of the way this bit of smoke, this fence post, this clay with a dead rodent for a tongue, becomes animate again and thus able to tell his story to the tribal elders. This growth is a series of discoveries: the discovery in himself of the ability to use words; the discovery that there is life to be derived from an infusian of Mexican blood; the discovery that evil and witchery can be resisted; the discovery that the white culture he has allowed himself to be absorbed by is really a culture of "dead objects: the plastic and neon, the concrete and steel. Hollow and lifeless as a witchery clay figure" (p. 204); the discovery that Betonie's ceremony can, indeed, cure; the discovery that there is life and resurrection in story and in the sense of community that the telling of a story implies; the discovery that "nothing was ever lost as long as the love remained" (p. 220); the discovery that change is necessary for life, because "things which don't shift and grow are dead things" (p. 126). Tayo's recovery of life is all these things and more. The best measure of that recovery, however, is Tayo's changed attitude toward animal life. The change in that attitude can be seen most emphatically in three areas: his respect for animals, his acceptance of the apparent evil they do, and his imitation of them.

The fly-squashing soldier becomes transformed at home into a man who once more shows respect for and kindness toward even that lowly form of animal life, the insect. When he leaves the cafe owned by the old Mexican man who adorns his place with spirals of sticky flypaper, who arms himself with a "red rubber fly swatter," and who makes a "serious business" of killing flies, Tayo finds himself "opening the screen door only enough to squeeze out and closing it quickly so that no flies got in" (p. 101) to be killed. His concern for the welfare of insects is even stronger after his visit with the medicine man Betonie. After leaving Betonie he takes a walk in the grass: "He stepped carefully, pushing the toe of his boot into the weeds first to make sure the grasshoppers were gone before he set his foot down" (p. 155). His friend and lover Ts'eh sets him a good example in this, as Emo had much earlier set him a bad one. After trampling a melon patch, Emo had "trampled the ants with his boots" (p. 62). Ts'eh, on the other hand, before spreading her shawl on the ground, "made sure no ants were disturbed" (p. 224).

One aspect of Tayo's respect for animals is his increasing awareness of them in the world around him. This awareness takes several forms. He begins to observe the world about him in terms of animal images: Betonie's humming is like "butterflies darting from flower to flower" (p. 123); dawn spreads "like yellow wings" (p. 181) across the sky; "the magnetism of the center" which pulls him toward the earth soothes his pain "like feather-down wings" (p. 201). Where he had earlier seen only a wasteland, he now begins to hear and to see animals. Going out to the ranch to take care of the cattle and to wait for Ts'eh, for example, he finds that now the world is "alive" (p. 221). He hears "the buzzing of grasshopper wings" (p. 219), "the big bumblebees and the smaller bees sucking the blossoms" (p. 220), "the rustle of the swallows" (p. 222), and a "dove calling from the mouth of the canyon" (p. 222). He sees a "yellow spotted snake" (p. 221), "shiny black water beetles" (p. 221), and "a small green frog" (p. 222). His awareness of animals is also evident in his remembering of the stories of his people. Some of those stories are his old Grandma's stories of "time immemorial" when "animals could talk to human beings" (p. 94), and they involve such animals as Fly, Hummingbird, Caterpillar, and Buzzard, who rescue the people from destruction.

Tayo's respect for animals leads to his acceptance of the apparently evil role they sometimes play. Again Ts'eh is his guide, for it is she who convinces him that the black ants which make trails "across the head, from the nose to the eyes" (p. 229) of a dead calf are not evil. He had hated the insects that had crawled on Rocky, but now he has a better perspective and sees that the insects are not bad but good. He learns that death is natural, that insects perform a useful function in living from the dead, and that true evil lies elsewhere, in people and witches like Emo, who seek to "destroy the feeling people have for each other" (p. 229).

Tayo also begins to be aware that he must imitate animals. When he goes to the ranch he takes a feather and helps the bees to pollinate the flowers: "He imitated the gentleness of the bees as they brushed their sticky-haired feet and bellies softly against the flowers" (p. 220). Earlier he had noticed how animals "drifted with the wind" and he recalled Josiah's having said that "only humans resisted what they saw outside themselves. Animals did not resist. But they persisted, because they became part of the wind" (p. 27). At that time he had not thought of himself as being able to imitate the animals because he then thought of himself as inanimate, as smoke "drifting away in currents of air" (p. 17) and as clay "slipping away with the wind" (p. 27). Only the animate can imitate the animate. By the end of the novel Tayo has changed and has learned that his earlier death-wish was really an attempt to resist what he had then seen as the terrible injustice of Rocky's death. By the end he has come to accept what life and death have given him and to drift with, rather than be eroded by, the winds of nature. He has come to accept the natural world of circumstance and to resist only the unnatural power of the witches, the power of those who would destroy love and freedom and forests and mountains and animals with their artificial instruments.

The animals he comes most dramatically to imitate, of course, are the hardy Mexican cattle, those cattle that are closer to nature than are the stupid Herefords. Silko's imaginery makes their naturalness obvious. These Mexican cattle hunt water like the "desert antelope" (p. 74). They run "like antelope" (p. 80) and "more like deer that cattle" (p. 197). They listen "like deer" (p. 226) and are "smarter than elk about human beings" (p. 197). And like the wild animals of nature, they are able to forage for themselves in the desert. Unlike the fat white-faced Herefords (acculturated Indians?), they do not stand stupidly around artificial water tanks (bars?). Instead, they find their own water in desert springs, their own food in desert grasslands. They trust their own instincts, drift to the south, and survive by their own native and natural abilities. By the end of the novel Tayo has learned his lesson from them. He finds his own water, avoids the trap Emo lays for him, and survives while others perish, others who, like Harley and

Leroy, are farther from nature than he is. It is no accident, incidentally, that the cattle are crossbreeds which, like Tayo, seem to combine the best features of two strains.

In *Ceremony*, then, Silko points the way for Indians of her generation. They must, if they are to survive, learn to know what to accept and what to resist. They must accept the natural world around them, the world the wild animals know and accept. They must accept a role that permits them to live as close to the way animals live as possible. And they must accept death when it comes, either to themselves or to those around them. What they must not accept is the power of the evil witches, the destroyers who substitute for the living things of nature the things of lifelessness: the juke boxes, the bulldozers, the fly swatters, the atomic bombs, the fences, the pavements. Like the spotted cattle which have not forgotten their southern origins, they must not forget their own natural origins, and they must strive against these love-destroying things of the witches. Betonie tells Tayo, "Don't let them stop you. Don't let them finish off this world" (p. 152). Because by observing the animals Tayo has learned what to accept and what to resist, the world stays intact. The phrase "it is not easy" becomes almost a refrain at the end of the novel. Silko has no easy answers to the problems that American Indians—and all of humanity—face in the contemporary world, but she does have answers for those of us who can remain animate.

Circular Design in *Ceremony*

ROBERT C. BELL

❖   ❖   ❖

THE STANDARD NATIVE AMERICAN myth pattern uses the
hero-quest as a framework in which to establish prototype ceremonial procedures for curing rituals called chantways. Mythic plot embodies
reasons for the diverse and intricate procedures and items of ritual and, in
addition, involves a detailed description of legendary events that explains
rite, properties, and behavior. Thus, the mythic narrative (text) itself is
figural and symbolic. So, in their New World variations on the hero-
quest pattern—the worldwide "monomyth" of separation, initiation, and
return—most american ceremonial myths provide a hero or heroine who
gets into a series of predicaments or suffer injuries (usually transformations in mind and body) that require supernatural aid—"Thus the hero
acquires the ceremonial knowledge and power essential for establishing a
chantway."[1]

The Red Antway of the Navajo, for instance, relates a series of preemer-
gence events which "are the basis for establishing the chantway, the prototype *Restoration Rites,* the *Coyote Transformation* essential for the [exorcistic]
Evilway ritual of the chantway . . . and the *Prototype Ceremonial,* the first
performance of the chant itself."[2] In the prototype Restoration Rite, First
Man suggests that some of their former weapons be given back to the
restored but now defenseless ants: "Let some of it be replaced in their

interior! It shall be a chant by which good shall be produced. . . . and when in the future earth surface people begin to come into being, it shall be in their chant."[3] Myth and ritual, idea and act, are inseparable; ceremonial ritual enacts mythology and legend as if for the first time.

The Coyote Transformation story and its attendant hoop ritual, in particular, are, as Wyman and others have shown, a major motif in numerous exorcistic chant legends, including those of Waterway, Excessway, Beadway, and Red Antway.[4] Such curing ceremonials consist of a mixture of procedures designed to symbolically recapitulate the events told in myth and legend, including rituals "intended to appease or to exorcise the etiological factors that are thought to have caused the patient's troubles,"[5] and, if they are to work their magic, the procedures must be recited exactly and in detail: "Repetition is compulsive and authoritative."[6] In part, this is what Silko has done in her novel; the hoop transformation ceremony in *Ceremony* recapitulates, in astonishing detail, the procedures set forth in the Coyote Transformation rite in *The Myth of Red Antway, Male Evilway*, recorded and translated by Father Berard Haile in the 1930s. Simple comparison of the two texts (see pp. 35–39)—and recalling that oral "texts" were always figural and symbolic—reveals a likely source for Silko's hoop ceremony at the middle of the book (pp. 138–53). And in as much as the act of telling and retelling traditional stories is itself part of prescribed ritual, it requires nearly perfect fidelity. Indeed, Silko's telling is as significant as what she tells; repetition of story is comparable to recapitualtion of ritual. Silko's remarkable faithfulness to the Red Antway text as we have it, is comparable to the ritualistic exactness required of the singer or medicine man; her implicit faith in the method of the ceremony's story makes storytelling a curative art form which can bring about restoration and renewal, as it always has been in Native American oral traditions. (Let us not forget, Aristotle, too, made catharsis, the purgation of pity and fear, the object of all literature.)

ACCORDING TO THE RED ANTWAY tradition, angry Ant people are ultimately responsible for certain categories of disease and disturbance, including "evil dreams" and "the influence of ghosts of animals or of other beings that travel in darkness ('witchery of the whirling darkness')"; it explains further that "the Ant People may be offended if a person disturbs, digs up, burns, spits on, urinates on, sleeps on, or merely walks over their house, even though the act may be inadvertent or accidental."[7]

In *Ceremony*, the evil curse set in motion by witchery—"Whirling / whirling / whirling / whirling" (p. 138; cf. pp. 260–61)—begins with "white skin people" who bring disease, destruction, and death, "swarming like larva / out of a crushed ant hill" (p.136). And immediately following the curse is the Coyote Transformation story, paralleling closely the prototype myth and ritual set forth in the Red Antway. In fact, "most of the Evil Chant myths have an episode relating how the hero was transformed by Coyote into a mangy coyote, because Coyote, coveting the hero's wife, hit him with a coyote skin. The [hoop retransformation] rite represents the change back to normal."[8] Silko imitates this mythical pattern as an imperative of oral tradition: "We do not know myth as a making, only as a telling; and there is, with myth, an element of unchangeability in the structure of the telling, the basic terms of which, as spoken, heard, repeated, have the authority of the ritually stabilized."[9] Similarly, the hoops, commonly used in exorcistic transformation rites among the Pueblo and Navajo, represent a space so narrowed down that it is under ceremonial control, an area from which evil has been ritualistically driven and within which power has been concentrated. Re-enacting mythological scenes exactly, observing carefully the sequence of prescribed movements and words, brings myth alive in ritual. As Betonie puts it to Tayo, " 'The ceremonies must be performed exactly as they have always been done, maybe because one slip-up or mistake and the whole ceremony must be stopped and the sand painting destroyed. That much is true' " (p. 126).

But it is also true, Betonie continues, that " 'in many ways, the ceremonies have always been changing.' " Indeed, change and growth are necessary for survival, for " 'only this growth keeps the ceremonies strong,' " and " 'things which don't shift and grow are dead things' " (p. 126). The storytellers's fidelity to the body of myth and ritual, while crucial in a curing ceremony where all the details must be repeated exactly, is not so important to the novel as is the symbolic circular pattern that the hoop transformation rite establishes in the structure of Silko's story. Through repetition and recapitulation, the novel itself describes a circular design going into and out of the hoop ceremony at the center of the book. Linear time—beginning, middle, end—dissolves into a cycle of recapitulation and repetition. The tripartite structure is actually a figural design in which persons, places, and events in the third part of the novel, following the hoop transformation ceremony, are prefigured in the first part in a series of figural signs of types and symbols; the second part is, of course, the ceremony in the middle of the book. This figural design breaks down the very notion of past, present, and future, and we have what Eliot referred to in a review of Joyce's *Ulysses* as a "mythical" rather than a strictly linear "narrative" structure.[10]

Moreover, certain rituals associated with the Native American curing ceremonies we are concerned with here require that the patient re-enact mythological events as a necessary means of identification. When the patient re-enacts the hero's adventure, identification is complete: time is stilled, this world yields to that of myth and legend, the natural and the supernatural meld; and the present moment, which joins past and future, becomes a centering process, a locus of consciousness and being forever becoming. An exemplary paragraph in *Ceremony*, quoted in full, shows us how the process works:

> He stopped on the edge of the clearing. The air was much colder. He had been so intent on finding the cattle that he had forgotten all the events of the past days and past years. Hunting the cattle was good for that. Old Betonie was right. It was a cure for that, and maybe for other things too. The spotted cattle wouldn't be lost any more, scattered through his dreams, driven by his hesitation to admit they had been stolen, that the land—all of it—had been stolen from them. The anticipation of what he might find was strung tight in his belly; suddenly the tension snapped and hurled him into the empty room where the ticking of the clock behind the curtains had ceased. He stopped the mare. The silence was inside, in his belly; there was no longer any hurry. The ride into the mountain had branched into all directions of time. He knew then why the oldtimers could only speak of yesterday and tomorrow in terms of the present moment: the only certainly; and this present sense of being was qualified with bare hints of yesterday or tomorrow, by saying, "I go up to the mountain yesterday or I go up to the mountain tomorrow." The ck'o'yo Kaup'a'ta somewhere is stacking his gambling sticks and waiting for a visitor; Rocky and I are walking across the ridge in the moonlight; Josiah and Robert are waiting for us. This night is a single night; and there has never been any other. (p. 192)

Tayo's search for the cattle becomes the mythical hero's quest for wholeness; even though the cattle and the land have been stolen, this does not mean the end; events following the hoop transformation only complete the ceremony begun in the opening pages of the book.

THE DISTINCTIVE PROPERTIES OF MYTH are structural, and because the ritualistic procedures of the Red Antway curing ceremony are based strictly on incidents in myth and legend, Silko must retell the story of the young hunter-hero whose mind and body were taken over by Coyote, and Tayo must symbolically recapitulate the mythological struggle through the rituals prepared and performed by Betonie. For it is only through identification with the mythological hero that Tayo is finally able to see "the pattern, the way all the stories fit together—the old stories, the war stories, their stories—to become the story that was still being told" (p. 246)—a pattern the reader, too, must come to see and understand.

The hoop ritual itself recapitulates the prototype curing ceremony given in myth by Bear People, and, as Father Haile noted, the ritual of passing through the hoops "symbolizes the removal of a shroud with which evil dreams and visions of ghosts have enveloped the mind, much as the dried skin of the coyote encased the hero's body in the legend."[11] Thus, through repetition and recapitulation—"it depended on whether you knew the story of how others before you had gone" (p. 19)—the myth comes full circle to touch Tayo; the natural and the supernatural are drawn together, "blurring the boundaries between the earth and sky" (p. 207). "He took a deep breath of cold mountain air: there were no boundaries; the world below and the sandpaintings inside became the same that night. The mountains from all directions had gathered there that night" (p. 125).

From this point forward, Silko rarely describes earth and sky separately: she intends for us to perceive in the duality of natural and supernatural a fundamental equivalence, the belief, integral to Native American philosophy, in the connection between present and the past, between the earthly and the transcendent, in the reconciliation of opposites. Tayo comes to see all of this, but only gradually, through the subtle processes of the ceremony. In the opening pages of the book, Tayo's lethargy and frustration nullify even his anger at Emo's bitter recriminations against himself and Indian people: "Emo liked to say, 'Look what is here for us. Look. Here's the Indian's mother earth! Old dried-up thing!'" (p. 25). Tayo's anger makes his hands shake ("Emo was wrong. All wrong."), but paralyzed by grief and guilt, haunted by his memories and his sense of loss, "he'd almost been convinced he was brittle red clay, slipping away with the wind, a little more each day" (p. 27). He cries helplessly: "It was him, Tayo, who had died, but somehow there had been a mistake with the corpses, and somehow his was still unburied" (p. 28). And in the allegorical story of the white shell beads, the tedium and linearity of Tayo's life—when he's not "going up to the line" with Harley and the others, he's "sitting at the ranch all afternoon, watching the yellow cat bite the air for flies; passing the time away, waiting for it to end" (p. 168)—is described in terms he knows are wrong, but he is helpless, hollow; dead, but "still unburied": "Every day they had to look at the land, from horizon to horizon, and every day the loss was with them; it was the dead unburied, and the mourning of the lost, going on forever" (p. 169). But as the influence of the hoop ceremony spreads like ripples in a pool of water, distinctions between a living mythical past and "the dead unburied" in the past, begin to blur. At the ranch again toward the end of the book, Tayo sees clearly, as a result of this blurring of distinctions, that "nothing is lost; all was retained between the sky and the earth, and within himself" (p. 219). Ts'eh camps at a nearby spring where Tayo's mythically structured dreams, which have displaced his terrifying nightmares, are nonetheless as real:

> He lay down beside the pool, across from her, and closed his eyes. He dreamed he made love to her there. He felt the warm sand on his toes and knees, he felt her body, and it was warm as the sand, and he couldn't feel where her body ended and the sand began. (p. 222)

Even after waking to discover her gone, he finds her again, shortly, as real as she was in his dreams; and "coming over the edge, the canyon and the rock of the cliff seemed suddenly gone as if he had stepped from the earth into the sky; where they were, the sky was more than half of the world; it enclosed the mesa top where they stood" (p. 223).

Indeed, even after Ts'eh has left him alone to struggle against the death-giving curse—"They were coming to end it their way" (p. 235)—and Tayo is running from Harley, Leroy, and Emo, earth and sky, the natural and the supernatural, circle together to enclose him in a protective, mythologically ordained and ritualistically prepared space that opens up to contain past and present, the earthly and the transendent, at sunrise:

> On the ridge south of Engine Rock, he stopped to look down at the Acoma valley and the road. Enchanted Mesa was a dark slivered shadow rising up from the valley into the sky. . . . A frail luminous glow pushed out between the edges of horizon and clouds. . . . All things seemed to converge there. . . . at that moment in the sunrise, it was all so beautiful, everything, from all directions, evenly, perfectly, balancing day with night, summer months with winter. The valley was enclosing this totality, like the mind holding all thoughts together in a single moment. (pp. 236–37)

This picture of cosmic order presents an image of perpetual stability and unchanging permanence, one that Tayo (and the reader) might like to delude himself into believing. But as Betonie instructs Tayo, these " 'balances and harmonies always shifting, always necessary to maintain' " order, are always a "matter of transitions, you see; the changing, the becoming must be cared for closely' " (p. 130). Change, which keeps the ceremonies strong, which characterizes life itself, is forever working through order, balancing opposites, restoring itself, "enclosing this totality" if tempo-

rarily, gradually reordering, rebalancing, restoring. Like the child of legend
who wanders off with the Bear People (pp. 128–30), like the mythological
hero who is transformed into a mangy coyote in the prototype Transformation Rite, Tayo must be brought back, restored to normal. But "They
couldn't just grab the child / They couldn't simply take him back / because
he would be in between forever / and probably he would die" (p. 130). And
even after Tayo "passed through the last loop" in Betonie's ceremony,

> it wasn't finished
> They spun him around sunwise
> and he recovered
> he stood up
> The rainbows returned him to his
> home, but it wasn't over.
> All kinds of evil were still on him.
> (p. 144)

So even the hoop ritual, which provided a key to Tayo's final restoration and to the circular narrative structure of the novel, is only a part of
the larger ceremonial pattern and accounts only partially for the complexity of the book. Just as gathering the spotted cattle is "only one color
of sand falling from the fingertips" (p. 196), "in the belly of the story / the
rituals and the ceremony / are still growing" (p. 2). " 'One night or nine
nights won't do it anymore,' " Betonie says; " 'the ceremony isn't finished
yet. . . . This has been going on for a long time now. It's up to you. Don't
let them stop you. Don't let them finish off this world' " (p. 152). This applies directly to Tayo's story from his point of view and from the novelist's;
Tayo imitates myth and ritual, but then so does his author.

Ritual identification and recapitulation operates on several levels in
most curing ceremonies: by absorption (evil is absorbed into the sandpainting, for example), by imitation (in telling stories and in making prayersticks,
sandpaintings, and other ritual paraphernalia), by transformation (from
animal form and sometimes into animal form and back again), by substitu-
tion (many mythical objects and personage are substituted for in ritual by
images in the sand), by recapitulation (of mythical place and circumstance),
by repetition (doing or saying the same thing a prescribed number of times
in prayer, song, or symbol), by commemoration (each performance of the
ritual celebrates all performances in the past and is timeless in its power to
alter events in the future), by concentration (especially in exorcistic rites, a
catharsis requires the singer's and the patient's undivided attention, an intensified form of commemoration). In short, if the division of myth and re-

ality, past and present, supernatural and natural is to be effectively removed, identification must be complete and nearly absolute. Through identification itself, then—in Tayo's case, identification with the hero-quest—there is a sense of return, of a restoration of a tradition.

To be sure, Tayo's identification with the legendary hero is gradual, just as the hoop ceremony itself emphasizes necessary caution in the process of retransformation: "Old Betonie might explain it this way—Tayo didn't know for sure: there were transitions that had to be made in order to become whole again, in order to be the people our Mother would remember; transitions, like the boy walking in bear country being called back softly" (p. 170). Only when he is with Ts'eh is the identification complete. But even as early as his guilt-ridden nightmares and terrifying visions of the dead in Korea, the ritual design of the story encircled him. Unwittingly, he is re-creating the myth when he is a patient in the veteran's hospital in Los Angeles, and even when he and Harley go "up the line." His alienation from himself and from his people, his seemingly futile efforts to create an identity for himself beside Rocky (and the memory of Rocky), his nightmares—all these are symbolic features of an ordeal prefigured in legend. In order to retrace the hero's separation and gradual return, Tayo has to get back to where he started from (see p. 123), and in his end (see p. 258) is his beginning (renewal). Tayo's story is, as it were, contained within the design of the legendary hero-quest; myth, legend, and history are thus enclosed within a circle. There is no end (a linear concept), but a beginning again (a circular concept); Tayo relives legend, from beginning to end to begin again.

Thus, when Tayo goes with Betonie and his assistant on horseback into Chuska Mountains (see pp. 138–39, juxtaposed between witchery's curse and the Coyote Transformation story), they are no longer just an old man on "a skinny pinto mare with hip bones and ribs poking against the hide like springs on an old car seat" (p. 138); a strange boy called Shush riding "a black pony hunching low over its neck with his face in the mane" (p. 138); and a troubled alcoholic war veteran on a brown gelding. They come to represent mythological victims, heroes, and healers. Time, the strictly linear progress of history, dissolves; the line between the present world and a supernatural world of the past narrows. When they stop for the night high in the mountains, Tayo looks down and "the world below was distant and small; it was dwarfed by a sky so blue and vast the clouds were lost in it" (p. 139).

> He could see no signs of what had been set loose upon the earth: the highways, the towns, even the fences were gone. This was the highest point on the earth: he could feel it. It had nothing to do with measurements or

heights. It was a special place. He was smiling. He felt strong. He had to touch his own hand to remember what year it was. (p. 139)

And once the hoops are set, the sandpaintings drawn, and the prayersticks prepared, Tayo, Betonie, and Shush, for the time being, *are* supernatural actors in a mythological drama. Shush becomes the child-bear[12] referred to earlier: "The helper stepped out from the shadows; he was grunting like a bear. He raised his head as if it were heavy for him, and he sniffed the air" (pp. 142–43). Tayo's role is symbolized by the young hunter in the Coyote Transformation Myth, and old Betonie becomes one of the "elders who belong to Bear People . . . at the summit of a place called Dark Mountain."[13] As he walks Tayo through the hoops, Betonie sings a prayer that begins:

> At the Dark Mountain
> born from the mountain
> walked along the mountain
> I will bring you through my hoop,
> I will bring you back.
> (p. 143)

Singing it, saying so, according to Native American ways of perceiving time and space, often makes it so; "saying a thing was true made it true."[14] The ritualistic phrases from Red Antway Silko imitates belong to a special ceremonial language based upon the idea that the word—that is, the formulation of sounds (sacred because associated with breath itself) into organized speech—has a "compulsive power" which brings about a "close identification of person, mind, word, and power and its extension to objects and means."[15] Because the words retell a traditional story, they function to create and reflect the efficacy of order, of repetition, and recapitulation; a circle of identification is completed in the enduring sanctity of the words of the ceremony. Tayo *is* the young hunter who has "lost his mind," who is "not himself" since Coyote slapped his mangy skin over him and breathed on him. But as Betonie and his assistant lead him through the five hoops, Tayo, like the young hunter, renews his mind and spirit. The words sung become reality:

> I'm walking home
> I'm walking back to belonging
> I'm walking back to happiness
> I'm walking back to long life
> (p. 144)

To James Welch's sardonic narrator in *Winter in the Blood*, "Coming home was not easy anymore. It was never a cinch, but it had become a torture" (chapter 1). And First Raise freezes to death in the snow—rather like a Big Foot in the infamous photograph taken at Wounded Knee in 1890: "he was on his way home when they found him. . . . He was pointing toward home" (chapter 9).

In James Welch's novel, *Winter in the Blood*, the pastness of the past, the sense of loss and of the remoteness of supernatural aid, are reflected in and embody the fragmented narrative method. And there is little doubt that Welch knows what he is up to: the sharp divisions he imposes on his material are integral, formalized part of the novel's meaning. In *Ceremony*, on the other hand, Silko involves the oral tradition of Native American myth and medicine in her method and as matter. The patterns of correspondence and concentric symmetry that she creates in so doing, compensate for (and finally reduce) the effects of the intentionally "disjointed quality of the plot. The sense of fragmentation yields finally to the force of the connectedness of the past with the present and to the future. We need the narrative digressions and dislocations to see the larger pattern, to understand the story. Indeed, they *are* the story. And they aren't really digressions or dislocations. Tayo makes it back home:

> They unraveled
> the dead skin
> Coyote threw
> on him
>
> They cut it up
> bundle by bundle.
>
> Every evil
> which entangled him
> was cut
> to pieces.
> (p. 258)

The hoop rite in the middle of the novel mediates events that come prior to as well as after the ceremony itself. It thus becomes the common symbol of form and content in *Ceremony*. For, as Betonie tells Tayo, " 'It is a matter of transitions, you see; the changing, the becoming must be cared for closely. You would do as much for the seedlings as they become plants in the field' " (p. 130). It is, moreover, through the cycle of the hoop ceremony that Tayo finally arrives "at a convergence of patterns" (p. 254):

The cloudy yellow sandstone of Enchanted Mesa was still smoky blue before dawn, and only a faint hint of yellow light touched the highest point of the mesa. All things seemed to converge there: roads and wagon trails, canyons with springs, cliff paintings and shrines, the memory of Josiah with his cattle; but the other was distinct and strong like the violet-flowered weed that killed the mule, and the black markings on the cliffs, deep caves along the valley the Spaniards followed to their attack on Acoma. (p. 237)

[In] . . . Los Alamos, only a hundred miles northeast of him now, still surrounded by high electric fences and the ponderosa pine and tawny sandrock of the Jemez Mountain canyon where the shrine of the twin mountain lions had always been. There was no end to it; it knew no boundaries; and he had arrived at the point of convergence where the fate of all living things, and even the earth, had been laid. (p. 246)

He could still see the stars. He had arrived at a convergence of patterns; he could see them clearly now. The stars had always been with them, existing beyond memory, and they were all held together there. Under these same stars the people had come down from White House in the north. They had seen mountains shift and rivers change course and even disappear back into the earth; but always there were these stars. Accordingly, the story goes on with these stars of the old war shield. (p. 254)

As a novel, *Ceremony* exploits the generic impulse of the form to explore the mysteries of individual history or biography (as does *Winter in the Blood*), but has fused it, in the ritualistic detail, to the quest of modern Native Americans for an identity of their own that begins where Indian history only apparently ended, that begins, that is, in the past, in tradition. The novel gains its peculiar wholeness by assimilating both the detailed particularity of the conventional biographical novel and "the drive toward absoluteness—completeness, autonomy, immunity to neglected contingencies—characteristic of myth."[16] Tayo thus provides a kind of antitype to Welch's nameless narrator, who is unable to control the constituent parts of an impinging world of contingency. *Winter in the Blood* ends "the way history ended" in Welch's poem, "Getting Things Straight":

> . . . history ended when
> the last giant climbed Heart Butte, had his vision
> came back to town and drank himself
> sick.
>
> (*Riding the Earthboy* 40)

But all stories, all ceremonies or rituals, secular and sacred, are attempts to confer "totality" or structure on experience: objects and events that would not otherwise be related to one another are given definite connection. According to even the most ancient of Western philosophers, it is almost a commonplace that there are, actually, no beginnings and no endings in the world's time, only an endless flow out of the eternity of the past and into the eternity of the future. It is the same in myth, in the stories and rituals of New World philosophers: time is flux and change, beginnings and endings are vague if not irrelevant. Native American myth and history move along a continuum, but it is cyclic, not according with a one-dimensional linear pattern of progress. As Simon Oritz has put it:

> In the ancient and deep story
> of all our nights, we contemplated,
> contemplated not the completion of our age,
> but the continuance of the universe,
> the travelling, not the progress,
> but the humility of our being there.
> ("The Significance of a Veteran's Day," *Going for the Rain*)

In the making of myths, in ritual storytelling, in ceremonies of any type, we remove a segment of time from the great flux and confer wholeness (roundness) upon it by controlling, by ordering, by giving a shape and significance to what Eliot (over 50 years ago) called "the immense panorama of futility and anarchy which is contemporary history." Eliot regarded Joyce's achievement in *Ulysses* as "a step toward making the modern world possible for art, order and form." In *Winter in the Blood* the vastness and shapelessness of the narrator's fragmented experience speaks for itself, but in the form as well as content.

In *Ceremony*, on the other hand, the disjointed parts are refocused through the power field created by the traditional hoop symbol and converge in a circular pattern of restoration and genuine renewal—for the reader as well as for Tayo, the half-breed Indian in contemporary America.

Coyote Transformation Prototype Ceremony
from
"The Myth of Red Antway, Male Evilway"
as
Told by Son of the Late Tall Deshchini
Recorded and Translated by Father Berard Haile (1933–1934)
Published in *The Red Antway of the Navaho,* Leland C. Wyman
(Santa Fe: Museum of Navaho Ceremonial Art, Inc., 1973)

And it happened that a girl, who was husbandless, married a young man
who was likewise (single). But the Coyote from somewhere cherished a desire for this woman, and many were the ways in which he began his
schemes. All sorts of things he tried on the young man in order to deceive
him, but always failed. Now this young man was exclusively occupied with
the chase. He was an expert at it and never returned empty-handed. . . .
In his accustomed manner he had one day not gone very far before he
came upon the tracks of a deer, which he began to track. After he overtook
it he wounded it with an arrow, then gave it chase yonder across Slim
Water. In the meantime, while he was following it, Coyote had waylaid
him and without being aware of it, he was running parallel with Coyote.
Thus it happened that he (Coyote) blew his own voice, his entire interior,
his breath, and his entire exterior, exactly as he was in appearance upon
the young man. This caused a change to come over him, he began to stag-
ger and in time fell over. The Coyote then approached him and clothed
himself in that person's appearance. In exchange he clothed the young
man in his own looks. He then lay there in the form of a coyote, while
Coyote walked away in the form of a man. This they call, he struck him
with a coyote's dried skin.

After this had so happened and the person lay here, the other returned
alone to the man's home where his wife was living. At sundown he arrived
there, and she thought he was her husband. Now it seems he returned
without venison. . . . In time food was brought to him from the other
hogan [his mother-in-law's] the basket with food was carried into him. He
ate all of it, while the young man had not been in the habit of consuming
all. The empty basket was carried back to the hogan. "Look, he ate it all!"
she remarked. Then after dusk she laid robes for him. While the young
man had been backward and reserved with his wife, this one was not so, he
bothered her constantly all night long. At dawn he dashed off, picking
up his arrows as he passed by. Here it seems the mother-in-law (custom)

originated again, which to this day regulates the practice of hiding from one's mother-in-law.

And at sunset he returned again without having killed even a single one all day long. The arrows with which he returned were grey with dust. Then food was brought to him in the basket, and again he consumed it all. The robes were spread for him again and he spent the night in the same manner as the previous one. "What is this? This one does not appear to be the same person. The other as we know was not in the habit of eating it all," the woman and the man said whose son-in-law he was. . . . thus he had spent three nights there. Meanwhile he gave chase over there to any large game that came his way. These would outrun him, so that he merely tired himself out with running among them until sunset, when he returned home. This night finally she was altogether unable to sleep on his account. On the morning of the forth night he left again. So she entered her mother's home. But when she warmed up, she clearly smelled of coyote urine. "So it is Coyote doing this, I see! Where is the place in which he has not yet schemed! From that time on it did not seem right to me!" the old woman said. "Suppose now, that you begin to track the young man from the place he left four days ago! There is no telling what he has done to him! He certainly did not leave him unharmed!" they said. At once four of them set out to track him. And they tracked him to the spot where he had found the deer tracks, then where it had been arrowwounded, then where he had given it chase. Then they followed him up to the point where Coyote had waylaid him and, sure enough, coyote tracks led along there. The signs were unmistakable that the man had lain there.

And from there on a human track led off, while the other way, towards the mountain, the person must have crawled. So they followed this track some distance and found that he had crawled below a hard oak, where evidently he had spent the night. From here he had crawled farther on below an oak tree, where again he had spent the night. From here he had crawled some distance farther under a pinyon tree, where he had spent the night. Again they found that he had crawled on until he had reached a juniper, below which he had spent another night. Then he had crawled on until he had crawled below the wild rose bush. There they overtook and found him lying below the wild rose bush. Here Talking God came and stood before him. "What has happened? Are you the person who left four days ago, my grandchild?" he asked him. Perhaps he would have replied, but a coyote sound alone was heard, the person's tail only twirled, digging a hole in the ground. He certainly was a sight, he was found suffering with thirst and hunger, and apparently in a very critical condition. He then repeated the same question, "Are you the one, my grandchild, that left here four days ago?" A coyote whine was the answer. Again he repeated the same question, "Four days ago you left here, are you that one, my grandchild?" he repeated. Again a coyote whine alone was heard, he only shook his head in consent, they say.

"Truly it is he!" they said. "How now? What shall be done? Go ahead, you who are fleet of foot, quickly spread the news in the holy places!" was said. This they did, and from these places they met here. "What in your opinion shall be done? Here your young man is lying!" they said. "Yonder beyond Hesperus Peak, at the summit of a place called Dark Mountain, is the home of four elders who belong to the Bear People. These, possibly, offer the only hope. They have hoops called once-they-are-to-be-seen, they have footprint figures, they have sitting place figures, they have hand prints with power to restore the mind time and again; notify them!" was suggested. Immediately Big Fly sped away. The elders arrived here in full number. "It is only this, that this happened here in some manner. That accounts for the news being sent to you." And the story of how it happened was related to them. "All right, we shall do as you wish! Bring some hard oak, also some ordinary oak, pinyon, juniper, and wild rose twigs!" Immediately they went to work on their preparation, and robes were spread for the hoops as they were being made. . . . Bundles of weeds were placed in four places and tied to them with yucca, namely spruce and burned-mixture-weeds (mixed charcoal), that is, snakeweed, gramma grass, and rock sage (for the four bundles). That completed the preparations.

Then a sandpainting was made inside the hogan. Rainbows lying in cross form only were made, because these had been his former traveling means and their purpose was to restore his travel means to him. At a point beyond where the hoops were to be placed the white corn sandpainting also was made, similar to a sun figure, inside of which Pollen Boy was drawn with pollen. Blue pollen was used for his eyes and mouth and the same for his neck. At the various joints too, pinches of it were strewn. After that, on this side of it, (small trenches) were dug in which hoops were to stand, with places left between them. The hoops were then lined up at a distance from the hogan and at the end farthest from the hoops, a dark mountain range was placed. The next range this side of it was blue, the next range this way was yellow, and the next range white. Beyond the dark mountain range, coming from its rear, bear tracks were set in black, resting their feet side by side, because he was to stand on these. On this side of them their paws were placed in blue. Next their footprints again were placed in yellow, and next to these paws again in white. And, stringing over the mountain ranges just mentioned, a rainbow was strewn, which represented his former travelling means. Then he (the patient) was placed upon the drawing in white corn mentioned before. There the talking prayersticks were laid upon him, while here inside, the turquoise arrow and white bead arrow were laid in a basket, and placed on the sandpainting here.

As soon as all was about ready, a song was intoned inside to fetch him and, at mention of the proper words, he (Bear, the singer) started walking towards him, and continued so until he reached the patient. After applying the talking prayersticks to him he pressed them against his heart. . . . With [a dark flint] a diagonal crosscut was made at the top of the person's head. From there they supported him in walking to the said foot place prints, on top of which they placed his right foot, then his left one. Then a prayer was recited for him, the Bear's own prayer. . . . This prayer proceeded on through the hoops, he was talked through the five hoops with it.

Bear's Prayer

At the Dark Mountain, who was reared in the mountain, who walks along the mountain, I have started through your red hoop! I have started through your dark hoop, I have started through your blue hoop, I have started through your yellow hoop, I have started through your white hoop, I have started through your sparkling (pink) hoop.
I have left on the foot place prints of white corn, I left on the trail of white corn.
In the rear recess of the white corn home zigzag lightning has dropped with me.
Happily I have returned to my home, happily I have returned belonging to my home, happily my home has become mine again.
The talking prayerstick instructs me as I return to my sitting place, I have returned to be long life (and) happiness again, I have returned to be long life (and) happiness again.
At Dark Mountain, reared in the mountain, who moves his hand along the mountain, I have started out through your dark hoop. ("Red hoop" is omitted in this part which otherwise repeats the first part until): In the rear recess of the white corn home straight lightning has dropped with me (etc., until the end).
At Dark Mountain, reared within the mountain, who shoves the dew (etc., as in the first part, but "dark hoop" is omitted, and "sunray dropped with me" is substituted for "zigzag lightning" of the first part).

At Dark Mountain, reared within the mountain, who leaves a path walking over nice flowers (etc., as in the second part, but "rainway dropped
with me" is pronounced here).

Notes

Coyote Transformation Prototype Ceremony reprinted from *The Red Antway*, pp. 129–35, by kind permission of the Wheelwright Museum of the American Indian (formerly the Museum of Navaho Ceremonial Art), Santa Fe, New
Mexico.

1. Leland C. Wyman, *The Red Antway of the Navaho* (Santa Fe, 1973), p. 65.

2. Wyman, p. 70.

3. Wyman, p. 128.

4. Gladys A. Reichard, *Navaho Religion: A Study of Symbolism* (Princeton, 1974),
p. 656; also Wyman, p. 74.

5. Wyman, p. 25.

6. Reichard, p. 118

7. Wyman, pp. 25–26.

8. Reichard, p. 656.

9. Werner Berthoff, "Fiction, History, Myth: Notes toward the Discrimination
of Narrative Forms," in *The Interpretation of Narrative: Theory and Practice*, ed. Morton W.
Bloomfield (Cambridge, 1970), p. 276; see also Robert Scholes and Robert Kellogg.
The Native of Narrative (New York, 1966), Chapter 2.

10. As Joyce himself put it in *Ulysses*: "Hold to the now, the here, through
which all future plunges to the past" (New York, 1961), p. 186; and Eliot in *Burnt Nor-
ton*: Time past and time future / What might have been and what has been / Point to
one end, which is always present, (I, 44–46). Eliot's short essay, " 'Ulysses,' Order,
and Myth," first appeared in 1923; it is reprinted in a number of critical anthologies,
including *Criticism*, ed. Schorer, Miles, and McKenzie, rev. ed., pp. 269–71.

11. Wyman, p. 31.

12. Shush, whose name translates from Navajo as "Bear," could also be performing the Shock Rite ritual of the Coyote Transformation rite. This part of the
ceremony involves impersonation of Bear by one of the medicine men's assistants
and is designed to test the effectiveness of the retransformation procedures. See
Wyman, pp. 56–58.

13. Wyman, p. 133.

14. Reichard, p. 289.

15. Reichard, p. 270; also pp. 33–34.

16. Berthoff, "Fiction, History, Myth: Notes toward the Discrimination of Narrative Forms," p. 269.

An Act of Attention

Event Structure in Ceremony

ELAINE JAHNER

◆　◆　◆

AFTER READING LESLIE SILKO'S NOVEL *Ceremony*, many readers know the novel possesses an energy that engages their sense of themselves as persons. That energy seems to elude discussion because the labeling required in any kind of analysis appears more than usually inadequate for describing the act of attention that is an essential part of the reader's experience. But then there are those like myself who sense that trying again and again to talk about the quality of attention evoked by the book can be an important part of developing more sensitive understanding not only of Leslie Silko's own work but of other Native American writers who might also require of readers a particular attention directed toward matters that their previous experience of novels may not have demanded. Perhaps one way of describing the magnetic field of attention is to say that the lodestone in this field is the experience of event[1] rather than sequentially motivated action as the determinant of plot coherence; but that is too cryptic a statement to have much meaning without explanation.

In this context the word "event" has a specific meaning that is best described through looking at Silko's novel. Once event has been defined, we can contrast the nature of its structuring force with that of other, more commonly experienced ways of developing coherence within any novel. Since giving event structure priority over temporal structure seems to be a

41

characteristic of art that is intimately related to an ongoing oral tradition, progress made toward understanding event may be progress toward understanding relationships between oral and written literatures.

One of the pivotal events in *Ceremony* is that which describes the protagonist Tayo singing the sunrise song after his first encounter with the mysterious woman. If we examine that passage, we can identify the essential features of Silko's sense of event:

> He stood on the steps and looked at the morning stars in the west. He breathed deeply, and each breath had a distinct smell of snow from the north, of ponderosa pine on the rimrock above; finally he smelled horses from the direction of the corral, and he smiled. Being alive was all right then: he had not breathed like that for a long time. . . .
>
> Coming closer to the river, faintly at first, faint as the pale yellow light emerging across the southeast horizon, the sounds gathered intensity from the swelling colors of dawn. And at the moment the sun came over the edge of the horizon, they suddenly appeared on the riverbank, the Ka't'sina approaching the river crossing. He stood up. He knew the people had a song for the sunrise. . . .
>
> He repeated the words as he remembered them, not sure if they were the right ones, but feeling they were right, feeling the instant of the dawn was an event which in a single moment gathered all things together—the last stars, the mountaintops, the clouds, and the winds—celebrating this coming. (pp. 181–82)

Almost every aspect of the long quotation is significant. Tayo's experience of event is precisely realized in language replete with the most exact sensuous detail. There are distinct smells, sounds, and colors, all qualities of definite and real places. Each detail shapes the way Tayo experiences this particular intersection of life and story. Ostensibly alone, Tayo does not experience the moment as isolation. He senses the presence of the Ka't'sina and knows he is in touch with very fundamental life forces. In this place, at this time, he gives them full recognition. His own act of attention is complete. We know from earlier developments in the novel that the place where he finds himself able to sing the sunrise song is a specific place, marked by the stars themselves. It is Tayo's center of the world, using that phrase in the sense in which it is used in American Indian ceremony. It is also an emergence place for him because he moves into a new level of experiencing his role in an all-encompassing story.

Tayo's participating in the sunrise event is both convergence and emergence. Past understandings of the meaning of experiences converge and permit emergence to new levels of comprehension, new parts of the story, and new aspects of ceremonies. Events are boundary experiences marking stages of life for the protagonist. They also mark stages of the story for the reader who can experience their impact by relating to their significance as primary human experiences that are at one and the same time, acts of recognition and experiences of renewal of energies. As recognition, event implies pattern, form that is enduring yet specific as to time and place. As experience, it implies conscious participation in the dynamic energies that generate and perpetuate life and form. Both the pattern and the experience are, by their very nature, culturally specific; and it is at this level that a reader must bring his or her own cultural experiences into relation with those of the protagonist.

There is nothing of chance or absurdity in the meaning and experience of event which can only be experienced by one who knows how to recognize its signs. Such knowledge is by no means universal, and the novel *Ceremony* has as its theme, the gaining of that knowledge. Furthermore, the novel itself is shaped by the processes that lead to the capacity to experience event in life or in art. The ebb and flow of narrative rhythm in the novel creates an event in the process of telling about event. The entire process is ceremonial, and one learns how to experience it ceremonially by achieving various kinds of knowledge attained not through logical analysis but through narrative processes that have their own epistemological basis.

Although many types of narrative function in *Ceremony*, jokes, personal experience stories, rumor, gossip, two major types of narrative shape the events of the novel and affect the way the other types interweave as they lead to different kinds of perception. These two types are the contemporary and the mythic tellings, the timeless and the time-bound narratives. The two are not independent of each other in that they constantly shape each other, but finding out how they interact is complicated by the fact that all which occurs in the time-bound framework is confused because the ways of knowing, the various kinds of narrative are all entangled. Reader and protagonist alike must learn to untangle, and the reader can follow Tayo from event to event by moving from poetry to prose and back again to poetry. Silko juxtaposes the mythic portions of the novel and the story of Tayo's efforts by starting the myth in poetic form to contrast with the prose that carries forward contemporary realizations of the meaning stated in poetic sections.

The first event of the novel occurs while Tayo is a soldier. The dense jungle rain, so different from rain in the desert, appears malevolent and Tayo curses it. When he returns home, there is drought and Tayo assumes responsibility for it, believing that his curse caused it. His belief derives from the fact that he knows or intuits the power of words in relation to myth but he follows the results of his powerful words to the wrong mythic prototypes. His experiences at this stage are like those of the character Auntie whose feelings are "twisted, tangled roots, and all the names for the source of this growth were buried under English words; out of reach. And there would be no peace and the people would have no rest until the entanglement had been unwound to the source" (p. 69). As the first poetic portion tells us, the mythic story is the source and it gives rise to ritual and ceremony, situations in which words bring things into being:

> See, it is moving.
> There is life here
> for the people
>
> And in the belly of this story
> the rituals and the ceremony
> are still growing.
> (p. 2)

At the beginning of the novel, Tayo is sufficiently in touch with the nature of mythic life to recognize the potential significance of the first event of the novel—his cursing the rain. What he cannot understand is the event's actual significance. Silko's description of the event clearly indicates both the convergence and the emergence aspects of its meaning. When Tayo acts out of a firm sense of event, he knows that his actions cannot be insignificant; there is the experience of gathering together and moving onward:

> He started repeating "Goddamn, goddamn!": it flooded out of the last warm core in his chest and echoed inside his head. He damned the rain until the words were a chant, and he sang it while he crawled through the mud to find the corporal and get him up before the Japanese saw them. He wanted the words to make a cloudless blue sky, pale with a summer sun pressing across wide and empty horizons. The words gathered inside him and gave him strength. (p. 12)

What Tayo cannot understand is the literal effect his words will have so he cannot emerge from his first event into new levels of understanding without help from medicine men—help he receives later in the novel. Alien ways of looking at the world prevent a full understanding of the event experience. Entanglement is Silko's main metaphor for describing obstacles to the event experience, and its use in early sections of the novel helps readers sense the feeling and meaning of Tayo's need to truly understand the connections among acts that will lead him to full event experience: "He could feel it inside his skull—the tension of little threads being pulled and how it was with tangled things, things tied together, and as he tried to pull them apart and rewind them into their places, they snagged and tangled even more" (p. 7).

Reader and protagonist alike go from event to event trying to learn the connection between contemporary action and the mythic prototype. To perceive the wrong bonds is to be caught up in the wrong boundaries of experience and to misunderstand the nature of cause and effect. After the first event, the main patterns of imagery in the novel have to do with vaguely understood or false boundaries and relationships. Tayo knows he is caught between different ways of seeing relationships, and he senses that the real boundaries have to do with mythic prototypes: "Years and months had become weak, and people could push against them and wander back and forth in time. Maybe it had always been this way and he was only seeing it for the first time" (p. 18). False boundaries lead to death and while he is in a state of confusion about the meaning of relationships, Tayo lives a kind of death in life: "He inhabited a gray winter fog on a distant elk mountain where hunters are lost indefinitely and their own bones mark the boundaries" (p. 15).

As he struggles with various conflicts and watches the drought-stricken land, Tayo remembers the actions narrated in the second poem of the novel which tells of the argument between Reed Woman and her sister Corn Woman, an argument that results in Reed Woman abandoning the present world and going to an earlier one so that the rain disappears. Because he knows that his actions have something to do with myth, Tayo blames himself for the drought. The relationship between cause and effect, though, is more complex than Tayo realizes; and the second section of the novel emphasizes what it means not to know the connections. In this section, the medicine man Ku'oosh helps Tayo understand both the fragility and the complexity of the connections and relationships. Both the imagery and the plot elements having to do with boundaries come together in the event that is the medicine man's ceremony. As always, Silko's description of time and place are specific. It is a windy afternoon: Tayo is at home but he must remember and mentally enter a cave near Laguna that he knows well. After the medicine man has led Tayo to an understanding of the meaning of his ceremony by making him remember the meaning of a particular place, he brings Tayo to a profound experience of not knowing. He explains the fragility of the world, the need for telling of the story behind each word, and he asks Tayo for his own story of the war—a story that Tayo cannot convey to him. According to the medicine man, telling the entire story is the human responsibility; Tayo realizes the difficulties of the responsibility and becomes ill once again.

The imagery and action that cluster in the third section of the novel have to do with trying to evade responsibilities seemingly too big to be understood. Tayo had learned that the medicine man does not know the right bonds anymore. Tayo himself must search for them because, as the medicine man says, "It is important to all of us. Not only for your sake, but for this fragile world" (p. 36). With the theme of responsibility for searching for new links between prototype and contemporary action, there is also concentration on the meaning of the process of transmission of stories. Silko shows us that the transmission of such knowledge is a far more complicated process than scholars usually describe. Transmission involves not only the sharing of knowledge but also the sharing of how the knowledge has been shaped through one's living with it. Any event by event analysis of the entire novel is impossible in a short essay, but since all the specific events have to do with the learning process that is part of the transmission of knowledge about stories, I will simply sketch the learning process for key events.

Some characters, like Harley, evade the responsibility that goes with the entire learning process. They accept quick solutions, quick magic, but they cannot perceive the right relationships and boundaries. As one of the poems says,

> They thought they didn't have to worry
> about anything
> They thought this magic
> could give life to plants
> and animals.
> They didn't know it was all just a trick.
>
> (p. 48)

Unlike Harley, Tayo has known and loved people who knew how to make the right stories relate to the right points in the ongoing movement of life. One important teacher was his uncle Josiah. The phrase, "Josiah said," introduces the many sections of the novel that narrate Tayo's childhood learning about the meaning that event can have: "'You see,' Josiah had said, '. . . there are some things worth more than money.' He pointed his chin at the springs and around at the narrow canyon. 'This is where we come from, see. This sand, this stone, these trees, the vines, all the wildflowers. This earth keeps us going'" (p. 45). Josiah understood the importance of the conjunction between the right place and the right time. Such respect for place and its relation to time is an important element in learning how to experience mythic knowledge which, in turn, leads to the event experience.

There was also a woman called the Night Swan who understood the need to seek for real boundaries in the life process. She understood too the need to relate one's understanding of real boundaries to one's capacity to feel. Her experiences with her first lovers had taught her only that some paths cannot lead to emergence from anything: "She kept him there for as long as she could, searching out the boundary, the end to the power of the feeling. She wanted to prowl those warm close places until she discovered the end because at the time she had not yet seen that the horizon was an il- lusion and the plains extended infinitely; and up until that final evening, she had found no limit" (p. 85). The Night Swan taught Tayo that the ex- perience I am calling event is the key to maintaining every form of life be- cause it relates change and continuity. Some people, like Tayo and herself, are different. These people are part of change and the way in which these "different ones" experience event is a fundamental part of the way the pro- totypical myths remain a vital part of human life. She says to Tayo, "'You don't have to understand what is happening. But remember this day. You will recognize it later. You are part of it now'" (p. 100).

Tayo does recognize it later when the teacher Betonie finally prepares him for the experience of event and brings home to him the fact that learning the transmission process of myth involves learning to bring the meaning of all the changes he has experienced in life to the way he feels the stories. If he can bring the meaning of his actions to the way he feels the stories, then he will be attentive enough to sense the subtle shifts and movements that define the way the story takes shape through the people who allow it to come into their lives. When the story comes into lives, it sets the important boundaries because it shapes events that relate past to present, prototype to immediate experience. Through the ceremonies that Betonie performs for him, Tayo realizes a little more about how to allow story to shape his experience as event so that both he and the story remain alive. Through ceremony he begins to learn to feel the gathering of mean- ing that occurs in story: "He remembered the black of the sand paintings on the floor of the hogan; the hills and mountains were the mountains and hills they had painted in sand. He took a deep breath of cold mountain air; there were no boundaries; the world below and the sand paintings inside became the same that night. The mountains from all the directions had been gathered there that night" (p. 145). In any event, space and time, inner and outer come together. The significant boundaries are between what and who are or are not part of the event; between what is gathered together and what is scattered.

Betonie also teaches Tayo that an important part of the experience of event is the experience of transitions: "'There are balances and harmonies always shifting, always necessary to maintain. . . . It is a matter of transitions, you see; the changing, the becoming must be cared for closely. You would do as much for seedlings as they become plants in the fields'" (p. 130). Transitions are a part of the emergence phase. During the transitional times, Tayo must nourish the feelings that enable him to respond fully to events when their time and place has come. That there is a right time and right place and that these are specific, real places is something that Silko carefully establishes. One could document references to the right time and the right place for all the event experiences of the book, but the major ones are set with special care.

Betonie explains to Tayo that he must watch for the right mountain, the right stars, and the right woman before he will be able to finish the Ceremony. When he finds the right conjunction of all, he is able to sing the sunrise song, the event quoted at the beginning of this essay. Once he comes to this intersection of time, place, and story, Betonie's teachings become "a story he could feel happening—from the stars and the woman, the mountain and the cattle would come" (p. 186). Once Tayo has come to this realization, he is a conscious participant in the development of the story. He can shape the story because he understands something about the real boundaries that relate and separate actions and persons. He has many kinds of new strength when he can untangle the twisted roots of his thoughts and he knows that some things outdistance death and destruction:

> The mountain outdistanced their destruction, just as love had outdistanced death. The mountain could not be lost to them, because it was in their bones; Josiah and Rocky were not far away. They were close; they had always been close. And he loved them then as he had always loved them, the feeling pulsing over him as strong as it had ever been. They loved him that way; he could still feel the love they had for him. . . . This feeling was their life, vitality locked deep in blood memory, and the people were strong, and the fifth world endured, and nothing was ever lost as long as the love remained." (pp. 219–20)

Understanding and participating in event is knowing that vitality and love endure. This is Tayo's healing experience. He re-creates himself in creating the new boundaries in his life, not those of logic, but the traditional ones of story. Even witchery can be handled within the boundaries of story. It is only those events that do not seem part of any pattern at all which are utterly destructive. They intrude upon lives without preparation and rearrange them so that there can be no transitions among events and all pattern seems irrelevant; even ceremony appears irrelevant. But once the true pattern is perceived by those participating in it, the story goes on and the right ceremonies are in the belly of the story. The story perpetuates life and love; and people experience the story as event.

Through the narrative events of the novel, protagonist and reader gradually learn to relate myth to immediate action, cause to effect; and both reader and protagonist learn more about the power of story itself. The reader seeks to learn not only what happens to Tayo but also how and why it happens. The whole pattern of cause and effect is different from most novels written from a perspective outside the mythic mode of knowledge. To employ myth as a conscious literary device is a quite different thing from employing the mythic way of knowing as the basic structural element in a novel as Silko does. But as they read the story, readers are not likely to analyze what kind of energy is at work; they continue because Silko is a skilled storyteller. Then in direct proportion to the degree of their belief in mythic reality, critical readers are likely to distance themselves from the novel's world and begin to consider the nature of its impact. It is at this stage of inquiry that the concept of event structure can have meaning. Perhaps the experience of event is something all people have but the novel poses interesting questions. What constitutes the experience for different people in different cultures and how is it shaped by different kinds of narrative? More specifically, how does the novel as a particular kind of narrative function in shaping and describing event experiences?

The critic Irving Buchen says that "the novel is not a defined but a discovered form."[2] In the context of Silko's writing we can carry this statement further and say that a certain type of novel is becoming a form (and forum) for rediscovering narrative potential in a contemporary context. For the traditional tribal artist, narrative forms have always had to do with particular ways of knowing and learning; they have not been mere objects of knowledge. The novel is a narrative genre well suited for examining how the traditional ways of knowing function in a multicultural world, where the meanings of narrative are often twisted and tangled. The novel can accommodate enough detail and can juxtapose enough different kinds of narrative to show how it is possible to untangle our responses to different ways of knowing and follow them to their experiential roots.[3] For that is what event is, a primary experience of sources of knowledge shaped not by logical concepts but by the action of story. Such an experience requires of readers a special act of attention that combines the oldest mode of attentiveness—the mythic mode—with a contemporary one shaped by our successive experience with novels. If we accept Dan Ben-Amos's characterization of any genre as a cluster of thematic and behavioral attributes,[4] then we can easily focus on the concept of event as a cluster of both thematic and behavioral attributes that are shaping an emerging type of American Indian novel, one that has interesting differences from other types of American novels because its emphasis is less on what is known than on how one comes to know certain things and because it demands an attentiveness from the reader that has less to do with grasping what the action is than it does with feeling how actions have meanings that live and grow according to the many different ways human beings have of knowing about them.

Notes

1. The term "event" has a long history in the criticism of narrative but it has no single, critical meaning. It is often used to refer to the duration of a given state of being. The following definition is typical. ". . . events are . . . complex structures consisting of states and a (change) relation over these states." Teunis van Dijik, *Some Aspects of Text Grammars* (The Hague, 1972), p. 308. The term, as defined in this essay, requires that particular elements be part of a state before that state is defined as event. But as in previous uses of the term, mine assumes that event is a basic unit of narrative structure.

2. "The Aesthetics of the Supra-Novel," in *The Theory of the Novel,* ed. John Halperin (New York, 1974), p. 102.

3. The whole concept of narrative modes as epistemological models that function in the novel is one that Barbara Hardy explores: "Narrative, like drama, lyric, or dance, cannot be regarded simply as an aesthetic invention used by artists in order to control, manipulate, order and investigate the experiences of that life we tend to separate from art, but must be seen as a primary act of mind transferred to art from life. The novel does not invent its structures but heightens, isolates and proceeds to analyze the narrative forms, methods and motions of perception and communication. Sometimes explicitly, always implicitly, the novel is concerned to analyze the narrative forms of ordinary life." *Tellers and Listeners* (London, 1975), p. 1.

4. "Analytical Categories and Ethnic Genres," in *Folklore Genres,* ed. Dan Ben-Amos (Austin, 1976), p. 231.

Blue Medicine

KENNETH LINCOLN

◆　◆　◆

the struggle is the ritual
—"Deer Song"

EARLY IN *Ceremony* Old Ku'oosh, a Laguna elder, comes to Tayo with
"his bag of weeds and dust" to counter Emo's rattling a Bull Durham
bag of Japanese teeth (a story heard in Silko's childhood when some reservation lands became internment camps). Old Ku'oosh speaks the ceremonial language of a dialect that enacts meanings, revealing thought by natural action, all with the gentle care of growing things: "He smelled like
mutton tallow and mountain sagebrush. He spoke softly, using the old
dialect full of sentences that were involuted with explanations of their own
origins, as if nothing the old man said were his own but all had been said
before and he was only there to repeat it" (*C* 34).[1]

This Pueblo medicine leads Tayo to a more arcane healer, Old Betonie,
the contemporary Navajo/Mexican breed. Betonie also is known by hazel
eyes, and he lives above the Gallup dump in an ancient hogan dug halfway
(again, fusional) into the foothill. Betonie collects times and places, calendars and phone books, from his travels among Indians all over America:
"all the names in them. Keeping track of things" (*C* 121). "All these things
have stories alive in them," Betonie claims. Tayo recognizes calendar pic-
tures from 1939 and 1940, predating his war sickness. The scene implies
that healing involves the right triggering of memory, a health within
things, natural to body and mind. And, similarly, to name things rightly is

51

to make medicine through memory, to heal and give strength. This right naming connects inner with outer forms, the ianyi ("breath") or spirit with matter, by way of living words. So, to remember and breathe, according to traditional memory, places one naturally in a naming ceremony, aligned with the things that are and always have been. "You should understand the way it was back then. Because it is the same even now," Silko has said of mythic storytelling.[2]

In Gallup. Betonie tells Tayo to look "east to Mount Taylor towering dark blue with the last twilight," where the story finally will heal him. "It is the people who belong to the mountain," Betonie corrects Tayo's white misconception, not the mountain to the deed holder behind barbed wire (*C* 128). And the people belong to the names they bear, the language they are born into and grow through, the stories they are known by. "That's how you know, that's how you belong, that's how you know you belong," Silko reasons, "if the stories incorporate you into them. . . . In a sense, you are told who you are, or you know who you are by the stories that are told about you."[3] The sickness, then, is to forget and blame others for the loss, to fall silent, not to remember the ceremony of the natural world. "It is that town down there which is out of place. Not this old medicine man," Betonie nods towards the infernal Gallup arroyos Ceremonial Grounds, where whites parade storefront Indians for tourists (*C* 118).

Not all "ceremonies" heal. Some are manipulations of the "witchery" started long ago, evil spirits showing off and competing their horrors. So it is recorded in the ritual legend of the shadow witch, who invented whites by telling a story of terror that came true.

> They fear
> They fear the world.
> They destroy what they fear.
> They fear themselves.
>
> (*C* 135)

But Indians cannot rule out whites, Betonie considers, for Thought-Woman created them all. Hating whites mirrors and feeds the Indian's own misery, as the white fears his own fear: "you don't write off all the white people, just like you don't trust all Indians" (*C* 128). For a mixed blood to condemn all whites is tantamount to historical parricide.

"The changing" always changes, in people and ceremonies they live by, and Tayo must complete the old rituals in order to "create new ceremonies." So the culture has always continued. It is not just the way things *were*, but how they *are*, evolving from the past; the past informs a living present, just as Spider-Old-Woman's web spins reality out of her aged abdomen. It is not object, but the life moving through things that matters most (*C* 135).

Betonie would have Tayo take responsibility for what is: his own life mediating several cultures, races, tongues, and times. The ceremonies of the stars and mountains and woman and rain, even rounding up the speckled wild cattle, account for everything without dehumanizing or denaturalizing any one part. They unify all people, bloods, breeds, bastards, whites, darks, animals, plants, spirits, and stones in patterns of cyclic continuity. The witchery starts opposedly, displacing one's own pain on others, "me" against "them," castigating, warring, killing, dividing the people.

So Tayo must make a healing pilgrimage north into the Chuksa Mountains under "a sky so blue and vast the clouds were lost in it" (*C* 139). Betonie and his helper, Shush ("bear," Pueblo animal-spirit ally of warriors, because of its courage, and of healers, because it digs for roots), take Tayo through an old-time Scalp Ceremony for returning warriors. They call the bear-child back from the "whirling darkness" of neither man nor animal, body nor spirit, lost "in between forever."

Like Grandmother Spider behind the story, and Auntie by *Ceremony*'s end, a hundred years ago Betonie's grandfather knew that "it never has been easy" to bridge transitions. In grandfather's time, a "blue lace shawl" was one day found under a tree, and Navajo traders brought Descheeny a Mexican outcast for his bride. A century of plotting began here to offset the "witchery" of warring American racisms. The curing requires three generations of transition between dark and white, native and immigrant: "It will take a long long time and many many more stories like this one" (*C* 150). To counter racial divisions, the Navajo medicine man Descheeny, and his Mexican bride a century ago made love and medicine and children, planning by the stars the ceremony that Tayo must one day complete: "He gazed into his smoky quartz crystal and she stared into the fire, and they plotted the course of the ceremony by the direction of dark night winds and by the colors of the clay in drought-ridden valleys" (*C* 150, 151).[4] All need "a safe return," the novel's cohering theme, as Rocky prays before going to war. Gallup survivors hunger their return home, as the desert thirsts for rain: the people turn again to the old ceremonies.

Old and new adaptations of ritual accommodate transitional change. The Night Swan's Mexican cousin sells Josiah "wild-eyed" longhorns, animals of mixed breeding and hazel eyes, more deer than cattle. "If it's going to be a drought these next few years," Josiah plans, "then we need some special breed of cattle" (*C* 75). And so the totemic stock range as Tayo's brown and white misfits, magically wild and mottled á la Faulkner's "Spotted Horses" and Iyetiko of the Laguna Fire Society: "Tayo watched them disappear over the horizon, their ivory hides shining, speckled brown like a butterfly's wing" (*C* 78). Tayo must round up these speckled mavericks, plunging through barbed-wired barricades with home "lodged deep in their bones" (*C* 188), headed "always south, to the Mexican desert where they were born" (*C* 197). He journeys south after the cattle, west to Old Betonie in Gallup, *down* east in a police car to Albuquerque after trying to gut Emo with a broken beer bottle ("east" here also in reference to his Oriental war duty and Rocky's death), *up* north to Ts'eh Montaño on Mount Taylor—the ceremonial six direction of Indian myth—and finally back to the middle in the Laguna kiva with the old cheani. Finding the cattle not south, but north on Mount Taylor (toward shipap origins and the land of the dead), at last Tayo realizes the significance of inverse transitions over the last one hundred years: "Gathering the spotted cattle was only one color of sand falling from the fingertips; the design was still growing, but already long ago it had encircled him" (*C* 196).

Tayo's quest north to the Keres place of mythic origin with Ts'eh, attended by her consort hunter on the sacred mountain, offers a mythological and somewhat mystical place of healing. This retreat grants him a measure of natural calmness and strength to resist the witchery ending a century-old transition between dark and light skins. The positive transition is coded chromatically: sunrise yellow highlights the blue emergence of night into day. The Keres see Yellow Woman, possibly Ts'eh's matrix, as goddess of the game, giver of women's dress, baskets, and place-names; she is attended by Arrow Youth, a brother or husband, friend of the Great Star. She is sometimes seen as Moon Mother of the War Twins, *Masewi* and *Oyoyewi*, who search for the sun, their lost father.[5]

The issue whether Ts'eh derives from the Pueblo goddess complex of Yellow Woman (K'o'tc'in^{Y}ina''k o), a mountain spirit with yellow face, as well as the generic term for mythic heroines of Laguna stories, or whether Emo and the others are possessed by witchery, stands secondary to the curative effect of the "plot" on Tayo. He comes to believe in the story of his life. The narrative resolves and heals. Silko layers one level of contrary events—love with a beautiful woman in the old ways, warring sadism among men crazed by their displaced Indianness in white America—with a second level of mythological overtone.

One culture's religion may register as another's superstition; between cultures, without ceremony, Tayo negotiates between belief and disbelief to purge his own schizophrenia. Instead of proving or disproving Ts'eh, then, Tayo simply witness her presence. Tayo's love is, after all, a giving of spirit, no less than religion. To believe in Ts'eh, to remember her healing effect on him, resists the despair that destroys young Indians through alcohol, drugs, car wrecks, suicide, and violence all across America. This love strengthens, whether a reader testifies to gods or witches, old medicine or new psychology. Belief, when it heals, contains good medicine, in any culture. "But as long as you remember what you have seen, then nothing is gone," Ts'eh tells Tayo. "As long as you remember, it is part of this story we have together" (*C* 231). The curative memory of love calms Tayo's nightmarish voices: his abandonment, dislocation, rejection, and battle fatigue. The orphan can then come home.

The mountain setting tonalizes Ts'eh's character and speaks for her in natural landscapes. Everywhere around this woman blooms a sky, clouds, stones, horizons, flowers, plants, and cloths of blue: the sky "a bright blue intensity that only autumn and the movement of the sun from its summer place in the sky could give it" (*C* 184). Blue signifies the traditional Laguna color of the west and the first of four worlds under ours, yellow the color of the north and the second world; bear lives in the blue west, mountain lion in the yellow north.[6] Mount Taylor rises northwest of Laguna, balancing the two directions, and from there Tayo scans the blue Pueblo crescent below, his people's homeland for some thousand years: "Years of wind and no rain had finally stripped the valley down to dark gray clay, where only the bluish salt brush could grow. Beyond the Rio Puerco, to the southeast, he could see the blue mountains east of the Rio Grande" (*C* 184). The land's blue threads tie back through the story: Josiah's blue-lined notepaper sends Tayo to the Night Swan's blue door and bed during the rain, and he goes on to find a third hazel-eyed outcast in Betonie, who wears a blue cotton workshirt in a hogan arched with "thick bluish green glass of Coke bottles" (*C* 120). Even the empathetic cowboy who wants to let Tayo go free on Mount Taylor is graced by a blue bandanna.

At Tayo's last meeting with Ts'eh, "blue-bellied clouds" hang "low over the mountain peaks," and he gathers "yellow pollen gently with a small blue feather from Josiah's pouch" (*C* 220). Ts'eh walks toward him through sunflowers, with her curved willow and "blue silk shawl" (recalling a century ago when the "blue lace shawl" lay under the Mexican outcast's tree). She collects blue-flowering roots of rain plants: "This one contains the color of the sky after a summer rainstorm. I'll take it from here and plant it in another place, a canyon where it hasn't rained for a while" (*C* 224).

Tayo and Ts'eh kneel at an ancient she-elk rock-carving, "a dark blue shadow on the cliff" (*C* 231), where they recognize the ceremony in the

[margin handwritten note: blue + yellow]

stars. They imagine themselves mythically and realistically to be characters in a story, as though somehow the living creations of this storytelling could stand outside looking in on themselves. Traditional to Indian myth, the storyteller's sense of ceremony frames the people's lives from within, casting the participant audience in tales that have always been tribal. Silko's personal relation as artist to her materials, both in and out of her novel, induces a similar kind of empathetic magic in the reader. Tayo's return to life initiates the reader's own sense of homecoming in the plot's resolution.

This lovely medicine woman, with relatives all over the Southwest, comes and goes like a spirit. She has a traditional Indian name stringing out so long that she goes by the nickname "Ts'eh," or water (a tie with *Tsi'-ty'icots'a* or Salt Woman, the pan-Pueblo spirit of pure water). Ts'eh Montaño, or "Water Mountain," seems a coded and composite reference to the spirit-woman who returns vitality to the arid desert for Indians, Mexicans, and whites alike, all embodied in Tayo, all sharing in the sickness and health of one another, many as one with the land.

Like the kurena, whose songs are sung from the corn harvest at the end of summer until the winter solstice, Ts'eh leaves going "uphill to the northeast" (*C* 234). Tayo witnesses a convergence of his mixed lifelines at the autumnal equinox, the celestial fusion of light and dark, analogous to this mixed blood, when summer and winter solstices balance zenith and nadir. Pueblo mythology is rich in this sense of changing balance.[7] In the four directions, plus the diagonal "south corner time" and "north corner time" (solstices) fusing up and down, appear the axes of the ceremonial six directions (see figure 1).

> The cloudy yellow sandstone of Enchanted Mesa was still smoky blue before dawn, and only a faint hint of yellow light touched the highest point of the mesa. All things seemed to converge there: roads and wagon trails, canyons with springs, cliff paintings and shrines, the memory of Josiah with his cattle, . . . Yet at that moment in the sunrise, it was all so beautiful, everything, from all directions, evenly, perfectly, balancing day with night, summer months with winter. The valley was enclosing this totality, like the mind holding all thoughts together in a single moment. (*C* 237)

A hundred years ago, Betonie told Tayo, the Indian holy men saw that "the balance of the world had been disturbed," when whites came buying land, logging, mining, killing bears and mountain lions for sport, not need. There would be "droughts and harder days to come" (*C* 186). So by Tayo's day, young Indian was heroes die "defending the land they had already

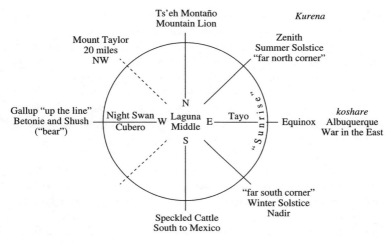

Figure 1

lost" (*C* 169), and Emo wears a bronze star on a blue ribbon for blowing up Japs (*C* 164), while whites run cattle on Indian lands: "the lie was destroying the Indian people" (*C* 204). Tayo cuts open the barbed wire fence to retrieve his stolen cattle on Mount Taylor, and Silko intrudes:

> If the white people never looked beyond the lie, to see that theirs was a nation built on stolen land, then they would never be able to understand how they had been used by the witchery; they would never know that they were still being manipulated by those who know how to stir the ingredients together: white thievery and injustice boiling up the anger and hatred that would finally destroy the world: the starving against the fat, the colored against the white. (*C* 191)

What is the lie? In the contemporary imagery of *Ceremony*, it is the pretense that peoples fenced apart can live by " the plastic and neon, the concrete and steel." More personally, the lie comes in forgetting ceremonial regards for all life forms growing in transitions. It is thinking to possess human as nonhuman, to kill for "things"; the destroyers "destroy the feeling people have for each other" (*C* 229). The Indian traditionally counters in offerings of corn pollen and turquoise, rain clouds and sandstone, squash and melons, myth and ritual—a ceremonial life beyond owning things, free of possessing land or other people. But Josiah and Betonie, surrogate fathers, remind Tayo of a simple Indian belief: everything that is *is*.

Indians cannot abnegate responsibility for their own lives maligning whites. To hate whites for their hatreds will destroy Indians.

All peoples stand accountable to all other peoples, the old ways hold; the mixed breed is living testimony to the transitions, the changes, the old ways evolving constantly into new variables. The ceremonies promise renewal out of the "end" of temporary life forms: continuity from one generation to the next, rain one day to end the drought, water to complement sun, a restoration of health after sickness, balance over time. The ancestral belief in natural benevolence through time orders the way-things-are, even when life seems lost in the moment.

The fear of destruction is real enough, witchery or not. As the Pueblos only too well know, uranium gorged from the Cebolleta land grant was first exploded over White Sands to the south. The threat of atomic annihilation unites all peoples again into "one clan," if nations are to avert "witchery's final ceremonial sand painting." Even grandma's "old clouded-up eyes," thinking she was seeing the sun rise, could see the initial holocaust over Trinity Site when the desert sand burned to glass under a nuclear cloud (*C* 245).[8] Nuclear devastation is witchery's inversion of the "sunrise" that begins and ends the story.

Back home the "destroyers" manipulate Indian people's despair. Tormented veterans drink cheap wine by night tumbleweed fires near the first uranium mine, blame and forget and wound their own brothers. Self-tortures stun them into destroying others, martyring the half-breed Harley over barbed wire fencing, cutting the whorls from his toes. The Indians' hatred of themselves and their oppressors fuels "witchery." This is a way of voicing a realistic state of fear, not just paranoia or superstition. It generates from an ominous sense of unreality and cultural dissociation that divides oppressed peoples among themselves.[9]

Nearing the autumnal equinox, then, Tayo at last knows his marginality must engender a courage to trust that "the pattern of the ceremony was in the stars": "The sun was nearing its autumn place in the sky, each day dropping lower, leaving more and more of the sky undilute blue" (*C* 238). He returns to a belief in himself, consistent with belief in the world that tells his story. His mixed blood fuses peoples divided over time: "He cried the relief he felt at finally seeing the pattern, the way all the stories fit together—the old stories, the war stories, their stories—to become the story that was still being told. He was not crazy; he had never been crazy. He had only seen and heard the world as it always was: no boundaries, only transitions through all distances and time" (*C* 246). The equinox is his ceremonial confluence: "A transition was about to be completed: the sun was crossing the zenith to a winter place in the sky, a place where prayers of long winter nights would call out the long summer days of new growth" (*C* 247).

A sense of ceremony, restored to Tayo, also instills positive abstinence, knowing what *not* to do. The curing for the poison in people's bellies comes in *not* countering bitterness bitterly, in gathering Ts'eh's rain root seeds to end the drought. By extension, Tayo's positive nonaction is not to kill Emo: the wise patience, the discipline, the informed waiting counseled by the care of ceremonial design. The alternative to violence rests where it always has: "They were taking him home." The stars group in patterns, the land grows in cycles, all peoples gather as families in a house made of pollen, rain, sun, earth, darkness, and dawn. "The transition was completed. In the west and in the south too, the clouds with round heavy bellies had gathered for the dawn. . . . The ear for the story and the eye for the pattern were theirs; the feeling was theirs: we came out of this land and we are hers" (*C* 255).

K'o·'tc'in^Yina·'k o shines among kachina spirits in the dawning sun's "yellow light across the clouds," the "yellow river sand," and in the "pale yellow" leaves of the cottonwood by the river (*C* 255). Just as his mother, Laura (from laurel for the victory of the century-old ceremony), returned naked at sunrise to cross the river, seeded with Tayo, so her son now comes home, across the river at dawn, to right her supposed waywardness. The kiva elders gather to confirm Tayo's story of the spirit-woman's fertile return. Inside the Pueblo now, the breed is acknowledged as one of "the people," a storied warrior who helped bring native life back into balance.

The novel moves from sunrise to sunrise, spring through a complete seasonal cycle to fall, on the promise of a new day returning. The threads of the web must be tied up: Harley and Leory dead in the wrecked pickup, Emo killing Pinkie and ostracized to California. A reader feels something hasty in this ending, the stars wheeling round while young men die pointlessly: but these names serve less as characters in the story, more as signs of the destructive self-hatred in young Indians encased in shells, veterans sucked empty over a century of foreign and civil wars.[10] Grandma is no longer interested in the gossip of these war stories. Her grandson has been taken into the reconstructed kiva. The "Whirling Darkness" has turned back on itself.

If words, truly regarded from Indian beliefs, act out their beings-as-they-are, witchery witches itself, devouring its own belly in the centripetal motions basic to Pueblo worldviews. Like comes from like, as Alfonso Ortiz observes.[11] "It is dead for now." Anticipatory of winter storytelling, the people face a new day, scatter pollen trails for spirits to travel, and chant blessings in the old ways at the end of the novel:

> Sunrise,
> accept this offering
> Sunrise.

Notes

1. Page numbers cited in the text refer to Leslie Marmon Silko, *Ceremony* (New York: Viking, 1977), cited as *C.*

2. Silko reading, MLA Conference for Teachers of Native American Literature, July 1977, Flagstaff, Arizona. Prologue talk to the poem "Storytelling."

3. Lawrence Evers and Dennis Carr, "A Conversation with Leslie Marmon Silko," *Sun Tracks* 3 (1976), 29–30.

4. Fred Eggan describes a *cheani* ceremony still practiced: "The shaman sets up an altar and uses a crystal to search for the heart of the patient which has been stolen by witches; with a bear's paw he rushes out and finds the patient's 'heart.'" Fred Eggan, *Social Organization of the Western Pueblos* (Chicago: University of Chicago Press, 1950), p. 281.

5. Hamilton A. Tyler, *Pueblo Animals and Myths* (Norman: University of Oklahoma Press, 1975), pp. 213, 227.

6. Franz Boas, *Keresan Texts*, Publications of the American Ethnological Society 8, pt. 1 (1928; reprint ed. New York: AMS Press Reprint, 1974), p. 282.

7. Against Tayo's sense of dislocation, place the ceremonial "attention to boundaries, to detail and order, and to the center," ideally speaking, in what Alfonso Ortiz sees as the Pueblo worldview:

> everything—animate and inanimate—counts and everything has its place in the cosmos. All things are thought to have two aspects, essence and matter. Thus everything in the cosmos is believed to be knowable and, being knowable, controllable. Effective control comes only from letter-perfect attention to detail and correct performance, thus the Pueblo emphasis on formulas, ritual, and repetition revealed in ritual drama. Among human beings the primary causal factors are mental and psychological states; if these are harmonious, the supernaturals will dispense what is asked and expected of them. If they are not, untoward consequences will follow just as quickly, because within this relentlessly interconnected universal whole the part can affect the whole, just as like can come from like. Men, animals, plants and spirits are intertransposable in a seemingly unbroken chain of being.

Alfonso Ortiz, "Ritual Drama and the Pueblo World View" in *New Perspectives on the Pueblos*, ed. Alfonso Ortiz (Albuquerque: University of New Mexico Press, 1972), p. 143.

In an interview with Dexter Fisher, Silko explains what it means for a storyteller to "make accessible certain ways of seeing things. This is the beauty of the old way": "Things about relationships. That's all there really is. There's your relationship with the dust that just blew in your face, or with the person who just kicked you end over end. That's all I'm interested in. You have to come to terms, to some kind of equilibrium with those people around you, those people who care for you, your environment." Leslie Marmon Silko and Dexter Fisher, "Stories and Their Tellers—A Conversation with Leslie Marmon Silko" in Dexter Fisher, *The Third Woman* (Boston: Houghton Mifflin, 1990), p. 22.

In 1957, four informants gave Florence Ellis a Laguna Origin Legend, including the statement:

> The Whites came out from the underworld, which we call Shipap, and went to Europe and South America as Your Father told them. Our Mother told her people they were to go south. She made a song naming all the places which they were to go. The people were in a kiva for several days trying to learn the song, which we still have today, but some went to sleep and when they awoke they heard only parts of it. When they left to go south they knew they would find Laguna because the song was like a map in their memory. Everything the people had done or were to do was in the song made for the Lagunas by Our Mother.

Florence H. Ellis "Anthropology of Laguna Pueblo Land Claims," *Pueblo Indians* 3 (New York: Garland, 1974), p. 13.

8. There are 43 uranium mines, 5 mills, and 31 mining companies digging up Indian lands in the Four Corners area, according to Simon Ortiz's *Fight Back: For the Sake of the People, for the Sake of the Land, INAD Literary Journal* 1, 1 (Albuquerque: Institute for Native American Development, 1980). The Jackpile open-pit uranium mine, on the Laguna Reservation, is the largest in the country. Grants, New Mexico advertises itself as "The Uranium Capital of the World," with a park dedicated to a Navajo, Paddy Martinez, who carried in a chunk of uranium ore lying outside his hogan one afternoon in 1953 (cf. Ortiz's "It Was That Indian" in *Fight Back*). Los Alamos, New Mexico, at the hub of the Pueblo crescent, is a small city of nuclear scientists spearheading the government's atomic energy research.

9. Pueblo witches or Two-Hearts are seen as "simply ordinary humans," Tyler notes, "who possess a special degree of supernatural power and direct it toward antisocial ends." Hamilton A. Tyler, *Pueblo Gods and Myths* (Norman: University of Oklahoma Press, 1964), p. 259.

10. An older oral tradition of type characterization may be at work here. The ethnopsychology of Pueblo narrative, Tedlock observes in Zuni tales, implodes character development in ritualized cultural types whose actions spell out their names. Dennis Tedlock, "Pueblo Literature" in Ortiz, ed., *New Perspectives*, pp. 230–37.

11. Ortiz, "Ritual Drama and the Pueblo World View" in Ortiz, ed., *New Perspectives*, p. 142.

The Transformation

Tayo's Genealogy in Ceremony

JOHN PURDY

◆　　◆　　◆

T AYO IS AN INTRIGUING and complex character, and thanks to Leslie Silko's abilities as a storyteller, his story is engaging. As we read of his search for a cure, we sympathize with his plight, and when Tayo confronts Emo and the evil forces he represents at book's end, we support him. Like Tayo, we come to recognize the responsibilities he has to his world, but also that meeting these responsibilities results in his gaining the power to survive the confrontation through his awareness of appropriate action, or inaction in this case. Like Laguna oral literature, *Ceremony* is concerned with entertainment and enduring cultural values, and when Silko writes of a man trying to come to grips with a chaotic world seemingly bent on self-destruction, she does what past Laguna storytellers have done: clarify the changes in their world and dramatize how old ways may be adapted to accommodate those changes. Tayo's story emerges from a longstanding literary tradition which continues to define and redefine the sources of power found in the Laguna landscape and to provide knowledge of the ways that these sources may be utilized. As Tayo moves through his narrative, his awareness of the relationship between his experiences and those told of in the stories of his people grows, and he in turn moves from an isolated, ill individual to a powerful, competent representative of his people. In a word, he becomes a hero.

Silko's use of traditional stories as bases for her fiction is easily demonstrated. One need only to look to her short works such as "Yellow Woman" to see how she acknowledges the relevance of the old stories to an understanding of the present. In it, a woman is carried away, quite literally, by a man she meets near the stream on the outskirts of Laguna, and throughout the story she continually asks herself if the man is actually a Mountain Katsina and if she is a modern incarnation of Kochininako or Yellow Woman. Silko never overtly answers the question, but the mere fact that another, updated version of the stories of Yellow Woman is being "told" is answer enough. Yellow Woman, the perennial heroine, lives through Silko's story. Tayo shares a similar life in that Silko conscientiously tells the stories that relate to Tayo's life and from which his story emerges. When she tells of Hummingbird's and Fly's endeavors to set the world right and bring the rains back, she establishes the ways that individuals may act for the people and work transformations through correctly ordered actions and perseverance. And when she tells of Sun Man's confrontation with the Evil Gambler, Kaup'a'ta, she provides both the genesis of the plot for Tayo's narrative and his genealogy as a fictional character.

Sun Man climbs a mountain to rescue the rain clouds from Kaup'a'ta. He is successful because Spider Woman tells him what the Gambler will do, so he can anticipate events and react accordingly, thus turning the Gambler's evil back on himself. Obviously, these characters have contemporary counterparts in Silko's tale; *Ceremony* has its own hero who climbs the mountain and who with the aid of mysterious beings—Ts'eh and the hunter—is able to bring the rains and turn evil into its own defeat. If there is doubt about Emo's nature, one need only remember the scene in which Silko describes him playing with the teeth of a dead Japanese officer. He rolls them like dice; he is quite literally gambling for Tayo's life, and he nearly wins. If there is any doubt about Tayo's character, one need only re-examine the stages in his story that speak of his identity and also the ways by which he comes to understand what is happening in his world and how to react to the changes he sees taking place. His strength comes from his awareness that his story is very similar to those he heard from Josiah as a child.

The earliest event in Tayo's life is quite revealing. As Silko carefully notes, Tayo was four when his mother, Laura, left him with her kin—Josiah, her grandmother, and Auntie. Four is a number often used in sacred contexts, and this is his age when his memory begins. He lives with the family from that point on, but Auntie (Laura's older sister) will not let

Tayo forget his questionable parentage nor his mother's wild behavior. After Laura's death, Auntie periodically draws Tayo aside to tell him stories about Laura that, at first, seem to be delivered with the sole, malicious intent of tormenting and humbling the boy by emphasizing his isolation and his inferiority to her son, Rocky. On one such occasion, however, Silko provides an added dimension to Auntie's burden as the self-proclaimed mediator between her family's actions and its reputation in the community. The event takes an interesting turn from the Christian morality that would seem to be Auntie's prime concern:

> "One morning," she [Auntie] said, "before you were born, I got up to go outside, right before sunrise. I knew she [Laura] had been out all night because I never heard her come in. Anyway, I thought I would walk down toward the river. I just had a feeling, you know. I stood on that sandrock, above the big curve in the river, and there she was, coming down the trail on the other side. . . . I am only telling you this because she was your mother, and you have to understand. . . . Right as the sun came up, she walked under that big cottonwood tree, and I could see her clearly: she had no clothes on. Nothing. She was completely naked except for her high-heel shoes." (73)

Readers might interpret this passage as proof of Auntie's narrow nature, as well as Laura's wild abandon. The younger sister could be viewed as another lost soul, an Indian going "bad." However, there is another possibility; by fulfilling her role as an older sister and family matriarch, Auntie helps—in her own way—her adopted child understand his character by emphasizing certain qualities of the scene she witnessed long ago.

In the first place, she notes that the event took place *before* Tayo was born. Likewise she is very specific about *where* it took place—"on that sandrock, above the big curve in the river"—as well as when—at dawn. The earliest events in Tayo's life story are tied to water and a specific place and time, all of which are associated with the Katsina. As Silko and Elsie Clews Parsons both note, the Katsina of Laguna are traditionally connected with water, either rainfall or the river (Parsons 176). Like Yellow Woman, Laura has gone to the river where meetings between humans and Katsina have been known to take place. Moreover, Auntie tells Tayo the exact place on the river, the same place, Silko suggests later, where the Laguna people wait for the arrival of the Katsina during a ceremony. Also, she sees Laura at dawn, a time associated once again with Katsina (Parsons 179). In brief, Silko implies that her protagonist may in fact be directly related to, and therefore aided by, Katsina; his conception and birth may very well conform to those of other heroes in the Laguna tradition.

This connection becomes clearer after Tayo visits Betonie. Through Betonie's help, Tayo initiates a journey that begins with a search for the spotted cattle on Mount Taylor, a place once again bearing numerous sacred associations with the Katsina (Boas 38). This is where he meets Ts'eh; since their meeting follows immediately Silko's telling of the Gambler story, the reader begins to draw parallels between the actions presented in it and those of the main narrative. Given Tayo's obscure parentage, the similarities are cause for wonder. Before Tayo begins climbing the mountain, however, he spends the night with the mysterious Ts'eh, and this act has a profound effect on his ability to complete his quest. Like the meetings between the Mountain Katsina and Yellow Woman, theirs happens near a river, and it provides him with a powerful accomplice; interestingly, their lovemaking is described in terms appropriate to Tayo's developing character: "it was the edge of a steep riverbank crumbling under the downpour until suddenly it all broke loose and collapsed into itself" (188). The drought is nearing an end, and this is a direct result of Tayo's dawning knowledge of appropriate action, as his movements the next morning indicate.

In her seminal article "An Act of Attention: Event Structure in *Ceremony*" (see this volume), Elaine Jahner focuses on Tayo's greeting of the dawn to support her contention that the novel's structure is based upon events that mark a pattern of convergence and then emergence. Her insight is intriguing, for such a pattern exists in Laguna oral tradition and ceremonialism. Stories tell of the people converging in a previous world and then emerging into this one (which is only one event in a long history of transformations), and when a ceremony is to begin, the people converge by societies, then emerge into public celebration. As Jahner points out, the major events in Tayo's story are those points where "time, place and story" intersect (44). These are times when Tayo makes crucial associations between his own experiences and those of his predecessors, and Jahner's definition suggests that an event is significant when it marks the convergence of the story of an individual with the perceptions and life ways of his people as related in their oral literature. Such moments lead to insight and knowledge and, in turn, to appropriate action.

On the morning Tayo begins his climb, he sings to the dawn. He also notes the "damp and cold" quality of the air. His actions and the conditions of his world mark a vast change from those described at the opening of the book, when he was passive and inert in the hot, dry, drought air. Things are changing, and Tayo is at the cutting edge of a transition. Significantly, he breathes deeply; breathing in Laguna ritualism is an act of blessing (Parsons 421). The effects on Tayo are obvious: "Being alive was all right then; he had not breathed like that for a long time" (189). Since his visit to Betonie and his night with Ts'eh, his cure has taken the form of a journey— a series of instances in which he perceives his own experience through the knowledge gained from Laguna oral literature.

As he waters his horse in the dawn, Silko provides another important connection between Tayo's story and Sun Man's:

> Before the dawn, southeast of the village, the bells would announce their approach, the sound shimmering across the sand hills, followed by the clacking of turtleshell rattles—all these sounds gathering with the dawn. Coming to the river, faintly at first, faint as the pale yellow light emerging across the southeast horizon, the sounds gathering intensity from the swelling colors of the dawn. And at the moment the sun appeared over the edge of the horizon, they suddenly appeared on the riverbank, the Ka't'sina approaching the river crossing. (189)

Tayo rises to sing his song, and by this point in her narrative, Silko has given her readers enough evidence to make crucial associations that will allow them to share in the event by recognizing its significance to Tayo's development and character. Again, water and the dawn are connected with his actions, but the readers also relate Tayo's memory of a ceremonial place by the river, where the Katsina appear at dawn with qualities of the earlier story Auntie tells about Laura. Strange forces are at work in the narrative and the minds of Silko's readers, for whom Tayo's song becomes an appropriate observance of an ancient relationship between his people and forces in their world. As Tayo rides into mountains, he looks at his world differently; his story now has purpose and direction through his renewed knowledge of the powers that have aided, or challenged, past heroes in their quests.

Tayo's experiences on the mountain are confrontational, like those of Sun Man in the story Silko tells; however, rather than confront the Evil Gambler at this point, Tayo confronts himself. Although he recognizes the sacred associations between this place and his people, he is hampered by his fear of the white rancher, Floyd Lee. Lee "owns" the mountain now and has the forces of law and order on his side, but there is another Laguna order that predates Lee's by generations and survives, despite expensive fences and other physical boundaries. Tayo's fear is so great that it threatens to turn him from his journey, but as a hero in the ancient tradition, he finds the courage to continue through the aid of another character who, like Ts'eh, appears somewhat mysteriously to play a crucial role in Tayo's development.

As he lies on the earth under a pine tree, Tayo has a vision. First he goes through a transformation, becoming "insubstantial" and therefore free from the fear of the riders Lee employs to guard his property. Then he sees a mountain lion:

> The mountain lion came out from a grove of oak trees in the middle of the clearing. He did not walk or leap or run; his motions were like the shimmering of tall grass in the wind. . . . Relentless motion was the lion's greatest beauty, moving like mountain clouds with the wind, changing substance and color in rhythm with the contours of the mountain peaks: dark as lava rock, and suddenly as bright as a field of snow. When the mountain lion stopped in front of him, it was not hesitation, but a chance for the moonlight to catch up with him. (204)

The lion's actions speak of his fitness to his surroundings; there is no hesitation on his part as he moves freely and confidently in "rhythm" or harmony with his world. And Tayo recognizes the importance of the meeting. He, too, needs confidence in the old ways of moving with ancient powers to help him face the Floyd Lees of the modern world. He must fulfill his responsibilities, so he immediately rises to his knees to address the being before him: "mountain lion becoming what you are with each breath, your substance changing with the earth and the sky" (204). Tayo learns a valuable lesson about the nature of change, and when the lion leaves, he pours pollen into the tracks in devotion to "Mountain lion, the hunter, Mountain lion, the hunter's helper" (205). It is a curious act, but one which is obviously full of meaning, and as readers attempt to fit it into the progression of Tayo's journey, Silko gives it significance by connecting it to subsequent events on the mountain.

First, Tayo finds his cattle. Has the hunter's helper responded to Tayo's actions? Then, Tayo is captured, but Lee's fence riders are drawn away from their prisoner by the lure of the mountain lion. The mountain lion's presence quite literally saves Tayo. Next, as Tayo moves down the mountain, a storm approaches, so he seeks shelter in a scrub-oak grove: "He lay in a shallow depression and heaped piles of dry leaves over himself until he felt warm again" (212). This event seems insignificant, compared with those preceding it, but it is the final step in a process—a sequence of events or actions—that transforms Tayo from a fearful, ineffectual individual into a traditional Laguna hero capable of confronting the evil forces at work in his world, and surviving.

There is another published version of the story of the Evil Gambler that provides further connections between past narratives and Tayo's. In John

M. Gunn's *Schat-chen: History, Traditions and Narratives of the Queres Indians of Laguna and Acoma*, it is Pais-chun-ni-moot, or Sun Youth, who undertakes the journey to the Evil Gambler's mountain stronghold to end the drought that threatens the people, and he is the offspring of the Sun and Yellow Woman. Pais-chun-ni-moot first climbs a mountain to meet his father, who then takes him to the people who, in turn ask the boy to perform four tasks to prove his birthright. For the last, they place him in a room full of lions, "and the lions fawned upon him" (Gunn 163). Then the people perform the initial ceremony to celebrate Sun's child:

> And when the sun saw that the people were convinced, he ordered them to go to the mountains and gather leaves. These they brought and made from them a bed for the youth; and they warmed him in the leaves until he was made in the image of his father.
>
> Then the people cried, "Behold Pais-chun-ni-moot! He will go to the mountain where Kai-na-ni [Gambler] dwells and release our people." (Gunn 163)

Silko constructs a similar process taking Tayo through a like transformation from a lost and wandering individual to a character who can perceive the significance of events and the forces that move people, and who can respond accordingly. This knowledge provides him with the power to succeed in his final confrontation with Emo.

Subsequent events progressively enhance the mythical implications of Tayo's story. As he walks off the mountain through the storm the following morning, Tayo realizes that he and the mountain lion have been saved by the falling snow, which Silko immediately associates with the lion: "the snowflakes were swirling in tall chimneys of wind, filling his tracks like pollen sprinkled in the mountain lion's footprints" (215). Almost immediately, he is joined by a mysterious man carrying a deer; he is dressed in traditional clothing: rabbit fur and, for a cap, a fur that "looked like mountain lion skin" (216). As the two men continue down the mountain, the hunter sings. The first song Tayo hears is from Laguna, but the man sings songs from other pueblos where, interestingly enough, Mountain Lion is also a powerful figure in literature and ceremony. When the two arrive at the cabin, the accumulating snow threatens to break the branches of a tree near the house, and the hunter makes a simple statement connecting the storm to Ts'eh: "The tree . . . you [Ts'eh] better fold up the blanket before the snow storm breaks the branches" (218). She goes into the bedroom where the "black storm-patterned blanket was spread open across the gray flagstone" (218). The storm ends when she folds it; she has brought her two men home safely after their successful trips onto the mountain.

By this point in the narrative, we can accept the possibility that Ts'eh's blanket may bring snow, and we can believe that Tayo walks with the same hunter we have already met on the mountain because we, too, have made the same associations that transform Tayo from a man lost in the fog into an effective hero. Like characters in other Laguna stories, Tayo has gained personal relationships with powerful beings in his world—beings similar to those Silko carefully describes in the traditional narratives she reproduces—and we know he will counter the influences of Emo and his cronies. Like his predecessors, the heroes of Laguna literature, Tayo is a responsive, and therefore powerful, human being who leads the way for his people as they try to react to vast changes in their land. A contemporary Laguna storyteller has written an imaginative narrative that has its basis in the narratives of her people—in the characters, landscape, motivations, and, most of all, the desire to provide a continuity between the past and the present. However, her narrative goes beyond what has already been told to address an audience that her ancient, and contemporary, oral counterparts could never reach. When Tayo moves in the imagination of a nontribal person, he brings to life the traditional Laguna possibility that one person may work a massive transformation in the world and bring about sweeping, beneficial change through close attention to forces in the world that respond to considerate and responsive actions. Silko brings the stories to life today and demonstrates their global significance.

Works Cited

Boas, Franz. *Keresan Texts*. New York: American Ethnological Society, 1925.

Gunn, John M. *Schat-chen: History, Traditions and Narratives of the Queres Indians of Laguna and Acoma*. Albuquerque: Albright & Anderson, 1917.

Jahner, Elaine. "An Act of Attention: Event Structure in *Ceremony*." *American Indian Quarterly*, 5:1 (1979), 37–46.

Parsons, Elsie Clews. *Pueblo Indian Religion*. Chicago: University of Chicago Press, 1939.

Silko, Leslie Marmon. *Ceremony*. New York: New American Library, 1978.

Forms of Biculturalism in Southwestern Literature

The Work of Rudolfo Anaya and Leslie Marmon Silko

REED WAY DASENBROCK

◆　◆　◆

O NE OF THE IMPORTANT ISSUES in the consideration of
any work by "minority" or "ethnic" writers is the question of catego-
rization: In what category does one place the work? Even more basically,
what does one call the work? Should one, to use the examples that will
concern us here, consider the work of Rudolfo Anaya as Chicano literature and Leslie Marmon Silko as Native American literature? Or are their
works more usefully considered as part of American literature? Such questions are often dismissed as trivial by those committed to the notion that
we should (and can) approach works of literature in themselves, that the
categories with which we organize literature don't really matter and
are only an administrative or institutional convenience. My sense—in
contrast—is that categories are never neutral or simply instrumental, that
the categories we use help shape the phenomena we perceive. So these
questions are not simply questions for booksellers or librarians. The assumption that such categories are unimportant depends upon the prior
assumption that we can perceive and describe literary works in some neutral way. But as critical descriptions are always generic descriptions and, as I
hope to show, generic descriptions are culturally grounded, we therefore
need to reflect critically on the categories we use in our criticism if those
categories are to enable—not disable—our criticism.

In this context, though there is a good deal that could be said in favor of
considering the work of writers such as Anaya and Silko in either the
broad, inclusive category of American literature or the narrower or more
precise one of ethnic identity, Chicano or Native American, I want to argue
that both such rubrics are likely to prove at least partially misleading. I
would want to call them Southwestern writers instead. This doesn't mean

that the term "Southwestern" literature refers to a group of works with a specifiable set of features. There is no genre of Southwestern literature. Nevertheless, as I hope to make clear, the term can retain a certain utility despite—or perhaps because of—its lack of precision. There is a characteristically Southwestern generic (or perhaps cross-generic) space.

The term Southwestern literature is, of course, not a neutral descriptive term. By naming a literature by reference to a region, it immediately places the phenomenon it seeks to describe within the context of American regionalism: we have had the New England local color movement of Mary E. Wilkins Freeman and Sarah Orne Jewett, the Midwestern regionalism of Hamlin Garland and later Willa Cather, the Southern Renaissance of Faulkner, the Fugitives, Eudora Welty, and others, and now yet another region finds its voice in the work of Frank Waters, Edward Abbey, N. Scott Momaday, Simon Ortiz, Anaya, Silko, and others.[1] To be a region of American literature is to be interesting because different from the rest of the country and yet not so different as not to seem part of America. The interest and tension of regional literature is that of a part-whole relationship, and historically speaking the literature of a given area has ceased to flourish when the part became enough like the whole that the tension between them ceased or at least ceased to be interesting. There is thus a tradition of regional literatures within American literature but no one regional literature has really created and sustained a tradition of its own. The history of regional literature in this country is that of a continual dying away or perhaps dying into the mainstream tradition.

Southwestern literature looked far more like these other regional phenomena before the explosion over the last fifteen years of Native American and Chicano writing.[2] The standard line about the Southwest is to call it tricultural, as all of the tourist brochures do, yet in the very way they say it, like Catholic theologians they seem to make the three into one, implying that a harmonious convergence has taken place producing a unified culture with tricultural origins. It was probably possible to maintain this view as long as Anglo writing about the area predominated: it is no accident the the tourist brochures sound like the primitivistic rhapsodies of Mary Austin and Mabel Dodge Luhan. But the emergence of Chicano and Native American writing has clearly established that the three cultures haven't harmoniously converged; the perspectives and voices of the different communities remain radically distinct. This does not imply that they have had no effect on each other; just the contrary. The Southwest is less a region with *a* culture of its own than a zone of cultural contact, as it has been at least since Coronado. But, as the mention of Coronado should remind us, cultural contact in the Southwest has meant above all cultural conflict. So I would say that Southwestern literature has less *a* single tradition than a heritage of conflict and contact. But this could be put the other way: by now its tradition is this heritage of conflict and contact.

In what follows, I would like to make these general considerations with which I have begun more precise, and I would like to do so by discussing the work of Rudolfo Anaya and Leslie Marmon Silko, arguably the best Southwestern Chicano writer and the best Southwestern Native American writer. This is admittedly only a small portion of the rich panorama of contemporary Southwestern writing, but it is an apposite one in that their work seems at the very center of contemporary Southwestern literature, affording many rich examples of such cultural conflict and contact. For example, Antonio Marez, the protagonist of Anaya's first and best novel, *Bless Me, Ultima* (1971), is caught among the conflicting authorities of the *curandera (or curer)* Ultima, the Church, and school, and it is easy to see these three as figures for the Indian, Spanish, and Anglo cultures. But of course Ultima is Spanish speaking, one sign of the synthesis between Spanish and Indian culture that has formed Mexican and Mexican-American culture.[3] But that Chicano culture is not completely unified in itself, as Anaya shows in the novel by the conflicts between the priest and Ultima, between the *vaqueros* of the *llano* (or plains) and the farmers of the valley, and finally between the more traditional and the more Americanized members of the community.

Tayo, the protagonist of Silko's masterpiece, *Ceremony* (1977), is of mixed blood, half-Laguna and half-white. His fellow Indians, particularly Emo, his *bête-noire*, taunt him by calling him a half-breed, but as the story evolves, it is Emo who is revealed to be the real half-breed, poisoned by the white ways, while Tayo turns or returns to his native tradition. And though *Ceremony*, like *Bless Me, Ultima*, is predominately about two cultures, the missing third enters in, if somewhat schematically, as if the authors feel they need all three. The cattle whose purchase by Josiah and rescue by Tayo are so central to the novel are Mexican; a Mexican woman plays an important role in Tayo's maturation; and Betonie, the Navajo medicine man who guides Tayo during his cure, is also of mixed blood, with a Mexican grandmother.

Thus, if we take these two novels as representative—which I think we can—Southwestern literature is a literature of cultures still in a contact which involves conflict. Even where a melding of cultures has taken place, that only sets up new conflicts in turn, as the Anglo influence on Indian culture creates anti-traditional Indians like Emo who then enter into conflict with more traditional Indians. The analogous theme of the pocho is a central theme in Chicano literature and is a major source of tension within the world depicted by Chicano writers.[4]

✻   So I would insist that no unified culture or voice has emerged that we can call Southwestern; the essence of the Southwest is a diversity that does not comfortably coexist, and there is in fact great diversity and conflict within each community as well as across the three major communities. But that is paradoxically one reason why the term Southwestern remains of use: we need a term to describe the literature that emerges from the cultural contact situation of the Southwest. Anaya's work can indeed be considered within Chicano literature; Silko's within Native American literature. But we need a term to show what these works have in common with, say, the work of an Anglo writer like John Nichols who has depicted in his work exactly the same conflict of cultures.[5]

I would therefore say that the term Southwestern literature remains a useful term if we use it, not to suggest an unequivocal, local colorist tradition, but to mark out a zone, existing in social life and depicted in literature, in which these differing traditions come into play. There is thus no single Southwestern literary tradition, but there is a space we can usefully call Southwestern.

NOW, WHAT USE IS THERE in calling that space Southwestern as opposed to dissolving these works into the constituent and far more precise categories of Native American, Chicano, and Anglo literature? One use we have already seen is that these works are profoundly about these cultural contacts and conflicts, so thematic analyses of these works should profit from keeping the larger Southwestern context in mind. But what I would also like to suggest is that formal or generic analyses of these works have only to gain as well. For example, something that has troubled readers of Anaya's collection of short stories, *The Silence of the Llano*, and Silko's collection, *Storyteller*, is that they reprint without alteration parts of Anaya's and Silko's earlier novels. (In Silko's case, the evolution is even more complex, as independently written poems and tales were woven into *Ceremony* and then published separately in *Storyteller*.) The reaction of an Anglo reader to this is easy enough to sketch: since Aristotle, a central notion of Western aesthetics has been that a work of art ought to possess organic unity or coherence, what Stephen Dedalus after Aquinas called *integritas*. It ought to be of one piece. From an Aristotelian perspective, taking material from one work and putting it in another is a failure of design and coherence. The integrity of each work is violated by such reuse. But Silko and

Anaya have a rather different notion of coherence, I think, and they give us in their works the terms with which to understand their practice. We need to understand their cultural context before we can understand the generic identity or coherence of their works.

These writers were born into societies with rather different notions and forms of narrative from that implicit in the tradition of the novel. Antonio in *Bless Me, Ultima* loves to go to his uncles' in El Puerto because there he can sit and listen to *cuentos* all night long. The Hispanic culture in New Mexico has a rich tradition of *cuentos* and *cuentistas*, tales and storytellers, and some of the *cuentos* that have been collected in rural New Mexico are in origin medieval Spanish, even Moorish, stories that have been transmitted orally across the centuries.[6] In such an oral tradition, material is of course freely reused, by one *cuentista* combining stories or by another retelling a *cuento* he has heard. T. S. Eliot wrote, "Immature poets borrow; mature poets steal," and Eliot's dictum perfectly expresses the attitude toward "originality" expressed by an oral tradition such as that of the *cuentistas*, except that Eliot's use of the term "steal" betrays his own consciousness of the normative Western attitude he is opposing. Anaya has himself gestured toward the importance of the *cuento* tradition for his work, not just in Antonio's occasional references but in his having translated a collection of *cuentos*.

This emphasis on the *cuento* form explains a number of formal characteristics of Anaya's work. The stories abstracted from his novels to form *The Silence of the Llano* are in fact much less *cuento*-like than many other self-contained narrative units of his novels, the passages about the Golden Carp in *Bless Me, Ultima* and the visions of Crispin in *Heart of Aztlán* and of Salomon in *Tortuga*. These take place in a frankly other-worldly realm in which cosmic/mythic powers reveal themselves to the protagonists and direct their actions in the "this world" of the rest of the novel. These are far more self-consciously written or literary than the *cuentos* and they don't tend to work within the orthodox Catholic landscape of the *cuentos*, but they share with the *cuentos* a sense that another more fundamental spiritual realm is out there waiting to be encountered and that this encounter can powerfully shape and redirect our actions in this world.[7] And the manner in which these *cuento*-like narratives interpenetrate with the rest of Anaya's more conventionally novelistic narratives is a reflection of the way the realm of the spiritual interpenetrates the world of the ordinary both in the *cuentos* and in Anaya's own fiction. The formal discontinuities and lack of Aristotelian coherence in Anaya's long works of fiction can thus be traced to the fact that another, *cuento*-based sense of narrative is operative in his novels.

Leslie Marmon Silko has been even more explicit about her culture's sense of narrative and how that informs her fiction. *Storyteller* revolves, as the title suggests, around storytelling and the figure of the storyteller, but *Ceremony* does this as well. Stories shape our lives, in her account, both by giving form to events and by suggesting in advance the form events will have. In a flashback at the beginning of *Ceremony*, Tayo is trying to inspire an Anglo soldier to keep going in their attempt to carry out the wounded Rocky, Tayo's cousin:

> Tayo talked to the corporal almost incessantly, walking behind him with his end of the blanket stretcher, telling him it wasn't much farther now, and all down hill from there. He made a story for all of them, a story to give them strength. The words of the story poured out of his mouth as if they had substance, pebbles and stone extending to hold the corporal up, to keep his knees from buckling, to keep his hands from letting go of the blanket. (11)

And despite the "as if " in this passage, Silko's view is that stories do have substance. We all script our actions in advance or else have them scripted for us, and the stories we hear and tell are these scripts. The climactic action (or rather nonaction) of *Ceremony* is when Tayo doesn't kill Emo in order to save his friend Harley. Tayo presents his choice as that between two stories, one plotted by the "witchery," the other by the ceremony Tayo has undergone:

> It had been a close call. The witchery had almost ended the story according to its plan; Tayo had almost jammed the screwdriver into Emo's skull the way the witchery had wanted, savoring the yielding bone and membrane as the steel ruptured the brain. Their deadly ritual for the autumn solstice would have been completed by him. He would have been another victim, a drunk Indian war veteran settling an old feud; and the Army doctors would say that the indications of this end had been there all along, since his release from the mental ward at the Veterans' Hospital in Los Angeles. . . . He had arrived at a convergence of patterns; he could see them clearly now. The stars had always been with them, existing beyond memory, and they were all held together there. . . . Accordingly, the story goes on with these stars of the old war shield; go on, lasting until the fifth world ends, then maybe beyond. (256–66)

And Tayo survives where the other Indian war vets do not because he has this faith in the old stories and ceremonies. He follows their plot; the others fall prey to white plots and die according to the end of the story they have chosen.

We thus get a far more explicit sense of the storytelling tradition and what it means for the characters from Silko's work than from Anaya's, even from *Ceremony* alone without the later volume *Storyteller*. This is because while Anaya is content to allude to the *cuento* tradition and put *cuento*-like stories, visions, and dreams in the minds and speeches of his characters, Silko runs much greater risk with the coherence of their work by putting her versions of traditional stories directly into *Ceremony*. Running throughout *Ceremony*, set off from the rest because printed as poetry and not given as the thoughts or speeches of any one character, are a number of traditional mythic stories, primarily about drought and how to end it.[8] These are the stories that we find in *Storyteller* as well, and each story is printed in a self-contained unit in *Storyteller*, whereas it may be dispersed through the narrative in *Ceremony*. The dispersal is far more powerful, especially when one recognizes the coherence of the dispersed story, because then one starts to look for (and find) connections between Tayo's story and the more explicitly mythical stories. Thus, Silko violates any Aristotelian notion of *integritas* because stories don't work that way in the world she is depicting. Precisely, the opposite of the Western tradition of closure and boundedness obtains: stories are valued for their overlap, for the way they lead to new stories in turn.

Thus, both Anaya and Silko tell us something about how they should be read, and it is important to listen for such clues, for if we approach their work with expectations based solely on Anglo-American cultural and narrative forms, we will misread because we will not understand their reliance on the different norms of their own culture. Forms and genres are culturally embedded, and the first step toward a proper appreciation and understanding of these Southwestern literary works is to recognize that we cannot impose our own cultural norms and forms on work with a different cultural context.

THAT IS THE FIRST and perhaps most important step. Yet it is crucial not to stop there, with a recognition of the otherness of these texts, for for if we concentrate exclusively on their otherness, on their roots in a culture foreign to us, then we may misread them in another, subtler way. First, we are much less likely to read them at all, as we will have categorized them as belonging to others, with little to say to us unless we are especially interested in that particular other. Second more important, though one must recognize the heritage of the literary forms of their own cultures in the work of Anaya and Silko (and other Chicano and Native American writers), it would be absurd to claim that such formal inheritances explain everything about the forms of these works. These works are after all novels with a fair number—if not all—of the typical characteristics of that Western form. *Bless Me, Ultima* is a classic bildungsroman, the account of a young boy's passage from innocence to experience. More specifically, it might be titled "A Portrait of the Artist as a Young Boy in a New Mexican Town," as it shares with Joyce's bildungsroman the voyage through the Church and an emerging—though in Anaya's case, far less explicit—sense of the protagonist's deeper vocation as in artist. *Ceremony* represents a latter, equally inevitable stage in the development toward maturity, which is the stage at which one has to cope—or at least try to cope—with the stresses and even disintegration experience can bring. This has been an important theme in American literature, and it had traditionally been the war novel (or, more precisely, the after-the-war novel) that has depicted this. *In Our Time* provides one familiar and apposite example of the kind of work I am referring to. Other works of Native American fiction have worked within this mode, which is unsurprising given the bleak landscape that Native American writers have to depict: D'Arcy McNickle's *The Surrounded* and James Welch's first two novels, *Winter in the Blood* and *The Death of Jim Loney*, are comparably naturalistic novels in which protagonists try—but fail—to cope with the stresses of their lives. And *Ceremony* clearly has generic affiliations with this naturalistic tradition of American literature.

Ceremony, however, is not entirely of this genre, for it breaks with it precisely where Tayo breaks with the story plotted by the witchery discussed above. The two breaks, in fact, are the same, for the story plotted by the witchery was a thoroughly naturalistic narrative of the war vet's failure to cope, of "a drunk Indian was veteran settling an old feud." Like Hemingway's Nick Adams or D'Arcy McNickle's Archilde but more violently, Tayo would have succumbed to the forces of disintegration, and *Ceremony* would have ended in a fitting manner for a naturalistic novel. But *Ceremony* invokes that kind of story only in the end to swerve deliberately away from it: the naturalistic mode is a representation of precisely what Tayo (and Silko with him) must transcend in order to achieve the wholeness of the ceremony. And Silko revises the naturalistic mode precisely to show Tayo's victory over it. Yet, that naturalistic mode has structured our experience of the novel for a long time, and that generic affiliation is therefore an important part of the book's meaning.

Moreover, it is important to realize as well that these works are in English, are part of English language literature simply by virtue of the language in which they are written. It is this fact more than any other that indicates the distance between them and their cultural roots: Silko is no traditional storyteller, Anaya no *cuentista*. Silko is certainly aware of this, as a major theme in *Ceremony* is how the ceremonies and stories must change in order to keep up with the changing circumstances the people find themselves in. The medicine man Betonie and the protagonist Tayo don't do things the old way, nor are they completely of the traditional culture, but their argument is that they are truer to the spirit of the old ceremonies than are the traditionalists who keep exactly to the letter of the old ways. As Betonie tells Tayo:

> The people nowadays have an idea about the ceremonies. They think the ceremonies must be performed exactly as they have always have been done. . . . But long ago when the people were given these ceremonies, the changing began, if only in the aging of the yellow gourd or the shrinking of the skin around the eagle's claw, if only in the different voices from genera-tion to generation, singing the chants. You see, in many ways, the cere-monies have always been changing. . . . things which don't shift and grow are dead things. They are things the witchery people want. (132–33)

In passages such as these, Silko is implicitly commenting on her own work, arguing that though she may not be a storyteller in the old way, she is nonetheless keeping that spirit alive in a new shape and form.

Anaya seems less alive to the difference between his situation and that of a *cuentista*. In his introduction to the volume of *cuentos* he translated, he argues for the continuous vitality of the *cuentos* tradition:

> Because the cuentos are alive! We hear them in the wind which sweeps across our mountains and deserts. We sense them in the work of the people—in the sweat of summer when the gurgle of muddy water brings life to the fields and at harvest gatherings when groups sit around the fire nib-bling the fresh roasted nuts of the pinon. The stories are in the people as they work and dance. They are in the vision of beauty and art which has been kept alive in the craft of the *santeros*, the colors of the painters, in the songs the native poets sing, and in the *colchas* and rugs the women weave! (8–9)

I find no note of irony in the passage, but it is hard to imagine it being writ-ten seriously in the 1980s. How many *santeros* are there today? How many *colchas* and rugs are woven in New Mexico? How many people are working and dancing in the fields while they nibble fresh-roasted pinon nuts? The society Anaya celebrates here is indeed the society from which the *cuentos* came, but I am afraid that Anaya's nostalgic celebration of it here dosen't manage to bring it back to life. And in general Anaya has had more diffi-culty in finding an appropriate modern equivalent for the *cuentos* than Silko has for the ceremonies. The blind singer Crispin, in *Heart of Aztlán,* could perhaps be seen as a contemporary re-creation of the *cuentista,* but Crispin isn't integral to the novel in the way Betonie is. Crispin at most comments on the story; Betonie is in the best storyteller tradition in that he helps to *make* the story, not just to record it or comment on it. And it may be that it is Silko's awareness of the vast gap between her and her tradition that helps her to find a way to bridge them; Anaya, seemingly oblivious to the existence of any such gap, is less successful at bridging it, at finding contemporary equivalents to the traditional forms he reveres.

I hope that by now I haven't undermined my earlier analysis of the debts each writer owes to his or her cultural roots as much as put that analysis in its proper perspective. Neither writer is unproblematically or unequivocally the voice of a cultural community. Both are in their very situation between two cultures, neither completely one nor the other, and they show this by their choice of protagonists, the bilingual Antonio who learns so well at school and with Ultima, and Tayo, the mixed-blood war veteran who nonetheless turns back to Indian ways. Both writers seek ultimately to use the language of the one culture, the dominant Anglo culture, to speak for and represent their own. But I think that Silko has been more successful in this endeavor to date because she realizes more acutely the situation she is in. To communicate in a language is at least partly to be caught in its forms, and so neither writer can be understood simply in terms of their own native cultural forms. But Silko relies upon Western forms only finally to have her protagonist break free of them and perceive them as Anglo forms: his perceptions are hers and should be ours as well. But if we feel by the end of *Ceremony* that she has re-created the narrative forms of her own culture, she has nonetheless done so in English, in a form communicable to us. She is still speaking to us in our language, even if in her own voice.

The temptations in studying such bicultural writers is to deny their biculturality, to privilege one of their formative cultures in the name of authenticity or the other in the name of universality. And the temptation is stronger when the cultures are so obviously not fused but still separate and in a state of tension and interaction. But finally we have to resist such a temptation and try for an analysis that sees these writers and others like them as a product of both cultures. If genres are cultural constructs, these bicultural writers create works of mixed genres as a way to represent that biculturality. These writers are where their formative cultures meet, and it is precisely for their representation of that meeting ground which can be a battleground that these writers are Southwestern, Southwestern in the sense of representing through that very conflict the meeting and battleground that is the Southwest.

Notes

1. No one history of American regionalism has been written, though the topic cries out for a book-length treatment. The best studied regional tradition is probably the Southern; for some of the classic studies, see Rubin, Rubin & Jacobs, and Holman.

2. This can best be seen by looking at a book like Gaston's 1961 study, which assumes a far more coherent and univocal tradition that one could do today and disposes of "non-Anglo-American literature" about the area (that in Indian languages, French, and Spanish) in a single long footnote (16–17). Even Powell's 1974 book completely ignores non-Anglo literature, whether contemporary or traditional. A good survey of contemporary Native American writing can be found in Wiget (70–120), of contemporary Chicano writing in Tatum (1982, 50–166).

3. This statement might have been challenged some years ago, for Chicano activists tended to stress the Indian roots of Chicano culture, as indeed Anaya has. But Elizondo puts the current consensus well: "Out of the ancient cultures of Spain and Mexico a new and distinct person has been formed, being neither 'pure' Spanish nor Mexican, but *Mestizo*" (17).

4. See, most notably, the "first Chicano novel," *Pacho* by José Antonio Villarreal and, for a discussion of the theme of the pocho in Chicano literature, Tatum, "Contemporary Chicano Prose Fiction," 245–48.

5. This is not to say that all Southwestern writers see things the same way. There is a tendency for Anglo writers to see the Southwest as the site of a conflict between man and nature; Chicano and Native American writers never lose sight of the cultural conflict. For a good reflection of this see Lensink, especially the contrast between Anaya's essay, "An American Chicano in King Arthur's Court" (113–18), and those by a number of Anglo writers including Nichols's "The Writer as Revolutionary" (101–12). This means, in terms of the special sense of the term Southwestern used here, that all writing by Chicano and Native American writers in the area is Southwestern; much Anglo writing, however, is more part of the thematic landscape of traditional Western writing, which is in important respects different. For a longer treatment of this issue than we have space for here, see my review of Lensink, in *Rocky Mountain Review* 42 (1988): 86–87.

6. See, in addition to Griego y Maestas, Espinoso (7–19).

7. For another, more orthodox Catholic body of fiction based on the *cuento* tra-

dition that may have helped Anaya see the relevance of the *cuentos* to his art, see the stories of Fray Angelico Chavez, now most accessible in Padilla.

8. See Wiget (88–89).

Works Cited

Anaya, Rudolfo A. *Bless Me, Ultima*. Berkeley: Tonatiuh, 1972.

———. *Heart of Aztlán*. Berkeley: Justa Publications, 1976.

———. *The Silence of the Llano*. Berkeley: Tonatiuh-Quinto Sol, 1982.

———. *Tortuga*. Berkeley: Justa Publications, 1979.

Elizondo, Sergio. "ABC: Aztlan, the Borderlands, and Chicago." In *Missions in Conflict: Essays on U.S.-Mexican Relations and Chicano Culture*. Ed. Renate von Bardeleben. Tübingen: Gunter Narr Verlag, 1986. 13–24.

Espinoso, Aurelio M. *Romanciero de Nuevo Mejico*. Madrid, 1953.

Gaston, Edwin W. Jr. *The Early Novel of the Southwest*. Albuquerque: University of New Mexico Press, 1961.

Griego y Maestas, José, ed. *Cuentos: Tales from the Hispanic Southwest*. Trans. Rudolfo A. Anaya. Santa Fe: Museum of New Mexico, 1980.

Holman, C. Hugh. *The Roots of Southern Writing: Essays on the Literature of the American South*. Athens: University of Georgia Press, 1972.

Lensink, Judy Nolte, ed. *Old Southwest/New Southwest: Essays on a Region and Its Literature*. Tucson: Tucson Public Library, 1987.

McNickle, D'Arcy. *The Surrounded*. 1936. Albuquerque: University of New Mexico Press, 1978.

Padilla, Genaro, ed. *The Short Stories of Fray Angelico Chavez*. Albuquerque: University of New Mexico Press, 1987.

Powell, Lawrence Clark. *Southwest Classics: The Creative Literature of the Arid Lands*. Tucson: University of Arizona Press, 1974.

Rubin, Louis D., Jr. *A Gallery of Southerners*. Baton Rouge: Louisiana State UP, 1982.

Rubin, Louis D., Jr., & Robert D. Jacobs, eds. *Southern Renascence: The Literature of the Modern South*. Baltimore: Johns Hopkins University Press, 1953.

Silko, Leslie Marmon. *Ceremony*. 1977; New York: New American Library, 1978.

———. *Storyteller*. New York: Seaver, 1981.

Tatum, Charles M. *Chicano Literature*. Boston: Twayne, 1982.

———. "Contemporary Chicano Prose Fiction: A Chronicle of Misery." In *The Identification and Analysis of Chicano Literature*. Ed. Francisco Jimenez. New York: Bilingual Press, 1979. 241–253.

Villarreal, José Antonio. *Pocho*. New York: Doubleday, 1959.

Welch, James. *The Death of Jim Loney*. New York: Harper & Row, 1979.

———. *Winter in the Blood*. New York: Harper & Row, 1974.

Wiget, Andrew. *Native American Literature*. Boston: Twayne, 1985.

Special Problems in Teaching
Leslie Marmon Silko's *Ceremony*

PAULA GUNN ALLEN

◆ ◆ ◆

BEFORE I GET TO THE SPECIAL PART, I want to make a few comments about classroom use of sacred materials. Maybe a good place to start is at the point a television commercial calls "book smart," then to what the same commercial terms "street smart." If we are "book smart" we will define "sacred," and if we are "street smart" we will check out the lay of the land.

For the purposes of this discussion, I'm taking "sacred" to refer to any material that is drawn from ritual and myth. This definition might extend to include "little stories," the kind that are told to children, and it certainly includes most arcane information that can be culled from a variety of scholarly or native sources.

"Street smart" is fairly simple in the commercial, but it's a bit complicated in a university setting. It's easy enough to discern the lay of the land from a white professor's point of view and teach ethically in the best academic tradition, unworried about treading on sacred ground. Ethically, a professor is responsible to provide students with the most complete, coherent information available, and in teaching Native American literature providing the best information includes drawing from ritual and mythic sources that have bearing on the text under consideration. Indeed, I myself have argued elsewhere that teaching a native text without recourse to ethnographic as well as historical glossing is an exercise in obscurity, because texts, either derived from or directly connected to tradition, are firmly embedded within the matrix of their cultural base. But to use the oral tradition directly is to run afoul of native ethics, which is itself a considerable part of the tradition. Using the tradition while contravening it is to do violence to it. The ethical issue is both political and metaphysical, and to violate the traditional ethos is to run risks that no university professor signed up for in any case.

The protectiveness of native people, particularly Pueblos, toward their tradition is legendary, but the reasons for that protectiveness are perhaps not so well known. Among the Pueblos, a person is expected to know no more than is necessary, sufficient and congruent with their spiritual and social place. One does not tell or inquire about matters that do not directly concern one. I was raised to understand that "street smart" around Laguna meant respecting privacy and modesty, and that to step beyond the bounds of the required propriety was to put myself and others at risk. One did not inquire about or tell about matters that were not hers or his to know or discuss. As my grandmother deftly phrased the requirements, one was to mind her p's and q's as well as her own beeswax.

Recently, I discovered that the sense of propriety I was taught is not confined to Lagunas or even the Pueblo world. As recorded in *Survival This Way*, Ray Young Bear tells Joe Bruchac about an experience he had that taught him the lay of the land in the Midwest. He had contracted with Harper & Row for a book of Indian folktales. He decided he didn't want to draw from published sources for his volume but would go direct to the source. To that end, he wrote a number of people inquiring after storytellers around the Midwest. In a year or so he still had not received a reply. "I took this as a sign that the whole concept of telling a story is still regarded with a lot of veneration among Native American tribes," he says (pp. 347–48). He wrote the publishers saying "there were a whole lot of Native American spiritual leaders throughout the United States who were becoming increasingly aware of people who were making profits out of Indian culture" (p. 348). He still thought he might do a book on only Mesquakie stories, so he checked with his grandmother and other people. Eventually, he came to the conclusion that it wasn't possible.

> The first and only stories we could have picked from Mesquakie people were published by William Jones, who was a protege of Franz Boas, in the early 1900s. I tried to tell my relatives that there had been previously published material on Mesquakie people by our forefathers. I thought it would still be

possible to, at least, try and share some stories now before they are forgotten. But this idea of trying to keep a culture free of what would be called cultural contamination is still very prevalent among the Mesquakie. It would be easier just to forget the stories and not publish them at all. If one attempts to do that, they are risking their lives. As my grandmother told me, "I used to hear stories about William Jones being here on the Settlement when I was young. He must have gone around with a bag over his shoulder, collecting these stories. But what happened to him? He went overseas and was killed by the Philippines or some other tribe in those islands in the Pacific." She uses that as a reference and I think it is a reference that must be heeded. (p. 348)

Young Bear raises a couple of issues: the distinction that is being made by his erstwhile contact is pretty much across the board. "If it's ours, it's not for sale." He also discovers that what was told to a white enthnographer is not to be retold by a Mesquakie, *lest tragic consequences ensue.* Preserving tradition in print is not worth the price.

Preserving tradition with the sacrifice of its living bearers seems at best reasonless, at worst blasphemous. If people die as a result of preserving tradition in the white way of preservation, for whom will the tradition be preserved?

But that's an Indian attitude. In his article "Life and Death in the Navajo Coyote Tales" published in *Recovering the Word*, the white folklorist Barre Toelken tells a similar though more elaborate tale about the risk of violating the traditional ethic. He was working with Dine on a cycle of Coyote stories when he came up against the same bottom line Young Bear stumbled on. Essentially, he was told to continue to probe the stories—perhaps even to recount them—he was courting not simply his own death but that of his children or wife, his loved ones. Toelken names two levels of meaning at which one might explore narratives of Dine only at one's peril as Medicine, which he lists as level III and categorizes as ritual of a restorative nature concerned with order, and Level IV, which he names Witchcraft, also categorized as ritual but destructive in nature. This level is, according to Toelken's scheme concerned with disorder, "(aimed at individuals, contrary to community values)." He comments that "Level III, while fascinating, involves such heavy implications for Level IV that I think it should also be left alone by outsiders" (p. 400).

"The Navajos believe that language does not merely describe reality, it creates it" (p. 390). Toelken comments, and adds "Since words and narratives have power to heal, they may also be used to injure and kill" through the selection of certain parts of the Coyote narratives for incorporation into "witch's" rituals but "instead of integrating the story with a model of order and restoration," they incorporate it into a structure modeled on disorder by using the elements "separately, divisively, and analytically" (p. 396).

Because of the power of language, and because one singer warned Toelken himself that he was flirting with becoming a witch or being seen as one asking, "Are you ready to lose a member of your family?" (p. 395).

> Since my questions had been selective and analytical, since I was clearly try-ing to find out exactly what was powerful about Coyote stories, since I stood to gain by this knowledge, the old singer wanted to warn me of two possible dangers: If I became a witch, I would lose someone from my family; if others *thought* I was a witch, someone might try to kill someone in my family. In ei-ther case, Navajo informants would assume that my detailed knowledge in-dicated witchcraft, and no one would be willing to tell me stories any more. (p. 396–97)

In the white world, information is to be saved and analyzed at all costs. It is not seen as residing in the minds and molecules of human beings, but —dare I say it?—transcendent. Civilization and its attendant virtues of freedom and primacy depend on the accessibility of millions of megabytes of data; no matter that the data has lost its meaning by virtue of loss of its human context. Yet traditional materials, sacred or social, have meaning within the traditional, day-to-day context of the people who live within it.

But the white world has a different set of values, one which requires learning all and telling all in the interests of knowledge, objectivity, and freedom. This ethos and its obverse—a nearly neurotic distress in the pres-ence of secrets and mystery—underlie much of modern American cul-ture. Witness the John F. Kennedy murder investigations, the bumper stickers that command us to Stop the Secret Government, the conspiracy fever that motivates right- and left-wing organizations, the Irangate hear-ings, the Watergate hearings, and the cry for full disclosure in political, personal, and scholarly arenas. Indeed, entire disciplines have been devel-oped on exactly the penchant for knowing everything possible that char-acterizes American ideas of adulthood though the earlier American belief in privacy is strongly at odds with this trend.

The dilemma in American culture is reflected in American institutions such as universities, where it is doubly dangerous to be short on particu-lars. It might do harm to oneself and one's dependents. In the field of Na-tive American Studies, the drawing card is largely exactly those matters that we are not to divulge. My students, usually "wanna be's" to at least some degree, are voraciously interested in the exotic aspects of Indian ways—and they usually mean by that traditional spiritual practices, understandings, and beliefs. Drawing their attention from the object of their longing to more mundane literary concerns and practices is troublesome. At every least opportunity, they vigorously wrest the discussion from theme, symbol, structure, and plot to questions of "medicine," sacred language, rituals, and spiritual customs.

Their interest isn't dampened by the arcane lore contained in much of the literature I teach. Numerous poems and novels such as *Cogewea, The Half Blood, Fools Crow, House Made of Dawn,* and *Ceremony,* as you all know, contain a number of references to arcane matters. My tendency is to feel ambivalent about the whole thing. I believe that to illuminate the works I must say something about the spiritual matters, the beliefs, practices, and ceremonialism the text is alluding to. On the other hand, I shy away from answering many particular questions because I find them offensive. It's not a reaction I plan ahead of time, by the way; in fact, it's not a reaction I have been more than peripherally aware of until working on this essay. But it's one I find myself in conflict with during every lecture and every discussion.

Ceremony is a novel that I find particularly troublesome, and I tend to nonteach it, if you can picture such a thing. I focus on the story, the plot, and action. I read the novel quite differently from how it is read by many. I believe I could no more do (or sanction) the kind of ceremonial investigation of *Ceremony* done by some researchers than I could slit my mother's throat. Even seeing some of it published makes my skin crawl. I have yet to read one of those articles all the way through, my physical reaction is so pronounced.

I teach the novel as being about a half-breed, in the context of half-breed literature from *Cogewea* on. Certainly, that is how I read the novel the first time I read it—as a plea for inclusion by a writer who felt excluded and compelled to depict the potential importance of breeds to Laguna survival. The parts of the novel that set other pulses atremble largely escape me. The long poem text that runs through the center has always seemed to me to contribute little to the story or its understanding. Certainly, the salvation of Laguna from drought is one of its themes, but the Tayo stories which, I surmise, form their own body of literature would have been a better choice if Silko's intention was to clarify or support her text with traditional materials.

Tayo is the name of one of the dramatic characters around Keresland. Perhaps in some story I am unfamiliar with, he is involved with Fly or Reed

Woman. But the story she lays alongside the novel is a clan story and is not to be told outside the clan.

I have long wondered why she did so. Certainly, being raised in greater proximity to Laguna village than I, she must have been told what I was, that we don't tell these things outside. Perhaps her desire to demonstrate the importance of breeds led her to this, or perhaps no one ever told her why the Lagunas and other Pueblos are so closed about their spiritual activities and the allied oral tradition.

Two instructive events were used as a reference to convey to me what behavior was expected with regard to passing on Laguna materials. I was told that an anthropologist, Elsie Clews Parsons, had come to Laguna to collect material for her study of Pueblo religion and social culture. They had given her information readily enough and everything seemed fine. But when Parsons published the material, Lagunas saw how she treated their practices and beliefs, and they were horrified. In accordance with her academic training, she objectified, explained, detailed, and analyzed their lives as though they were simply curios, artifacts, fetishes, and discussed the supernaturals as though they were objects of interest and patronization. Her underlying attitude for the supernaturals, the sacred, and the people who honored them didn't evade notice. The Lagunas were "red-haired" as my mother would say. Coincidently (or not so coincidently) the terrible drought deepened—the same drought Silko depicts in *Ceremony*—and in its wake many other ills visited the Pueblo. Personal horrors and societywide horrors ensued: the discovery of uranium on Laguna land, not far from where the giantess's head and her headless body had been flung by the War Twins, the development of nuclear weapons near Jemez, the Second World War, jackpile mine, water and land poisoned by nuclear waste, the village of Paguate all but surrounded by tailing-mesas almost as perfectly formed as the natural mesas all around. It's hardly any wonder that they shut it down. All entry by nontraditionals to dances and stories was cut off. They witnessed first-hand the appalling consequences of telling what was private for reasons that far exceed simple cultural purism.

While Silko details these horrors in *Ceremony*, she does not attribute them to security leaks. She is poignantly aware of the closure of village life to outsiders and depicts the pain such exclusion brings; she is aware of the discovery of uranium used to bomb Hiroshima and Nagasaki; she is aware of the devastating drought, the loss of self that the entire Pueblo suffered in those years; yet she is unaware of one small but essential bit of information: the information that telling the old stories, revealing the old ways can only lead to disaster.

Growing up in Cubero, I was not told all these details about the Parsons affair and its repercussions; it is only upon reflection that I can connect the uranium and the bomb as one of the disasters that ensued. But to bring the story even closer to home, I was told about my cousin, from another Pueblo, who had written about her life in the Pueblo as a school exercise. The exercise was published, and she was somewhat lionized locally, being a child and having notably developed writing skills. She was to do another book, one that told some stories from her Pueblo, but before that project got well underway, she was called before the tribal council and told in no uncertain terms that she must not complete it. I remember being told a person who told those stories might wake up dead in a ditch somewhere. I no longer remember the details clearly, but I think there was another story about exactly that happening to someone who had carried tales.

Now, I've been to college, even to graduate school. I suppose I should be like Rocky in *Ceremony*, able to dismiss these things with a wave of my hand, attributing them to superstition, or seeing them as quaint reminders of a lost past. What's the use in being educated if you still believe in such things? Besides, unlike Rocky, I am a breed. I have even less reason to honor the traditions and heed the references I've been given. And I suppose that, valuing my career and my job—which is a very good one—I have even less reason to honor the Laguna way.

But childhood learning dies hard. In the classroom or before the keyboard, I find myself physically ill when I attempt to override those early lessons. My body, breed as it is, rebels against the very idea that such violations might proceed from me. For years I have had a somewhat different attitude toward materials from other tribes, like those in the Midwest. But reading Young Bear's comments, I realize that even that territory—which for reasons of ignorance coupled with the availability of information from Midwestern native communities I had seen as open to such use—is not.

Reading Young Bear's comments have required me to see that my difficulties in teaching *Ceremony,* which are considerable, are extended to every writer and work I teach. Being faced with the ethical dilemma caused by my modicum of native awareness, I have specialized in teaching contemporary literature to avoid as many ethical violations as I could, believing that I might teach it and evade or avoid queries about arcane matters. By and large I have succeeded in doing so, giving a few generalized lectures on native spiritual systems and avoiding discussing any in particular detail. I have gone so far as to learn as little ritual or myth as possible in any particular detail to further buttress my defense against ethical violations.

But satisfying my ethical concerns poses a serious ethical problem:

pedagogically, I believe I should give specific information to students; discover and teach what the directions of Tayo's movements mean, what constellations figure in the story, and what their significance at Laguna is, what prayers, rituals, and spiritual activities occur at the Pueblo that have bearing on the novel, and how these elements propel the narrative and combine to form its overall significance.

Ethically, as a professor, I see this kind of methodology as necessary; but ethically, as an Indian, I can't do it. Contemplating my dilemma in cold, hard prose here, I begin to despair; no, I begin to understand some of the reasons for my extreme ambivalence in doing what I do, some of the reasons I find teaching in Native American Studies so painful, and some of the reasons why some of the poems and fiction I've been working on for years is stymied.

At this point I don't have any solutions or resolutions in mind, Sadly— and frustratingly—a human life isn't a television commercial OR a novel; it seldom structures itself along classical lines of conflict, crisis, and resolution. Probably I will continue to teach and write, more aware of the source of my conflict, perhaps more able to render that conflict articulate. I think I will feel more secure about my tendency to fail at my professional responsibilities by choosing my native obligations over my academic ones, and find more precise ways to teach away from forbidden territory while illuminating the texts in more prosaic, less titillating ways. For make no mistake, many students come to be titillated by Indian lore, seeing—however unconsciously—native spiritual life as a curious artifact, as they've been conditioned to see all things Indian. They will find themselves disappointed, but then that's not new. Perhaps they will find themselves ever more aware that native people are people, and their ways are not a spectacle but simply and significantly, a way of life.

Works Cited

Bruchac, Joseph, ed. *Survival This Way, Interviews with American Indian Poets.* Tucson: University of Arizona Press and Sun Tracks, 1987.

Swann, Brian, and Arnold Krupat, eds. *Recovering the Word: Essays on Native American Literature.* Los Angeles: University of California Press, 1987.

"The Very Essence of Our Lives"
Leslie Silko's Webs of Identity

LOUIS OWENS

◆ ◆ ◆

L IKE JAMES WELCH'S *Winter in the Blood* and, more fully, *Fools Crow,* Laguna author Leslie Marmon Silko's novel *Ceremony* is a remembering, a putting together of past, present, and future into a coherent fabric of timeless identity.[1] In Tayo, Silko's protagonist, the novel features yet another in the long line of liminally displaced mixed bloods who inhabit American fiction and fiction by Indian authors in particular. Tayo's mother, whose death has preceded the novel's opening, was Indian; the identity of his white father remains a mystery. Seemingly abandoned between generations and identities, Tayo lives with his aunt, grandmother, and uncle, his internal and external landscapes equally barren. About her own Laguna heritage, Leslie Silko has said: "The white men who came to the Laguna Pueblo Reservation and married Laguna women were the beginning of the half-breed Laguna people like my family, the Marmon family. I suppose at the core of my writing is the attempt to identify what it is to be a half-breed or mixed-blooded person; what it is to grow up neither white nor fully traditional Indian."[2]

At the core of *Ceremony* is the author's attempt to find a particular strength within what has almost universally been treated as the "tragic" fact of mixedblood existence. The central lesson of this novel is that through the dynamism, adaptability, and syncretism inherent in Native American cultures, both individuals and the cultures within which individuals find significance and identity are able to survive, grow, and evade the deadly traps of stasis and sterility. Simon Ortiz has accurately praised *Ceremony* as a "special and most complete example" of "affirmation and what it means in terms of Indian resistance," particularly the characteristically Indian creative incorporation of "foreign ritual, ideas, and material in . . . Indian terms."[3] Rather than undertake a clear-cut recovery project such as that in Welch's fiction, Silko attempts to demonstrate the possibility for authenticity and a coherent identity available to those like herself who might otherwise fall prey to the familiar malaise of mixed-blood alienation. In this aim, Silko's work most clearly resembles the more radically theoretical constructions of Gerald Vizenor. At the same time, Silko moves far beyond anything imagined by T. S. Eliot when he wrote of the usefulness of mythological structures in literature. Rather than a previously conceived metaphorical framework within which the anarchy and futility of "real" (as opposed to mythic) existence can be ordered, as often occurs in modernist texts, mythology in *Ceremony* insists upon its actual simultaneity with and interpenetration into the events of the everyday, mundane world. Holy Persons are not metaphors used to imply a "holistic" system of ecological values in this novel, like the sacrificial deities of Eliot's *The Waste Land;* they are very simply part of the reality into which Tayo is subsumed.

Throughout the novel, Silko works carefully to ensure that such binary oppositions are impossible to construct and that readers seeking to find distinct "realities," "planes," "dimensions," or "times" operating within her text will find that the text refuses to divulge such divisions. Rather than interweaving "planes" definable as "human," "myth/ritual," and "socio/cultural"—or working in several "dimensions" we might label "myth," "history," "realism," and "romance"—Silko spins an elaborate web that makes distinguishing between such concepts impossible. For example, Tayo's actions and experiences have "socio/cultural" significance only within the context of his mythic role, while history is shown to be the product of mythic consciousness and have no meaning outside of this consciousness. In the end, when the elders in the kiva recognize the mythic narrative that has determined Tayo's experience, they comprehend the timeless significance of Tayo's story for everyone. The romantic impulse that conventionally subsumes the "not me" into transcendent "me"— that evolves into the heroic quester in all his individual glory—is inverted in the culture-hero paradigm operative in Tayo's story as the "me" is subsumed into the "not me" and Tayo discovers that the two are one. Tayo's individual identity disappears as he journeys toward the communal identity ultimately pronounced by the Pueblo elders within the kiva—the center of their world.[4]

Ceremony begins with Ts'its'tsi'nako, Thought-Woman, "the spider," thinking and thereby creating the story we will read: "Ts'its'tsi'nako, Thought-Woman, / is sitting in her room / and whatever she thinks about appears. / . . . I'm telling you the story / she is thinking." The feminine creative principle and form for thought or reason, Thought-Woman is regarded by the Keres (Pueblo) people as a supreme creator who has existed from the beginning.[5] Paula Gunn Allen has suggested that "Locating events within the ritual context that supports them, [Silko] relies on accretive structuring to build toward comprehensive significance in her novel, as do traditional storytellers."[6] Silko at once associates primal creation with storytelling, underscoring, like Momaday in *The Way to Rainy Mountain,* the essential creative power of story and discourse to "bring into being." Implicit within Silko's prefatory "poems" is the Indian certainty that through the utterance of stories we place ourselves within and make inhabitable an ordered universe that without stories would be dangerously chaotic. The complex webs of language called stories become ceremonial acts performed in order to maintain the world as both knowable and inhabitable.

By announcing in what amounts to textual superscript her own subordination as author to the story-making authority of Thought-Woman, or Spider Woman ("I'm telling you the story / she is thinking"), Silko affects a deft dislocation of generic expectations, placing her novel within the context of the oral tradition and invoking the source and power of language found within that tradition. She simultaneously, and self-consciously, rejects the egocentric posture of the modern author in favor of what could be defined as an ecocentric orientation and attempts a culturally determined heteroglossia in which her text serves as transmitter rather than originator of voices and meanings. As a result, *Ceremony,* more than any other novel I know of, approaches the category of "authorless" text. In response to Foucault's rehashed questions, "Who really spoke? Is it really he and not someone else? With what authenticity or originality?"—Silko's text points toward the polyvocal oral tradition that predates the "privileged moment of individualization" marked by the coming into being of the notion of author. In the oral tradition, stories are never original and always have the "duty of providing immortality"—of preventing death of a culture; the very absence of author illuminates their authenticity. In the present age of author as icon, one can easily imagine a work such as *Ceremony* published with no author's name attached, a delightful possibility.[7]

By thus resituating her text and authority as author, Silko assumes a traditional role as storyteller in the context described by Dennis Tedlock (writing about the Lagunas' near neighbors, the Zuni), in which "the relationship between text and interpretation is a dialectical one: he or she both respects the text and revises it." Silko places the reader in the traditionally interactive position of coparticipant, taking part, as postmodern theorists would have it, "in the production of significations and meanings."[8]

More simply put, this framing device makes Silko—even more so than Momaday in *The Ancient Child*—the vehicle for a story that is older than she, as old as the consciousness of the people. The unmistakable message is that though Silko, like a traditional storyteller, is remaking the story, reforming it, molding it to fit new situations and times, she is not inventing it. The story, and all of the stories within it, are part of the primal matrix that cycles and recycles infinitely, as Old Grandma indicates when at the novel's end she says, "It seems like I already heard these stories before . . . only thing is, the names sound different" (260).

In the second framing poem of the novel, one seemingly entitled "Ceremony," Silko introduces a second voice that explains, "I will tell you something about stories, / . . . They aren't just entertainment. / Don't be fooled. / They are all we have, you see, / all we have to fight off / illness and death. "He," possibly an anonymous clan elder, defines the role and significance of the story we are about to read under the title of *Ceremony*—Tayo's story. Within her story of Tayo's journey toward wholeness and health, Silko—as did Momaday in *House Made of Dawn*—conducts a healing ceremony for all of us, for the world at large. The implications are serious, not to be taken lightly. Self-reflexively, the life-giving story is within the belly of the storyteller while the rituals and ceremony from which the "he" voice arises are found within the belly of the story. A blurring of gender definitions, "he" both gives birth to the story and is born from the story, while both are contained within Thought-Woman. "She," possibly a clan mother or Thought-Woman reentering the text, responds in the final lines of this poem set apart on the facing page: "The only cure / I know / is a good ceremony, / that's what she said." The male-female dialogue here emphasized the inextricable interrelatedness of story, ceremony, and cure while also pointing toward the male-female balance that is the desired state in Pueblo ritual.[9] The dissolution of generic distinctions affected by Silko's interweaving of poetry and prose throughout the novel further underscores the permeability of all boundaries, the interpenetrability of "conceptual horizons" within all discourse.

At this point in the novel, Silko has given the reader sufficient clues to the fact that the novel they are already embarked upon in is not within the conventions of the Euro-American genre. The novel is a multivalent ceremony, and it is designed to "cure." As an elder from the Tewa pueblo of San Juan has explained, the purpose of ceremonies in Native American cultures "is not entertainment but attainment. . . . Our dramas, our songs, and our dances are not performed for fun as they might be in the white world; no, they are more than that; they are the very essence of our lives; they are sacred."[10] Within the total context of the ceremony entitled *Ceremony* are other ceremonies: the story/ceremony charting Tayo's movements within the boundaries of the Keres world, the precisely orchestrated movements, events, and recognitions that lead to Tayo's being healed; the older story/ceremony of which Betonie is aware and of which Tayo's is merely a part; the healing ceremonies performed for Kayo by Ku'oosh and Betonie; the overall "witchery" ceremony woven by Emo and the destructive forces that would prevent Tayo from arriving at understanding and harmony and prevent balance from being restored within the Pueblo universe; and the several destructive ceremonies conducted in places such as bars and puckup trucks. Haunting the total ceremony of the novel, like figures in a sandpainting, are the dimly perceived physical presences of Holy Persons dispersed throughout the text in the physical dimensions of the poems/stories that bridge the distance between oral and written narrative. In an intriguing reading of *Ceremony,* David Hailey has taken this idea a step further, arguing that the structural—textual—forms of the oral materials placed in the novel as poems/stories actually evoke the presence of spiritual helpers within the text. "Silko fills *Ceremony* with a new dimension of conceptual life," Hailey suggests. "She adds more stories, being lived under the stories that are lived on the surface."[11]

Ceremony is a novel of demanding complexity, a work that, like other works by Native American writers, challenges readers with a new epistemological orientation while altering previously established understandings of the relationship between reader and text. Finally, *Ceremony* is a "cure" for all of us—inhabitants of a Western world that has, for more than a century, been increasingly acknowledging and even embracing its own fragmentation, deracination, and inauthenticity—dangerously out of harmony with the world we inhabit. Carol Mitchell has discussed this aspect of *Ceremony* perceptively, declaring that "Silko's novel it itself a curing ceremony." Kenneth Lincoln also makes this point, writing that the novel "tells Tayo's story as a curative act."[12] Rather than functioning from a merely rhetorical basis, to inform the reader, Silko creates an accretive and achronological experience for the reader, placing us in the center of the ceremonial cycles like the patient in a Navajo sandpainting.

Effective understanding of Silko's novel requires at least minimal familiarity with the Pueblo world. The universe of the Pueblos is a carefully controlled and balanced one with its boundaries precisely established by reference to the landscape in the four cardinal directions—most often marked by sacred mountains or, at times, bodies of water. Within these recognized boundaries the world is ordered and defined in reference to the center, the earth navel or, as the Tewa call it, the "Earth mother earth navel middle place."[13] As the pueblos conceive of their world, all orientation is centripetal, toward the sacred center, an imaginative construct evoked in the inward-spiraling form of a ceremonial sand painting. Furthermore, things beyond the boundaries of the fully imagined Pueblo world are dangerous and defiling. This conceptual orientation stands in rather interesting contrast to the centrifugal energies identified by Mikhail Bakhtin at the core of the modern, heteroglossic novel, a fact that further underscores the unique direction of Native American fiction.

According to Pueblo cosmology, everything in the universe—whether animate or inanimate—is significant and has its ordered place and is knowable and therefore controllable. Such knowledge and control, however, require extreme vigilance and attention to detail coupled with proper action, thus the Pueblos'—like most other tribal peoples'—insistence upon formula, ritual, and ceremony. Implicit within the Pueblo worldview is the belief that men and women have immense responsibility for the world we inhabit, a lesson that Tayo, along with the reader, will fully learn in the course of Silko's novel. And, concomitantly, the individual has little significance alone; an individual such as Tayo has identity and a coherent self only insofar as he is an integral part of the larger community. Discussing this communal basis for identity among Native American cultures, the American Indian writer and editor Elizabeth Cook-Lynn suggests that a Sioux greeting often translated as "What is your name?" should more correctly be translated as "Who are you in relation to all of us?" "When we ask each other this question," Cook-Lynn explains, "it's historical."[14] This is precisely the question confronting Tayo: "Who are you in relation to all of us?" By the end of his story, Tayo's ceremony will have moved him in a centripetal spiral toward the heart of his community until he is finally in the very center, within the kiva itself.[15]

Like *House Made of Dawn*, Tayo's story begins and ends with sunrise, a cycle suggestive of completion and wholeness. When we first encounter Tayo in the novel's opening lines, however, he is having a nightmare in which he is tormented by a confusion of voices rolling him "over and over again like debris caught in a flood." Amidst the voices he hears a refrain from "a familiar love song: *"Y volveré."* Immediately, Silko has introduced the motif of water—the symbol of fertility and life which Tayo will seek throughout the novel—but water uncontrolled and dangerous. At the same time, in the words of the Spanish love song, she introduces the theme of cyclical, accretive time and recurrence, the continuum which Tayo must discover and consciously enter in the course of the novel. This discovery will come to Tayo through love and will simultaneously re-awaken him to the possibilities of love; in that sense, like the song the novel is a "love story" of transcendent scope.

In addition to opening with a traditional Pueblo sunrise prayer, *Ceremony* begins in spring, the time when purification and healing ceremonies are held in the pueblos.[16] And it is at once obvious that Tayo is in need of both. Mixed up with the words of the Spanish song in Tayo's dream are Japanese voices and the Laguna words of his mother and his Uncle Josiah calling to him. The carefully ordered and infinitely interrelated world of the Pueblos has become confused and tangled for Tayo: "He could get no rest as long as the memories were tangled with the present, tangled up like colored threads from old Grandma's wicker sewing basket. . . . He could feel it inside his skull—the tension of little threads being pulled and how it was with tangled things" (6).

Another of the numerous Indian veterans in Native American fiction, Tayo has returned from World War II suffering from posttraumatic shock, what at the time was termed "shell-shock." Like the traditional culture hero in Native American mythology, Tayo has left his home and suffered almost to the point of annihilation. The experience of war has left him in a veterans' hospital seemingly schizophrenic. Like Abel in *House Made of Dawn,* Tayo is inarticulate, unable to put the pieces of himself back together in meaningful sentences. "He can't talk to you," he tells an Anglo doctor. "He is invisible. His words are formed with an invisible tongue, they have no sound." Silko adds: "He reached into his mouth and felt his own tongue; it was dry and dead, the carcass of a tiny rodent" (15). Tayo's sense of self has collapsed into a kind of bifurcated inarticulateness that has been defined as an almost quintessentially postmodern condition: "If personal identity is forged through 'a certain temporal unification of the past and future with the present before me,' and if sentences move through the same trajectory, then an inability to unify past, present, and future in the sentence betokens a similar inability to 'unify the past, present and future of our own biographical experience or psychic life.'" The effect of such a collapse, or "breakdown in the signifying chain," is to reduce experience to "a series of pure and unrelated presences in time."[17] Such a temporal breakdown is almost precisely what Tayo is experiencing. Before Tayo can be articulated, he must become articulate—he must be able to tell his story and thereby put his life into a coherent order—and by implication Silko suggests the same for all American Indians who must discover, once again, how to tell their stories. Tayo must discover, through the aid of an array of helpers, the relatedness and contemporaneity of all "presences in time." The order Tayo must come to understand is not a syntagmatic "signifying chain of meaning" but a paradigmatic signification of ceremonial, nonlinear time, a "web" of meaning.

Compounding Tayo's predicament is the fact that his cousin, Rocky, has been killed in the war. Like the unnamed narrator in *Winter in the Blood*, Tayo also suffers from survivor's guilt. Perhaps most significant here, however, is the possibility that Tayo's belief that his invisible self's words are formed "with an invisible tongue" and are without sound suggest his unconscious sensitivity to the enormous pressures brought to bear upon Native American speech by the monologic forces of colonization. Systematic, institutionalized attempts to eradicate Native American languages have formed a common denominator in Indian relations with European invaders from the colonial beginning to the present. Silence without cunning, "dry and dead" tongues are an easily anticipated result. In her writing Silko is attempting to return to Tayo, and to all Native Americans, the power of speech.

When, during Tayo's experience of war, American soldiers are ordered to shoot Japanese prisoners, Tayo believes that one of the executed men is his uncle, Josiah. To calm Tayo, Rocky says, "Hey, I know you're homesick. But, Tayo, we're *supposed* to be here. This is what we're supposed to do" (8). Although Tayo's vision of Josiah is dismissed as "battle fatigue," as Tayo comes to understand the world according to Pueblo values, he will realize that in a crucial sense the executed man actually was Josiah, that all men and women are one and all phenomena inextricably interrelated. What is dismissed as a form of insanity is, Silko ultimately argues in the novel, the only sane view of the world. The alternative is universal death. And in Rocky's words Silko introduces the "witchery" story/ceremony that works toward the destruction of the world. Rocky has fallen victim to the "authoritative discourse" of Euramerica, which "strives to determine the very basis of our behavior." This is the language of the privileged center Rocky encounters in school and in texts, a language "indissolubly fused with its authority—with political power"; the language of that privileged discourse tells a story, too, a metanarrative of westering, manifest destiny, and individualism that separates humanity from the world we inhabit. Precisely who, we are led to ask in this scene, has *supposed* Rocky and Tayo to be there in the midst of such evil? Whose story is this? Ultimately, Tayo must comprehend the web of meaning in his world through what Bakhtin calls "internally persuasive" discourse, that which is "affirmed through assimilation, tightly interwoven with 'one's own word.' "[18] Through ceremony, Tayo is able to "live into" the complex coherence of Pueblo reality and escape the metanarrative of the Western world with its story of separation and ultimate destruction. Were he simply "told" the truth by Betonie or anyone else—instead of living into that truth—he would once again be the object of externally imposed "authoritative discourse."

As Rocky lies dying in the jungle, Tayo curses the rain: "He damned the rain until the words were a chant. . . . He wanted the words to make a cloudless blue sky, pale with a summer sun pressing across wide and empty horizons" (12). Though he has been excluded from traditional teachings because of Auntie's manipulations, Tayo knows nonetheless the power of words and stories: "He made a story for all of them, a story to give them strength" (12). When he returns home to his desiccated reservation, he believes that his words have caused the drought; by damning the rain in a chant, ritualistically, he has dammed the waters of life. "So he had prayed the rain away," Silko writes, "and for the sixth year it was dry; the grass turned yellow and it did not grow. Wherever he looked, Tayo could see the consequences of his praying . . . and he cried for all of them, and for what he had done" (14).

Immediately following Silko's account of the war and Tayo's chanted curse, the author introduces the poem/story recounting a disagreement between Reed Woman and Corn Woman. Resentful of Reed Woman's constant bathing, Corn Woman becomes angry and drives Reed Woman away with the result that "there was no more rain then." By introducing this Pueblo myth at this point in the novel, Silko implies that Tayo has committed the same error as Corn Woman: through partial vision he has failed to see the necessity for every thread in the web of the universe, even the maddening jungle rains. His vision is unbalanced and has immediate effect upon his environment. The traditional story also underscores human responsibility for every aspect of existence, that responsibility Josiah had earlier explained to Tayo: "These dry years you hear some people complaining. . . . But the wind and the dust, they are part of life too, like the sun and the sky. You don't swear at them. It's people, see. They're the ones. The old people used to say that droughts happen when people forget, when people misbehave" (46). That Tayo and the land will be healed, that the vital rain will return once again to inner and outer landscapes, is clearly indicated here in the opening pages of the novel—as in *House Made of Dawn* and in traditional stories, we know from the beginning how this story will turn out. That the drought has continued for six years means that the number seven—in Pueblo tradition a powerful number comprehending the four cardinal directions plus zenith and nadir—will soon be invoked. Like Abel's journey in *House Made of Dawn,* Tayo's movement from fragmentation and alienation to wholeness and integration will require seven years. Furthermore, as Tayo steps outside the shack at his family's sheep camp, we are told, "The air outside was still cool; it smelled like night dampness, faintly of rain" (9). And as he wanders about the camp, Tayo steps inside a barrel hoop buried in the reddish sand. With the circle of the hoop, Silko suggests the continuum, the cosmos, the Native American concept of time and space and wholeness, the form of the sand painting that will figure later in Betonie's ceremony for Tayo. Tayo's brief step into the hoop, like the faint smell of rain, prefigures his eventual cure. In an interesting parallel to this passage, Hamilton Tyler suggests that "the place of the Pueblo in his cosmos might be compared to that of a hoop-dancer in relation to his numerous hoops which he must keep circling around himself."[19] As with traditional storytelling, our foreknowledge of how the story will "turn out" should shift our attention and interest to the performance of the story: How is this mixed-blood storyteller adapting the traditional materials to fit the present context? How are be being involved in the story? Our interest shifts from the "telling of a story" to the "story of a telling."

Tayo's movement toward full comprehension of his role and responsibility starts at once as he begins "to understand what Josiah had said. Nothing was all good or all bad either; it all depended" (11). His memories of childhood, memories he has attempted to repudiate, also serve to open him to the understanding that will prepare for healing:

> Distances and days existed in themselves then; they all had a story. They were not barriers. If a person wanted to get to the moon, there was a way; it all depended on whether you knew the directions—exactly which way to go and what to do to get there; it depended on whether you knew the story of how others before you had gone. He had believed in the stories for a long time, until the teachers at Indian School taught him not to believe in that kind of "nonsense." But they had been wrong. Josiah had been there, in the jungle; he had come. Tayo had watched him die, and he had done nothing to save him. (19)

But witchery—the evil that strives to separate and thereby destroy—
surrounds Tayo here in the beginning, as is suggested in the wind that "was
getting stronger; it made a whirling sound as it came around the southwest
corner of the ranch house" (21). This whirling sound, and whirling in general, as the reader will soon realize, is associated with witchcraft.

All of the veterans have returned from the war damaged and displaced.
Ku'oosh, the Pueblo medicine man summoned for Tayo by his grandmother, says, "I'm afraid of what will happen to all of us if you and the
others don't get well" (38). Earlier, the medicine man has explained:

> "But you know, grandson, this world is fragile." The word he chose to ex-
> press "fragile" was filled with the intricacies of a continuing process, and
> with a strength inherent in spider webs woven across paths through sand
> hills where early in the morning the sun becomes entangled in each fila-
> ment of web. It took a long time to explain the fragility and intricacy be-
> cause no word exists alone, and the reason for choosing each word had to be
> explained with a story about why it must be said this certain way. That was
> the responsibility that went with being human, old Ku'oosh said, the story
> behind each word must be told so there could be no mistake in the meaning
> of what had been said; and this demanded great patience and love. (35–36)

Words grow out of stories and stories out of words; stories tell the people
who tell the stories who they are. Tayo cannot be healed alone, for no one
and nothing within the cosmos has its existence and meaning alone. "You
understand don't you?" Ku'oosh asks Tayo. "It is important to all of us. Not
only for your sake, but for this fragile world" (36). Thus, Tayo is made to
understand his responsibility to his community and to all of creation; in
this sense, he becomes the archetypal questing hero familiar to Native
American and world mythologies.

An outsider, a half-blood who, like the Old Woman K'yo's son in one of
the traditional stories in the novel, "didn't know who his father was" (46),
Tayo has not been taught the necessary rituals: "He wished . . . they had
taught him more about the clouds and the sky, about the way the priests
called the storm clouds to bring the rain" (49). However, unlike Welch's
Jim Loney, Tayo has unconsciously absorbed much from those around
him, especially Josiah and Old Grandma, who offer him humor as well as
philosophy, and he is ready for the teachings of the helpers who will soon
enter his life. He even anticipates Betonie's message when he tells the white
doctor about his illness, "It's more than that [the effects of war]. I can feel
it. It's been going on for a long time. . . . I don't know what it is, but I
can feel it all around me" (53).

Within the bar, the veterans conduct their own ceremonies. Emo rattles his bag of human teeth and damns mother earth, saying, "us Indians deserve something better than this goddamn dried-up country. . . . They've got *everything*. And we don't get shit, do we?" (55). In the spirit of witchery, Emo seeks to divide not only Indians from mother earth (in a recognizably European pattern of thought) but also Tayo from the community and from himself; "He thinks he's something all right. Because he's part white. Don't you, half-breed?" (57). Led by Emo, the veterans tell stories of war and sex, "But in the end, they always came around to it" (61). "It" is the killing experienced in war. Taking on the form of stories from the oral tradition, the bar stories—at times even structured typographically by Silko to resemble the oral materials interspersed throughout the novel—serve to define the veterans and their world. "They repeated the stories about good times in Oakland and San Diego," Silko writes; "they repeated them like long medicine chants, the beer bottles pounding on the counter tops like drums" (43). With words the world is made and remade, and the veterans' stories, paralleled by the stories of witchery Silko interjects in the form of oral material, become dangerous and threatening. When Tayo attempts to kill Emo, he commits the same error committed by Abel in *House Made of Dawn*; he believes foolishly that he can destroy evil: "he felt that he would get well if he killed him" (63). He still must learn the lesson Josiah had tried to teach him—that good and evil must coexist in a delicate balance.

Tayo's mother, Laura, has been lost to the world of white men, alcohol, and promiscuity and, finally, to death. The disappearance and death of his mother is an enormous loss for the half-white Tayo, for in a matrilineal culture such as that of the Pueblo, clan identity and a secure knowledge of one's identity within the community is conveyed most firmly through the mother.[20] Without that essential connection, and rejected by his mother's sister, Tayo seems cut adrift at the borders of his culture. In her shame—both at her sister's corruption and at her own failure to bring Laura back into the community—Auntie has ostracized Tayo from family and community, committing essentially the same sin as Emo, that of separating what should be inseparable. "You know what people will say," Auntie tells Grandmother. "They'll say, 'Don't do it. He's not a full blood anyway'" (33). Like Corn Woman and Reed Woman, Auntie and Laura have quarreled, and, like Reed Woman, Laura has gone away. In this division, Silko suggests, may be found yet another reason for the drought afflicting the reservation.

Although Silko includes a variety of traditional stories in various permutations in the course of the novel, the primary unifying myth is the story of the people's failure to pay proper respect to the Corn Mother altar and the resulting anger of "Our mother / Nau'ts'ity'i." Drought and sterility are the result, and the people must seek help from Hummingbird and Fly in order to propitiate the Corn Mother and restore the rain and fertility of the earth. Like these mythic persons, the Indians of Silko's novel have failed to maintain the proper respect and understanding in relation to mother earth. Perhaps because of pressures from the dominant Euramerican culture, they have forgotten the stories that serve to reinforce correct behavior and to remind them of who and where they are. While no one has strayed as far as Emo, Tayo and the others have been taught in white schools that Indian beliefs are "nonsense." The stories have been confused; the orderly strands of Spider Woman's web have become tangled in the people's minds. Ironically, it is Tayo, the half-blood, who not only assumes responsibility for his people's well-being but also remembers, more effectively than the full-blood veterans, the traditional stories and, therefore, correct behavior. When he goes into a bar and sees flypaper "speckled with dead flies," for example, he leaves and closes the door "quickly so that no flies got in" (101). He is protecting Fly, the people's helper, because he remembers a story Josiah had told him as a child.

The difficult undertaking of Hummingbird and Fly obviously parallels Tayo's quest. Just as Hummingbird and Fly are seeking to bring back the Corn Mother, who has abandoned the people, Tayo is unconsciously awaiting the return of his own mother and thus his identity. At one point in the novel, Tayo remembers the experience of living in the filthy squatters' camp of cast-off Indians in Gallup. When the camp is burned and sprayed to kill flies and other unsanitary creatures) by whites, the infant Tayo hides in the tamarisk bushes, curled into a fetal position and thinking, "He would wait for her, and she would come back to him" (113). Like all abandoned children, the adult Tayo is still waiting, feeling that he has somehow offended his mother, that he is at fault, an attitude mirrored in the people's belief that drought is the result of a trespass they have committed against the Corn Mother.

Just as Hummingbird and Fly are the people's helpers and intermediaries with the Holy Persons, Tayo's helpers are Night Swan and Ts'eh Montaño. Night Swan, a Mexican with the distinctive hazel eyes of the mixed blood, has come from the New Mexican town of Socorro ("comfort") and has mysteriously appeared in Cubero at the edge of the reservation, drawn, she explains, to the vicinity of the sacred mountain, Tse-pi'na, "the woman veiled in clouds." Tse-pi'na (Mount Taylor on modern maps) is blue in the distance, the color associated by Keres people with west, the direction of rain. In Laguna Pueblo mythology, colors are associated with the fourfold underworld from which the people emerged through an opening the Laguna refer to as *shipap* and which is conceived of as filled with water. The lowest level of these worlds is white, and the succeeding levels red, blue, and yellow. Similarly, the Keresan Pueblos associate the six sacred directions with distinct colors, with north represented by yellow, west by blue, south by red, and east by white. The zenith is associated with darkness or black, while the nadir is identified as "all colors." With the addition of the center, the six directions form seven sacred reference points, a powerful orientation in Pueblo and Navajo cosmology.[21]

While the color blue figures as a positive motif throughout the novel (Ku'oosh, for example, wears a blue wool cap, the "good" cowboy who will later sympathize with Tayo wears a blue bandana, and it is a "blue lace shawl" that attracts the hunters' attention to Betonie's grandmother), Night Swan is most explicitly linked with this color and with rain itself. Wearing a "blue silk dress," the Night Swan lives in a room with a bright blue door. Josiah, Night Swan's lover before Tayo, drives to see her in a blue GMC pickup. When Tayo goes to her, she is wearing a blue kimono which outlines "her hips and belly" and she seats Tayo in a "blue armchair with dark wooden feet carved like eagle claws" in a room with "blue flowers" painted on the walls and blue sheets upon the bed. Tayo thinks of her as being "like the rain and the wind," and when they make love he feels "her rhythm merging into the sound of the wind shaking the rafters and the sound of the rain in the tree" (99).

Prior to his meeting with Night Swan, Tayo had speculated about prayer:

> He knew the holy men had their ways during the dry spells. People said they climbed the trails to the mountaintops to look west and southwest and to call the clouds and thunder. They studied the night skies from the mountaintops and listened to the winds at dawn. When they came back down they would tell the people it was time to dance for rain. Josiah never told him much about praying, except that it should be something he felt inside himself. (93)

In the course of the novel, Tayo will perform all these acts and will become one of the Holy Men. Following this speculation, he recalls a visit he had made before the war to a spring. He remembers watching as a spider comes to the water to drink: "He remembered stories about her. She waited in certain location for people to come to her for help. She alone had known how to outsmart the malicious mountain ka't'sina who imprisoned the rain clouds in the northwest room of his magical house" (94). And he sees the frogs which are "the rain's children." "Everywhere he looked," he realizes, "he saw a world made of stories, the long ago, time immemorial stories, as old Grandma called them. It was a world alive, always changing and moving; and if you knew where to look, you could see it, sometimes almost imperceptible, like the motion of the stars across the sky" (95). He remembers also dragonflies that were "all colors of blue—powdery sky blue, dark night blue, shimmering with almost black iridescent light, and mountain blue," and he remembers seeing "a bright green hummingbird" (95).

It is following this passage with its intense association of the color blue with rain, its invocation of Grandmother Spider and, thus Thought-Woman, and its introduction of the helper, Hummingbird, that Tayo first meets Night Swan. Just before going to Cubero, where she lives in a room over the bar, Tayo hears thunder from the direction of Tse-pi'na and sees rain "spinning out of the thunderheads like gray spider webs and tangling against the foothills of the mountain" (96). When he enters her room, she is playing a record with the refrain *"Y volveré."* And in her role as helper, Night Swan teaches Tayo about himself and his part in the larger ceremony. "I have been watching you for a long time," she tells him. "I saw the color of your eyes" (99). What she has seen are the telltale hazel eyes of the mixed blood—a hybrid color that results from the melding of blue and yellow, colors associated with rain and pollen.

Like other mixed bloods in Native American fiction, Tayo feels displaced. "I always wished I had dark eyes like other people," he tells Night Swan. She replies: "Indians or Mexicans or whites—most people are afraid of change. They think that if their children have the same color of skin, the same color of eyes, that nothing is changing. . . . They are fools. They blame us, the ones who look different. That way they don't have to think about what has happened inside themselves" (98–99). Finally, she says, "You don't have to understand what is happening. But remember this day. You will recognize it later. You are part of it now" (100). When Tayo leaves the Night Swan's room, he sees that "the sacred mountain was a dusty, dry blue color" (101).

Through Night Swan, Silko lays out her rationale for the power of the mixed blood to introduce a new vitality into the Indian world. And in Night Swan's words, Silko makes it clear that the evolution of Indian people and culture is a part of this cosmic ceremony designed to ensure both spiritual and physical survival. Her message responds to the facts of contemporary Indian life that James Welch underscored in a 1986 interview: "The people are going to be getting further and further away from their culture, so actually the reservation will be just a place to live. There will always be Indians, but they won't be very traditional, I don't think, on these small reservations."[22] It is a thesis in direct opposition to the more common image of the suffering half-blood caught between cultures.

The spotted cattle serve to further Silko's theme of renewed vitality and viability through a dynamic syncretism. The spotted "desert" cattle, crossed first with Hereford and later with the yellow bull Josiah has acquired from rodeo stock, are mixed bloods. At the time of purchase, the cattle are branded with a mark that "looked like a big butterfly with its wings outstretched, or two loops of rope tied together in the center" (81). This Mexican brand is the symbol for infinity, the continuum. Butterflies are also identified with the Pueblo personification of Summer, Miochin, as well as Yellow Woman, a fact that will serve to associate Tayo more closely with this mythological figure when, later in the novel, Tayo encounters Ts'eh Montaño and her husband, the hunter.[23] To this Mexican brand Josiah and Tayo add Auntie's brand, a rafter 4, the number of completion, balance, and harmony.

Like Thought-Women, Josiah has made a story about the cattle that seems to compel the special breed into existence. "I'm thinking about those cattle Tayo," he says. "See things work out funny sometimes" (74), and Silko adds, "They would breed these cattle, special cattle, not the weak, soft herefords that grew thin and died from eating thistle and burned-off cactus during the drought. The cattle Ulibarri sold them were exactly what they were thinking about" (74). These cattle, repeatedly associated with deer and antelope (and therefore with rain), are physical and spiritual hybrids and survivors. For Tayo, the cattle hold a special place, for it is obvious that Tayo has a unique relationship with and a reverence for the deer.[24]

When Ku'oosh's ceremony is insufficient, Tayo is taken to Betonie, a mixed-blood Navajo medicine man. An unusual medicine man—a mixed blood like Tayo, with the familiar hazel eyes—Betonie lives alone in a hogan cluttered with the paraphernalia of both traditional Navajo healing and modern American culture. And just as the patterns of a sand painting conform to the shape of a hogan and are formed centripetally, Tayo notes that "the boxes and trunks, the bundles and stacks were plainly part of the pattern: they followed the concentric shadows of the room" (120). Illustrating the nonlinear conception of time central to Native American cosmology—that time suggested in the infinity brand on the spotted cattle—the layers of old calendars in Betonie's hogan have "the sequences of years confused and lost as if occasionally the oldest calendars had fallen or been taken out from under the others and then had been replaced on top of the most recent years" (120).

In a monologue asserting the central theme of Silko's novel—the essential need for change and adaptation and the place of both within the traditional Indian world—Betonie confirms the sense Tayo has had all along that he is involved in a story much larger than himself:

> "You've been doing something all along. All this time, and now you are at an important place in the story." He paused. "The Japanese." The medicine man went on, as though he were trying to remember something. "It isn't surprising you saw him [Josiah] with them. You saw who they were. Thirty thousand years ago they were not strangers. You saw what the evil had done: you saw the witchery ranging as wide as this world." (124)

Like the Night Swan, Betonie teaches Tayo about himself and change: "The people nowadays have an idea about the ceremonies. They think the ceremonies must be performed exactly as they have always been done. . . . But long ago when the people were given these ceremonies, the changing began. . . . Things which don't shift and grow are dead things" (126). Tayo says, "I wonder what good Indian ceremonies can do against the sickness which comes from their wars, their bombs, their lies," and Betonie replies, "That is the trickery of the witchcraft. . . . They want us to believe all evil resides with white people. Then we will look no further to see what is really happening. . . .And I tell you, we can deal with white people. . . .We can because we invented white people; it was Indian witchery that made white people in the first place" (132).

Betonie's words and the story of witchery underscore an element central to Native American oral tradition and worldview: responsibility. To shirk that responsibility and blame whites, or any external phenomenon, is to buy into the role of helpless victim. We make our worlds, Silko is suggesting, and we thus have enormous responsibility. With this story, set in the same form as that of the stories from oral tradition in the novel, Silko also demonstrates how the stories evolve to meet new conditions and needs.

Following this recounting of the witchery ceremony responsible for the creation of whites and the ultimate destructiveness represented by the atomic bomb, Tayo rides deeper into the mountains with old Betonie and the medicine man's helper, Shush. Silko inserts here a story about a man transformed into a coyote and the precise actions necessary to bring the man back into the world of the people. Again, Big Fly is the messenger of the people, and the ceremony reenacts the emergence from the four worlds. At the end of this story/poem, Tayo is described sitting "in the center of the white corn sand painting" (141). Quite obviously, like the man stolen by the coyote, Tayo must be carefully brought back into the world of his people. The spirit of bear, the great curer for Keres peoples (as we have seen in Momaday's *The Ancient Child,* and other Indian cultures as well), is summoned to aid in Tayo's restoration, and the ceremony ends with the words "The rainbows returned him to his / home, but it wasn't over. / All kinds of evil were still on him" (144). Betonie reinforces this message when he tells Tayo, "One night or nine nights won't do it any more . . . the ceremony isn't finished yet," and he makes the extraordinary nature of Tayo's undertaking clear when he says, "Remember these stars. . . . I've seen them and I've seen the spotted cattle; I've seen a mountain and I've seen a woman" (152). When the sandpainting ceremony is completed, Tayo sleeps and dreams of the spotted cattle, and when he awakens he comes to a cosmic understanding:

> He stood on the edge of the rimrock and looked down below: the canyons and valleys were thick powdery black; their variations of height and depth were marked by a thinner black color. He remembered the black of the sand paintings on the floor of the hogan; the hills and mountains were the mountains and hills they had painted in sand. He took a deep breath of cold mountain air: there were no boundaries; the world below and the sand paintings inside became the same that night. The mountains from all the directions had been gathered there that night. (145)

Tayo is now living the ceremony fully, and Silko returns to the story of Fly and Hummingbird briefly at this point to remind us that the pattern of Tayo's quest has long been established in the oral tradition of the Pueblo.

As he heads home, Tayo is picked up by his friends and fellow veterans, Harley and Leroy, in their newly acquired truck. Also along for the ride is a young Indian woman named Helen Jean. An example of what must have gone wrong with Tayo's mother, Helen Jean is a long way from her tribal home, displaced and confused, drinking with drunken Indians in a battered pickup. When Harley says about Tayo, "Hey Leroy, this guy says he's sick! We Know how to cure him, don't we Helen Jean?" (156), and then repeats, "We'll give you a cure!" (158), we are given a sense of the inversions that constitute witchery in the novel and of the competing "stories" that seek to remake the world along opposing lines.

To make Tayo's role as questing hero still more obvious as he prepares to go into the mountains seeking the cattle, Silko interjects the traditional

Pueblo story of Sun Man's journey into the mountains to rescue the storm clouds from the Gambler. Like the other stories, this one is about the restoration of proper order and a coming home to harmony and balance: "Come on out," Sun Man says to the storm clouds. "Come home again. / Your mother, the earth is crying for you. / Come home, children, come home" (176).

At the foot of the sacred mountain (Tse-pi'na, the home of the keres rain deity), Tayo meets his second helper, Ts'eh Montaño. Ts'eh's eyes are ocher, her skirt is yellow (the color associated with the north), and silver rainbirds decorate her moccasins. On her blanket in four colors are patterns of storm clouds and black lightning. The constellations Betonie has foreseen revolve in the sky above her cabin. Dominating the imagery surrounding her are the colors yellow and blue, the colors of north and west, pollen and rain. So closely is Ts'eh identified with water that even the lovemaking between her and Tayo is described in water imagery, culminating in a "downpour." And when she folds up the storm blanket to stop the snow, it is very obvious that Ts'eh is a supernatural being, a Holy Person.

At this point in the novel, another fragment of the story of Hummingbird and Fly enters the text and it is obvious that, since they have now acquired the necessary tobacco as an offering, they are close to the successful completion of their quest. By implication it seems that Tayo, too, as he heads up Northtop, is close to completion of his own quest. Looking for the cattle, Tayo stops by a lightning-struck tree, a powerful and sacred place, and he gains a clearer understanding of cyclical time, a kind of eternal present in which mythic and mundane, sacred and profane, are woven together like the inseparable strands of Spider Woman's web: "The ck'o'yo Kaup'a'ta somewhere is stacking his gambling sticks and waiting for a visitor; Rocky and I are walking across the ridge in the moonlight; Josiah and Robert are waiting for us. This night is a single night; and there has never been any other" (192). And as Tayo is abruptly overcome with a sudden sense of despair, a mountain lion appears, "moving like mountain clouds with the wind, changing substance and color in rhythm with the contours of the mountain peaks" (195–96). Tayo offers a prayer and yellow pollen to mountain lion, the hunter, "the hunter's helper."

Fleeing from the white cowboys who have stolen Josiah's cattle, Tayo is thrown from his horse and stunned. As he lies upon the pebbles and cinders of the mountain, "The magnetism of the center spread over him smoothly like rainwater down his neck and shoulders. . . . It was pulling him back, close to the earth" (201). Tayo has already journeyed in the four directions, and here at last he has reached a center—one of the mountaintop "earth navels" which, according to Alfonso Ortiz, "gather in blessings from all around and direct them inward toward the village."[25] He is reconnected with mother earth. And at this moment the mountain lion reappears to lead the threatening cowboys away from Tayo and allow him to escape. Subsequently, snow begins to fall, "filling his tracks like pollen sprinkled in the mountain lion's footprints" (204).

As he descends the mountain, Tayo meets a hunter who carries a deer slung across his shoulders and wears a cap that "looked like mountain-lion skin." The hunter is Mountain Lion, who has come to Tayo's aid. He is also Winter, who lives on North Mountain in Keres tradition, and in this particular story Tayo is Summer. Tayo is reenacting a role in a story from Pueblo mythology, in which Yellow Woman, winter's wife, meets Summer one day and invites him to sleep with her while her husband is out hunting deer. When Winter returns home in a "blinding storm of snow and hail and sleet,"[26] he is angry, and the two spirits withdraw to prepare for battle, the result of which is an agreement that Yellow Woman will spend part of the year with Winter and part with Summer. A reader familiar with the traditional paradigms of the story will recognize what is happening to Tayo and will know, of course, the outcome of the story. If he renders his role accurately, "remembers the story," Tayo will succeed in restoring balance to his world.

A reader familiar with this "time immemorial" story will understand why in March of the spring following his recovery of the cattle Tayo dreams of Ts'eh and "he knew he would find her again," and why Tayo and Ts'eh know instinctively where to find each other at the beginning of summer. If the story is told correctly, with whatever variations the storyteller may affect, it will always end this way. With his love for Ts'eh comes wholeness and health for Tayo, who now realizes that "nothing was lost; all was retained between the sky and the earth and within himself. . . . Josiah and Rocky were not far away. They were close; they had always been close" (219). Silko repeats the word "love" four times: "And he loved them then as he had always loved them. . . . They loved him that way; he could still feel the love they had for him" (219–20). Harmony is achieved in both the four-part repetition and the careful balance of complementary pairs essential to Pueblo thought: "he loved them," "he had always loved them"—"They loved him," "the love they had for him."

Beneath "blue-bellied clouds," Tayo walks through flowers that are "all colors of yellow" as he gathers yellow pollen and moves toward the yellow and orange sandrock cliffs in the north. He sees a "yellow spotted snake"— a messenger to the people—and he meets Ts'eh "walking through the sunflowers, holding the blue silk shawl around her shoulders." In the distance the spotted cattle graze near Romero's yellow bull. Tayo sees the cattle "listening like deer" to his approach, and as he watches the calves play, "he could see Josiah's vision emerging, he could see the story taking form in bone and muscle" (226). He is almost fully integrated into the world of his people; even his hair "had grown below his ears and touched his neck" (229).

But Tayo's ceremony is not completed yet. Ts'eh tells him, "They have their stories about us—Indian people who are only marking time and waiting for the end. And they would end this story right here, with you fighting to your death alone in these hills" (232). "They" are the ones who would insist upon the Indian as victim, those who insist upon the "vanishing American" image of the Indian as incapable of change and invariably defeated. This is the impulse that drove Archilde down a naturalistic path in McNickle's *The Surrounded* and left Jim Loney only the option of choosing "a good day to die" in *The Death of Jim Loney*. And like Archilde and Loney, Tayo is as yet not certain of who he is, a fact underscored when Ts'eh tells him that the elders in the pueblo "are trying to decide who you are" (233).

As the novel draws toward its end, it is clear that the drought is over, an end that was foreseen in the novel's beginning. The quest has succeeded and "the land was green again" (234); in an archetypal pattern Tayo, the questing hero, has "freed the waters." Tayo's story is not yet finished, however, for he must still learn the final lesson taught by Emo's evil witchery ceremony. Underscoring a supreme irony of the modern world, Silko brings Tayo to a realization of the place of the Pueblos within the destructive "story" of nuclear holocaust:

> He had been so close to it, caught up in it for so long that its simplicity struck him deep inside his chest: Trinity site, where they exploded the first atomic bomb, was only three hundred miles to the southeast, at White Sands. And the top-secret laboratories where the bomb had been created were deep in the Jemez Mountains, on land the Government took from Cochiti Pueblo: Los Alamos, only a hundred miles northeast of him now, still surrounded by high electric fences and the ponderosa pine and tawny sandrock of the Jemez mountain canyon where the shrine of the twin mountain lions had always been. There was no end to it; it knew no boundaries; and he had arrived at the point of convergence where the fate of all living things, and even the earth, had been laid. (245–46)[27]

In the mouth of a uranium mine, Tayo sees, finally, the overall pattern as he kneels and looks closely at a piece of ore: "The gray stone was streaked with powdery yellow uranium, bright and alive as pollen; veins of sooty black formed lines with the yellow, making mountain ranges and rivers across the stone" (246). Within the stone, inextricably intertwined, are the colors of good and evil. The uranium itself, essential to the most destructive idea man has yet conceived, is the color of life, "bright and alive as pollen." The uranium comes from mother earth and cannot, therefore, be evil. The evil results in separating the rock from the earth and in separating the elements within the ore; "But they had taken these beautiful rocks from deep within earth and they had laid them in a monstrous design" (246). Separating and dividing are the tools of witchery. Auntie has sought to separate Tayo from the tribal community; Emo has not only sought to intensify Tayo's separation from the community but has also attempted to divide Tayo against himself by insisting upon Tayo's liminal mixed-blood status. Ceremonies seek to heal by compelling wholeness within the individual and between the individual and his world, including the earth itself. Capable of seeing the truth at last, Tayo cries "at the relief he felt at finally seeing the pattern, the way all the stories fit together . . . to become the story that was still being told. He was not crazy; he had never been crazy. He had only seen and heard the world as it always was: no boundaries, only transitions through all distances and time" (246).

Just before the scene in which Emo brutally sacrifices Harley as Tayo watches, Silko reintroduces the story/poem about witchery. This time, however, Arrowboy watches as the witches attempt to complete their ceremony, and by watching he prevents the completion. "Something is wrong," the witchman exclaims. "Ck'o'yo magic won't work / if someone is watching us" (247). The clear message is that it is our responsibility to be conscious, to watch and thus control evil the way Francisco is acutely aware of the albino's evil presence in *House Made of Dawn*. Evil cannot be destroyed, and to attempt to do so is to commit a dangerous error that would upset the delicate balance of the world. Tayo's temptation to destroy Emo—a temptation to which he succumbed early in the novel—would have merely fueled the witchery: "Their deadly ritual for the autumn solstice would have been completed by him. He would have been another victim, a drunk Indian war veteran settling an old feud" (253).[28]

As he stumbles back toward the pueblo after Harley's murder, Tayo dreams a waking dream of remembrance and reintegration: "He dreamed with his eyes open that he was wrapped in a blanket in the back of Josiah's wagon. . . . Josiah was driving the wagon, old Grandma was holding him, and Rocky whispered 'my brother.' They were taking him home" (254). Like the narrator in *Winter in the Blood,* Tayo has finally come to terms with his brother's (or, in this case, cousin's) death and feels himself forgiven. At the same time he realizes the meaning of his love for Ts'eh Montaño: "He thought of her then; she had always loved him, she had never left him; she had always been there. He crossed the river at sunrise" (255). The abandoned child on a circular journey in search of the mother, in search of the coherent center and sense of self located within community, Tayo has found what he sought. Laura, too, had crossed the river at sunrise, and now Tayo, like Hummingbird and Fly, has brought "our mother" home, a journey that will be repeated by Lipsha Morrissey at the end of Louise Erdrich's *Love Medicine*. In Laguna tradition the dead have a significant role as rain-bringers. As Tayo comes to understand his place in the ecosystemically determined "story" of Indian—and mixed-blood—identity, his mother is reclaimed into a place within his personal story and the interdependent story of their tribal culture. Once Tayo is able to comprehend that "she" had never left him, had always loved him—once he overcomes his feeling of abandonment by his mother, by his family and culture, by the land itself, his dead mother returns in the rain that revitalizes the barren landscape, both internal and external.

And now Silko completes the story of Hummingbird and Fly's endeavor to have the town purified and thus bring the Corn Mother (and fertility) home again. "Stay out of trouble / from now on," she tells the people. "It isn't very easy / to fix up things again." Auntie, who had finally accepted Tayo into the community, comically repeats this refrain at the novel's end: "'I'll tell them, 'It isn't easy. It never has been easy,' I say" (259).

As a final act, the returning culture hero must deliver his new knowledge to the people, and Tayo does this when he is invited into the kiva by the elders. The spiritual center of the pueblo, the kiva indicates that Tayo has indeed come home; no longer alienated, or schizophrenic, he can tell his story and thus articulate his fragmented self. And when he speaks, the elders understand at once. "You have seen her" they cry, "We will be blessed / again." As the voice at the beginning of the novel warned us we must, the elders have remembered the story.

Like virtually every novel written by an American Indian, *Ceremony* describes a circular journey toward home and identity. For some protagonists, too much has been lost for the journey to be completed; for those who succeed, the key is remembrance.

Notes

1. A number of critics have written about the nonlinear temporality in this novel. James Ruppert, for example, has suggested that the structure of *Ceremony*

"discourages the reader from imposing a strict chronological order on the narrative, thus reinforcing the perception the novel is a simultaneous, unified moment that circles like the waves around a rock dropped in a quiet pond, rather than a linear progression of events"—a way of testifying to the novel's place within the patterns of the oral tradition. James Ruppert, "The Reader's Lessons in *Ceremony*," *Arizona Quarterly*, 42, no.1 (1986): 80. See Elaine Jahner, "An Act of Attention: Event Structure in *Ceremony*," *American Indian Quarterly* 5 (1979): 37–46; Jarold Ramsey, ed., *Reading the Fire: Essays in the Traditional Indian Literatures of the Far West* (Lincoln: University of Nebraska Press, 1983); and Carol Mitchell, "*Ceremony* as Ritual," *American Indian Quarterly* 5 (1979): 27–35.

2. In Joseph Bruchac, ed., *The Next World: Poems by Third World Americans* (Trumansburg, N.Y.: Crossing Press, 1978), 1730.

3. Simon Ortiz, "Towards a National Indian Literature: Cultural Authenticity in Nationalism," *MELUS* 8, no. 2 (1981): 11.

4. For readings that do stress such distinctions, see Ramsey, *Reading the Fire*, 189ff.; Mitchell, "*Ceremony* as Ritual"; and Per Seyersted, *Leslie Marmon Silko* (Boise, Idaho: Boise State University Press, 1980).

5. Leslie Marmon Silko, *Ceremony* (New York: Viking, 1977), 1 (subsequent references to the novel will be to the 1977 edition and identified by page number in parentheses in the text). "Keres" refers to the seven Pueblos whose language is identified as Keresan: Acoma, Laguna, Santa Ana, Zia, San Felipe, Santo Domingo, and Cochiti. The other two linguistic identifications among the pueblo are the Zuni and the Hopi. See Hamilton A. Tyler, *Pueblo Gods and Myths* (Norman: University of Oklahoma Press, 1964), xix. For discussion of Thought-Woman, see Paula Gunn Allen, *The Sacred Hoop* (Boston: Beacon Press, 1986), 13ff.

6. Allen, *Sacred Hoop*, 95.

7. See Michel Foucault, "What Is an Author?" in Robert Con Davis and Ronald Scheifer, eds., *Contemporary Literary Criticism* (New York: Longman, 1989), 263–75.

8. Dennis Tedlock, "The Spoken Word and the Work of Interpretation in American Indian Religion," in Karl Kroeber, ed., *Traditional Literatures of the American Indian: Texts and Interpretations* (Lincoln: University of Nebraska, 1981), 48; David Harvey, *The Condition of Postmodernity: An Inquiry into the Origins of Cultural Change* (Cambridge: Basil Blackwell, 1989), 51.

9. See Harold S. McAllister, "Be a Man, Be a Woman: Androgyny in *House Made of Dawn*," *American Indian Quarterly* 2 (1976): 14–22. See also Allen's discussion of pairing and balance in *Sacred Hoop*, 12ff.; and Kenneth Lincoln, *Native American Renaissance* (Berkeley: University of California Press, 1983), 12.

10. Quoted in Peggy V. Beck and Anna Lee Walters, *The Sacred: Ways of Knowledge, Sources of Life* (Tsalie, Ariz.: Navajo Community College Press, 1977), 38–39.

11. David Hailey, "Visual Elegance of Ts'its'tsi'nako and the Other Invisible Characters in *Ceremony,*" *Wicazo Sa Review* 6, no. 2 (1990): 1–6.

12. Mitchell, *"Ceremony* as Ritual," 27–35; Lincoln, Native American Renaissance, 237.

13. Alfonso Ortiz, *The Tewa World: Space, Time, Being, and Becoming in a Pueblo Society* (Chicago: University of Chicago Press, 1969), 21. For a very useful discussion of traditional elements permeating the novel, see Edith Swan, "Laguna Symbolic Geography and Silko's *Ceremony,*" *American Indian Quarterly* 12 (1988): 229–49.

14. Conversation with the author, Dec. 3, 1990.

15. Any critic should be hesitant, I believe—for propriety's sake and out of respect for Native American cultures, if not simply for fear of misrepresentation—to go very far in explicating sacred and ceremonial materials. However, for a more thorough discussion of the Pueblo worldview, the reader may consult Tewa anthropologist Alfonso Ortiz, *Tewa World and New Perspectives on the Pueblos* (Albuquerque: University of New Mexico Press, 1972), and Tyler, *Pueblo Gods and Myths.*

16. Mitchell, *"Ceremony* as Ritual," 29.

17. Harvey, *Condition of Postmodernity,* 53.

18. Mikhail Bakhtin, *The Dialogic Imagination: Four Essays by M. M. Bakhtin,* ed. Michael Holquist (Austin: University of Texas Press, 1981), 342, 345.

19. Tyler, *Pueblo Gods,* 173.

20. For a discussion of gender and female significance in particular in Pueblo cultures, see Allen, *Sacred Hoop.* See also Paula Gunn Allen, ed., *Studies in American Indian Literature* (New York: Modern Language Association, 1983) 127–33; "A Stranger in My Own Life: Alienation in American Indian Prose and Poetry," *MELUS* 7, no. 2 (1980): 3–19; Judith A. Antell, "Momaday, Welch, and Silko: Expressing the Feminine Principle through Male Alienation," *American Indian Quarterly* 12 (1988): 213–20; and Kristin Herzog, "Thinking Woman and Feeling Man: Gender in Silko's *Ceremony,*" *MELUS* 12, no.1 (1985): 25–36.

21. Tyler, *Pueblo Gods,* 105, 175. See also Swan, "Laguna Symbolic Geography."

22. Ron McFarland, ed., *James Welch* (Lewiston, Idaho: Confluence Press, 1986), 16.

23. Tyler, *Pueblo Gods,* 166. See also Swan, "Laguna Symbolic Geography," 243.

24. For a thorough discussion of this subject, see Susan Blumenthal, "Spotted Cattle and Deer: Spirit Guides and Symbols of Endurance and Healing in *Ceremony,*" *American Indian Quarterly* 14 (1990): 367–77.

25. Ortiz, *Tewa World,* 21.

26. Tyler, *Pueblo Gods,* 167 (for the complete story, see 166–68). Silko has used this myth in a fascinating contemporary way in the short story "Yellow Woman" in her collection *Storyteller.*

27. For anyone who has spent a significant amount of time in and around New Mexico's pueblos—with their profoundly ecosystemic worldview—the irony of the region's involvement in nuclear technology strikes deeply. For the people of Laguna Pueblo and places near Laguna, living in sight of uranium tailings and the results of open-pit mining, the irony is a constant reminder.

28. In an essay highlighting the humorous elements in this novel, of which there are many, one critic attempts to find humor even in this horrific inverse ritual, suggesting that "Tayo's refusal to be caught up in the dynamics of mutual destruction is comical because it seems cowardly, as whites judge bravery" (Elizabeth N. Evasdaughter, "Leslie Marmon Silko's *Ceremony*: Healing Ethnic Hatred by MixedBreed Laughter," *MELUS* 15, no. 1 [1988]: 83–95).

The Semiotics of Dwelling in
Leslie Marmon Silko's *Ceremony*

CATHERINE RAINWATER

◆　◆　◆

A READER OF LESLIE MARMON SILKO'S *Ceremony* must recognize two concepts that are fundamental to Native American epistemology as Silko (and various other contemporary American Indian writers) represents it.[1] First, what we call "reality" is partly a product of semiosis, for many aspects of "reality" yield to human thought and imagination expressed through art and language. Thus, *Ceremony* opens by invoking "Thought-Woman," who "is sitting in her room / and whatever she thinks about appears. / . . . She is sitting in her room / thinking of a story now / I'm telling you the story / she is thinking" (1). According to Silko's narrator, thought becomes story and story, in turn "tak[es] form in bone and muscle" (226). For Silko, material reality originates, to some extent, in the imaginal realm of consciousness.

A reader of *Ceremony* must also acknowledge a second concept that Silko and other contemporary Indian writers suggest is fundamental to American Indian epistemology: there are profound, inextricable linkages among self, community, and the physical and metaphysical dimensions of the land. Three brief statements by N. Scott Momaday, Paula Gunn Allen, and Louise Erdrich succinctly outline such a relationship to the environment. Momaday's statement emphasizes an aesthetic perception and valuation of land that he sees as characteristically "Indian." He writes,

[W]estern man doesn't really perceive the world as beautiful. He perceives it, rather as useful. . . . I believe that unless we change our view, we will simply destroy the earth. . . . To preserve the natural landscape is desirable whatever the motive, I suppose. But it would be better if the motive were aesthetic as well as whatever else, and I don't think that's always the case even among environmentalists. . . . Use is not the first truth. (in Woodard 1989:69, 71)

Paula Gunn Allen emphasizes the spiritual bonds between Native Americans and the land, bonds that ought to be respected by all people. She says that

[t]he land is not really a place, separate from ourselves, where we act out the drama of our isolate destinies. . . . The earth is not a mere source of survival, distant from the creatures it nurtures and from the spirit that breathes in us, nor is it to be considered an inert resource on which we draw in order to keep our ideological self functioning, whether we perceive that self in sociological or personal terms. We must not conceive of the earth as an everdead other that supplies us with a sense of ego identity by virtue of our contrast to its perceived non-being. (1983:128)

Finally, in light of Momaday's and Allen's remarks, we may better understand Louise Erdrich in her poem, "Runaways," when she emphasizes many contemporary Indians' feelings of displacement in the universe. She writes, "Home's the place we head for in our sleep. / . . . The rails, old lacerations that we love, / shoot parallel across the face and break / just under Turtle Mountains. Riding scars / you can't get lost. Home is the place they cross. / . . . The highway doesn't rock, it only hums / like a wing of long insults. The worn down welts / of ancient punishments lead back and forth" (1984:13). Among other griefs, Erdrich laments her people's appropriated land, now "scarred" by the railroads and highways that mark it as U.S. national space. Her language reveals how Euro-American commodification of land violates the aesthetic and spiritual as well as the material dimensions of Native American life. In sharp contrast to the Westerner, who is often portrayed in the bildungsroman and other traditional, Eurocentric genres as running away *from* or leaving home in search of self, Erdrich's displaced, "runaway" Indian heads *for* home.[2]

No mere "horizontal" or geographical dwelling space of an isolated ego, "home" for the Indian characters populating much contemporary fiction by Native American writers includes the "vertical" or metaphysical space which the landscape informs and to which the self is inextricably connected. A Navajo collective work describes this vertical dimension of the land and its immediate linkage with personal knowledge: "A piece of land is like a book. A wise person can look at stones and mountains and read stories older than the first living things" (Rock Point 1982:1). The story of a self emerges from the land in which the story of one's people has arisen.[3] Consequently, when home no longer exists, the self is incomplete. As we shall observe, Silko's protagonist, Tayo, suffers from precisely this kind of homelessness and lack of secure identity. His recovery from illness involves nothing less than the recovery of his own story and the reintegration of this story with a larger encompassing story not only of his people in their ancestral lands, but of all people in our ancestral home which is earth.

In this context of Silko's and other Native Americans' apparent beliefs about story and place, we may begin to discuss the semiotics of dwelling in Silko's *Ceremony*. Dispossession of "home" is a primary feature of all Native American experience (in the sense that all Indians, whatever their tribal differences, have lost their lands to the dominant society). Therefore, most contemporary Indian narratives semiotically encode as "given" a "crisis of *habitare*," William Boelhower's term describing a "quest for a dwelling" in a place (like the idealized America of the immigrant's dream) that "does not exist" (119). Silko inscribes in her novel what she apparently sees as a uniquely Indian variety of such a crisis over a "home" that *once* existed. Furthermore, she attempts to resolve in textual space what cannot be resolved in geographical space: though Native Americans can never take back America as it existed before the European invasion, they can appropriate the textual space of the novel; and if "story" precedes reality, perhaps American Indian writers may begin through semiosis to reconstruct and reinhabit their home.[4]

A crisis of dwelling establishes the structural dynamic of Silko's novel. Encoded primarily through two textual features—conflicting codifications of space and competing forms of discourse—this crisis registers as semiotic instability. Indeed, the episteme of *Ceremony* is instability and, consequently, Silko's text commands especially active readers—participants in the crisis as well as in the "ceremony" of reclamation—whose ultimate role is to change our way of living in the world by recognizing and transforming our linguistic relationship to it.

SEVERAL KINDS OF MATERIAL and nonmaterial space appear in *Ceremony*: the public or federal space of the United States; the ostensibly Indian space of the reservation; the "vertical" or metaphysical spaces of the physical environment that for Silko's Native Americans are both communal and personal; the personal and psychological spaces of individual characters, including the space of the physical body; and finally, the space of the text itself—the ground on which Silko attempts her radical revision of the world.

On any road map of New Mexico, a reader may trace the geographical dimension of Tayo's journey as well as observe the ways in which federal space subsumes Native American space. On the map, thin and thick lines representing county, state, and national thoroughfares connect small and large dots representing towns; in letters appearing to lie underneath the more prominent lines and circles, one deciphers the names of reservations—"Navajo," Jémez," "Acoma," etc. Silko's novel likewise represents Euro-American space as written or superimposed over Indian lands, just as Native American culture seems "buried under English words" (69); indeed, homeless Indians live under the Route 66 bridge outside Gallup.[5] According-ing to Silko's code of the highway, United States space is defined by a series of gas stations, motels, and road signs urging the traveler to move over the land rather than settle into it. Cities are merely intensified versions of the road with their railroad depots, truck stops, tourist traps, rodeo grounds, and garbage dumps full of wrecked cars and other objects people throw away to make room for new things in their quest for an ever-postponed fulfillment of vague, commercially inspired desire. Noting this restlessness in his cousin, Tayo recalls that Rocky lived only for the future ever "since he first began to believe in the word 'someday; the way white people do" (73). While on the road, Tayo hitches a ride with a truck driver, who stops

at San Fidel to dump a load of diesel fuel. Tayo went inside the station. . . . The room smelled like rubber from the loops of fan belts hanging from the ceiling. Cases of motor oil were stacked in front of the counter; the cans had a dull oil film on them. . . . Above the desk, on a calendar, a smiling blond girl, in a baton twirler's shiny blue suit with white boots to her knees, had her arms flung around the neck of a palomino horse. She was holding a bottle of Coca-Cola in one hand. . . . [T]he horse's mane was bleached white, and there was no trace of dust on its coat. The hooves were waxed with dark polish, shining like metal. The woman's eyes and the display of her teeth made him remember the glassy eyes of the stuffed bobcat above the bar in Bibo. (153–54)

Components in Silko's code of the highway, the humanly made objects in the gas station (fuel, fan belts, motor oil, Coca-Cola) are metonymic equivalents of automobiles and their drivers who stop merely to buy what they need to move on.

Likewise packaged for consumption, the natural objects represented on the Coca-Cola calendar are unnaturally clean. Horse and twirler alike are "bleached," "waxed," and free of the "dust" which "connect[s creatures] . . . to the earth" (104). The ad depicts an American hyperreality[6]—a scene that does not exist as depicted but which nevertheless fuels consumer desire. Half-white and heavily influenced by the dominant culture, Tayo often "imagine[s] movie images of himself" in situations and settings more appealing than those of his actual existence (154).

Throughout *Ceremony,* Silko describes Euro-American space in terms of such hyperrealities. She suggests that for the dominant culture, American space must become artificial—*re-presented* and commodified—to be valuable and that, consequently, satisfaction is forever deferred into an imagined space which, according to advertisements, lies just ahead in the next purchase. The advertisement on the wall equates drinking Coca-Cola with living the idealized life depicted in the "American-girl-with-horse" scene. Likewise, when Tayo looks at the label on a Coors beer, he sees "the picture of the cascading spring on the bottle. He didn't know of any springs that big anywhere. . . . He drank the beer as it is were the tumbling ice-cold stream in the mountain canyon on the beer label" (55–56). Tayo is thus twice manipulated, first by the commodity—alcohol—the ruin of many Indian lives, and second by manipulative advertising, which distracts consumer attention away from the present into some forever deferred future that promises contentment but delivers only additional manufactured desires.

Silko encodes Euro-American space through syntagms of the road, whether this is the literal highway or the figurative "road" to some promised hyperreality. Silko's codifications of Euro-American space emphasize restless, horizontal movement away from the implied emptiness of the present toward an elusive "someday" offered by culture in lieu of vertical space—a metaphysical dimension of existence making the present moment *meaning-full* and inhabitable. Her codification of Native American space, however, suggests her Indian characters' different relationship to time and place.

Betonie, for example, has no doubts about his place in time and the landscape. When he is asked why he lives "so close" to the "filthy town" of Gallup, his answer reveals a sense of rootedness and belonging: "this hogan was here first. . . . It is that town down there which is out of place. Not this old medicine man" (118). Aware of the relative ephemerality of Euro-American culture, Betonie remains in his long-held horizontal and vertical space; moreover, Tayo's healing quest in the Southwestern desert teaches him the value of Betonie's way of being.[7] Home at Laguna and ready to tell his story, Tayo knows that "we came out of this land and we are hers" (255). Silko attributes stillness and connection to the Indian and juxtaposes these traits with Euro-American motion and alienation.

This juxtaposition, however, is more than simply a means of signaling cultural difference. The two conflicting codifications of space highlight the instability at the heart of a country which people inhabit in radically different ways. Such difference is not merely descriptive, but potentially threatening. The dominant culture's threat to the Native American, to the land and, indeed, to humanity in general is always impending: "In the distance [Tayo] could hear big diesel trucks rumbling down Highway 66 past Laguna" (255). Also in the distance lies the world's first atomic bomb crater at Trinity Site, a fearsome reminder of the white man's way of inhabiting the earth and (as we shall presently see) the central icon of Silko's episteme of instability.

Native American space is further encoded through a chain of accumulated associations with the color blue that define an Indian relationship to the earth. Moreover, this pattern contributes to Silko's generation of a double sociolect, since the color blue signifies within Navajo as well as Euro-American, extratextual frames of reference. This double sociolect, in turn, creates a cross-cultural field within which Silko's ideal reader develops an expanded interpretive framework and thus a new perspective on both text and world.

The color blue is important in the basically Navajo cosmology informing this novel and comprising one part of its double sociolect. Fundamental to the Navajo cosmology is an all-pervasive concern with health, a state of harmony among forces in the universe expressed on individual, communal, and environmental levels of experience. Navajo ceremonies aim beyond the particular symptoms of physical illness and other signs of disorder at their metaphysical causes. Indeed, Navajo traditional medicine classifies and treats maladies according to such causes rather than according to particular symptoms. Silko's "ceremony" follows suit. Presenting a range of symptoms of collective illness (from that of Native Americans as expressed through Tayo to that of all humanity expressed through war and nuclear bombs), Silko tells a story designed to restore proper equations between nature and earth's inhabitants.

Extremely important in the ritual process that Silko inscribes in her text are sandpaintings and chantways—ceremonial healing rites that invoke powers associated with colors.[8] Blue appears most often in rituals concerned with healing disharmonious relationships with the earth—especially the land in its maternal aspects. In *Ceremony*, Tayo's relationship to nurturing forces in the land needs healing. Among his many problems, he has offended Reed Woman by cursing the rain. To be cured, he must discover his proper role (of shamanic storyteller) in the Native American community and help make the land "green again" (234).

Betonie's healing ritual places Tayo in the middle of a ceremonial painting invoking the powers of the Bear People. Embodying the forces which Tayo most needs to internalize, Pollen Boy occupies "the center" of the painting with his eyes, mouth, neck and joints drawn in blue pollen (141). To restore Tayo's connection with the appropriate Holy People, Betonie also paints a rainbow with a blue stripe, a blue mountain range, and blue bear tracks, in which Tayo carefully steps as he walks "back to belonging / . . . home to happiness / . . . back to long life" (144).

Even for the reader who is relatively ignorant of the Navajo context of Silko's references to the color blue, these references evoke some common romantic ideas about therapeutic nature and the American landscape; such a reader, though ignorant of Navajo cosmology, will nevertheless usually be acquainted with color symbolism in Western culture. Thus, in addition to the Navajo context, Silko evokes a second (Western) sociolect through her code of the color blue. In *Ceremony,* the color blue directly describes the sky, mountains, and the apparel of two women characters. One woman's name is "La Montaña" (Spanish for "mountain") and thus overdetermines the equation of "blueness" with earth (specifically with the sacred mountains where the Holy People dwell). Silko's female, nurturing characters in *Ceremony* signify within the typical, Euro-American reader's[9] sociolectic conception of the earth as female. The color blue—especially as associated with female presence and power—becomes a key term in Silko's revisionary semiosis: if woman and earth are equated (both sociolects), and if woman and blueness are equated (Navajo sociolect), then the equation of blueness and earth becomes axiomatic in an expanded or "revised" reader frame of reference.

Guided by such textual clues, a careful reader is drawn back to the Navajo material; this time, however, such a reader is better prepared to decode Silko's references to blue in their "ceremonial" context, where the "ceremony" concerns healing the earth by reconnecting with its vertical, metaphysical, and "female" or nurturing dimensions. At this level of semiosic reader-participation, Silko affords the reader an experience parallel to, if not the same, as her protagonist's. Both the reader and Tayo must expand their vision. They must find a new way of interpreting experience within a metaphysical frame of reference that is, in particular, respectful of nature and the human capacity for environmental destruction.

Rife with meaning in both sociolects, Silko's blue code becomes a semiotic bridge between dually inscribed cultural contents. Therefore, no
matter which sociolect a reader possesses, Silko's blue code will not only signify, but will also deliver the alert reader into a wider interpretive field.
Within this field, what Silko has presented as Native American vision is
overdetermined. For example, blue equals woman equals earth, where both
woman and earth are defined for the reader primarily in Native American
terms. Though *Ceremony* is not polemical in its message—indeed, it straight-
forwardly states that both Indian and non-Indian must change—this
strategy of overdetermination almost certainly precludes a one-sided,
Euro-American reader-response. The novel both evokes and provides a cor-
rective for the Euro-American romantic vision of the earth that typically
equates woman and nature, but that also typically commodifies both. Silko
employs elements from the Euro-American sociolect, deploys them within
an interpretive field "widened" by an alternative sociolect consisting essentially of Navajo cultural material, and thus expands the reader's vision.
Through such an achievement, Silko becomes the consummate ritual artist
described by Victor Turner and other cultural anthropologists. The ritual
art of liminality, like Silko's novel, sets out to expand cultural "metapat-
terns"—interpretive frames of reference through which new experience is
both achieved and explained (Turner 1988:103).

An especially striking synecdoche of this process of "metapattern" ex-
pansion through double coding is Silko's Coca-Cola calendar. (Incidentally, Betonie collects Coca-Cola calendars because, he says, they "have
stories alive in them" [121].) The advertiser's image of the girl in the blue
twirler's suit reminds Tayo of a stuffed bobcat and almost speaks for itself as
an icon of Euro-American commodification of woman and the American
West. Responding to Silko's code of blue, however, a reader might find the
following "story" in the calendar: the dominant culture commodifies
woman (the twirler) and nature (waxed and bleached horse) by using
them for the purposes of advertisement, which sells not only Coca-Cola
but also a hyperrealtiy—an image of the West full of blond girls and perfect
horses. Made-up and packaged as an "American girl," the twirler is like the
bleached and waxed horse who who is unnaturally represented; the twirler
is also, in fact, a "dead bobcat," for both girl and cat are "trophies" hung on
a wall. However, in light of Silko's code of blue, the girl's blue suit connotes
her vestigial female power, though it is nearly eclipsed by the dominant
culture's countersigns, just as Native American culture is eclipsed (or
"buried," as we saw earlier) by the Euro-American. Nevertheless, this vesti-

gial trace of Silko's Native American sociolect is perhaps just enough to alert the reader to the full "story" in the calendar.

Through sociolectic doubling, Silko potentially expands the interpretive frame of reference of her readers in a way that affords a perspective on both cultures. Like Momaday's storyteller who "creates" his listener (Woodard 1989:113), Silko "invents" her reader, complete with a point of view unavailable within either one of the original (Native or Euro-American) "frames." Not coincidentally, this frame of reference resembles that of the half-blood Indian who, like Tayo, must constantly negotiate between cultural worlds (Scheick). Indeed, Tayo shouts, "I'm half-breed. I'll be the first to say it. I'll speak for both sides" (42). Generated partially through the code of blue, Silko's expanded interpretive frame of reference amounts to a cross-cultural bridge between Native and Euro-American worlds. It also outlines an alternative, transcultural set of values. The aesthetic, humane, and spiritual values inscribed through Silko's blue code prevail over the material values inscribed in the codes of Euro-American colonized space.

Two other kinds of Indian space that reward attention to Silko's encoding of them are the reservation and Tayo's Native American body. In *Ceremony*, both are sites of Euro-American violation of Native American sacred space. Just as roads, highways, and towns surround and even overlay the areas of the map marked "reservation," federal space in *Ceremony* semiotically obtrudes into land ostensibly "reserved" for the Indian. Paradoxically, Indian land is defined and managed by the U.S. government. In semiotic terms, the reservation is a prime example of what Hodge and Kress call an ideological complex—"a functionally related set of contradictory versions of the world, coercively imposed by one social group on another on behalf of its own distinctive interests or subversively offered by another social group in attempts at resistance in its own interests" (1988:3).

Betonie's conversation with Tayo about Gallup reveals the profound ironies underlying the "set of contradictory versions of the world" that is the "reservation." The Gallup Ceremonial is an annual event. It is a ceremonial in name only, however, for it mostly involves the Gallup merchants making "a lot of money off the tourists" (116). White merchants exhibit and sell Indian cultural artifacts, and then the Indians return to the reservation, or to the "alleys between the bars" in Gallup. Implying that Indian lands are little more than a place to store the Indians until they are needed in tourist season, Betonie tells Tayo that "this is where Gallup keeps Indians until Ceremonial time" (117). A site of "contradictory versions of the world," the reservation is on the one hand, "reserved" as a space where Native American culture may flourish or at least prevail; on the other hand, as Betonie shows, the "reservation" is a place where Indians are held "in reserve" until such time as they may serve the economic interests of the dominant culture.

"Coercively imposed by" the U.S. government on Native Americans "on behalf of its own distinctive interests," the reservation is also a place where the Native Americans "attempt . . . resistance in [their] own interests," where Native Americans like Betonie attempt to preserve their culture against the incursions of the Other. Silko shows that Indians do not necessarily fare well on the reservation, but their fate seems worse outside their communities. Whereas Betonie waits patiently in his hogan which "was here first," many off-reservation Navajos merely "dream . . . for wine, looking for it somewhere in the mud . . . crouching outside bars like cold flies stuck to the wall" (107). Defined as federal space or as Indian space, the reservation shapes Native American behavior by defining it within a binary set of on- and off-reservation alternatives. One may be an Indian in "reserve" until Ceremonial time, or a displaced "cold fly stuck to the wall."

As a half-blood, Tayo has been both. Part of his healing quest involves transcending the limits of vision imposed by cultural definitions of what it means to be white as well as what it means to be Indian; in other words, like Betonie he must choose deliberately how to live, how to dwell in the world. Once he is rehabilitated, Tayo's responsibility is to tell a new and radical story that will free whites and Indians alike from the unhealthy constraints imposed by the old "story."[10]

To succeed, Tayo must first reclaim another kind of space—the space of his own body that is, like the reservation, ambiguously defined in both white and Indian terms. As a half-blood, he must decide which half of himself to realize. Conflicting codifications of the space of Tayo's body include the white doctors' description of Tayo's illness versus the medicine men's description. Underlying these descriptions are profoundly different ways of seeing and being in the world. Tayo's recovery entails a struggle over the naming and meaning of illness and health, and over Tayo's ultimate definition of his body as Indian or white "space."[11]

While Tayo lies ill in the veteran's hospital, the white doctors "yell" at him because he does not define himself "correctly," according to their psychological model of self. They see him as a particular "individual" with a specific symptoms of "battle fatigue." In the "ontological" tradition of Western medicine, their aim is to make the symptoms disappear, not to waste time thinking about the metaphysical cause of the malady.[12] "[T]he Army doctors . . . told [Grandma] and Robert that the cause of battle fatigue was a mystery, even to them," but that Tayo's recovery depends upon his forgetting about the war and the death he saw there, and thinking only of himself (31). Ku'oosh and Betonie, however, define Tayo's illness in a traditional "medicine" way which treats primarily causes, not symptoms. His sickness is a part of a larger pattern of events that "ha[ve] been going on for a long time" (53). World War II is only one of many symptoms of global ill health. Because the Army doctors do not treat the cause of Tayo's sickness, their "medicine drained memory out of his thin arms and replaced it with a twilight cloud behind his eyes" (15).

Indeed, the Native American according to Silko suffers especially from a kind of general "drain" of cultural identity through contact with whites. Western European violence, dominance, and materialism are reflected in global warfare and are the source of much destruction—material, spiritual, and aesthetic. Silko iconizes this debilitating cultural contact between Indians and whites, again by generating a double sociolect, through references to the golden eagle, an emblem of America for the U.S. Army and an embodiment of sacred medicine for the Navajo.

The army eagle signifies Euro-American appropriation of Native American sacred symbols for nonsacramental purposes; it also signifies U.S. appropriation of Native American bodies to fight in the war. Under the sign of the eagle, Army recruiters come to the reservation to declare that "anyone can fight for America . . . even you [Indian] boys" (64). The eagle signifies doubly for Tayo as a half-blood soldier returned to America with "battle fatigue." Service in the army under the sign of the eagle leads to his need for a healing ceremony; this ceremony, in turn, awakens him to his shamanic role of making changes in the old ceremonies that began and continue with "the aging of the yellow gourd rattle [and] the shrinking of the skin around the eagle's claw" (126).

In his healing quest, Tayo must rediscover (for himself and others) the sacramentality of the signs and symbols of his culture. Like the eagle emblazoned across the property of the U.S. Army, the desacralized symbols of Native American culture that are displayed in stores and at annual tourist events at Gallup must be reclaimed and reinvested with sacramental value. The new ceremonies, says Betonie, will have to be powerful enough to heal the planet. They will have to reach across continents and cultures, lest those who remain sick should "take this world from ocean to ocean . . . [and] explode everything" (137). These new ceremonies amount to new stories told by shamanic storytellers such as Tayo, whose primary task is to continue the story begun about him by the narrator; moreover, Silko implores the reader to "accept this offering" (262)—the written novel—and, with Tayo, to help make a new story of humanity in an inhabitable land.

SILKO'S DRAMA OF CROSS-CULTURAL REGENERATION through semiosis takes place within yet another kind of space—the space of the written text—which has not been "home" to the Native American storyteller until recently. Of the spaces available to the contemporary Indian, the space of the text is perhaps most profoundly appropriated, for as we have seen, semiosis precedes reality, according to Silko's opening invocation of Thought-Woman, the Spider. Silko transforms the genre of the novel even as she writes, for she cross-codes her narrative with both the dominant and marginalized culture's interpretive conventions, and though she assists the reader, she commands an extremely energetic reader who is willing to "relearn" some ways of making and receiving meaning.[13]

Besides the conflicting codifications of space that oblige the reader to negotiate semiotic instability, the novel develops several different kinds of discourse that presuppose different agendas of production and reception. The structural dynamic that develops from such competing agendas restates the spatially encoded episteme of instability. The model reader's negotiation of such instability not only approximates the experience of the bicultural individual who lives, in a sense, between differently constructed worlds, but it also, and more important, underscores the main point of Silko's book: reality is the direct result of the versions of the world we construct. We may construct the story of reality carefully or carelessly, and we may either revise an uninhabitable reality of become its victims. As a responsible Native American storyteller with a cross-cultural mission, Silko also provides her readers with a metatextual set of instructions for participating in the re-creation of the world through storytelling.[14] This feature of *Ceremony* renders her novel paradigmatic among contemporary Native American written works, most of which encode as "given" what Silko makes explicit for readers.[15]

We may identify at least three large categories of discourse in *Ceremony:* lyric chantways, narrative (consisting of "narration" and "story"[16]), and dialogue. Moreover, each type of discourse may be subcategorized according to contrary "logonomic systems" that govern its production and reception. All three kinds of discourse are at all times encountered by the reader in terms of the double sociolect that *Ceremony* generates; this fact especially affects the reader's response to the "Indian" sociolectic material, which may be judged "true" or "mythical-imaginary," depending upon the reader's epistemological frame of reference. Both chantways and narrative, more-over, incorporate material originating in an atemporal, mythico-spiritual realm and material originating in temporal-historical experience. Espe-cially for the Euro-American reader, myth and history presuppose quite dif-ferent "logonomic systems" or "set[s] of rules . . . prescribing the condi-tions for production and reception of meanings."

Such rules "specify who can claim to initiate or know meanings about what topics under what circumstances and with what modalities" (Hodge and Kress 1988:4). (That is to say, logonomic rules specify who may with credibility say what to whom and in what form. A historian, for instance, may authoritatively relate to a Western audience the "truth" about the past in the form of historical narrative. Both historian and audience pre-sumably understand the rules governing the production and reception of historical knowledge, which differ from the rules governing the produc-tion and reception of fiction.) A variety of logonomic systems operate within *Ceremony,* a culturally cross-coded text which (as we have seen) ap-pears designed to devise and expand the "rules," first by bringing them into various oppositional relationships. Consequently, whether she is Indian or not, the reader must actively participate in a complex dialogical process. The reader must learn how to "dwell" within the space of the text as de-fined by Silko's revisionary semiotic practice.

Ceremony opens with a four-page lyric passage. Questions immediately arise concerning the identity and the source of authority of the speaker in these pages. The speaker declares, "Thought-Woman, the spider, / . . . is . . . thinking of a story . . . / I'm telling you the story / she is thinking" (1). If the story told in *Ceremony* originates with Thought-Woman, then it originates in the mythico-spiritual dimension, despite its narrative con-cern with the temporal-historical particulars of Tayo's life. However, the speaker, the "I" of the passage who speaks for Thought-Woman, is also the narrator of *Ceremony* (it is reasonable to assume that this narrator is Silko herself), who is presumably an inhabitant of the present, material world. Thus, from the outset, the ontological status of the narrating voice in *Cere-mony* is ambiguous, as are the truth-claims of the different types of dis-course (the average Western reader sees myth as "imaginary" and narrative as mimetic, if not literally true[17]).

Consequently, the protocol for decoding the text—as cultural myth or as fictional narrative—is problematic, at least for the average Western reader who accepts the conventional boundaries between these forms. Pointedly raising doubts in the reader about which interpretive frame of reference or set of logonomic rules to engage, Silko's text forces the reader to confront questions of origination and legitimation of knowledge. Silko apparently attempts to make her reader aware of the logonomic rules that govern meaning, and challenges the reader to help change some of these rules, which ultimately pertain not only to storytelling but also to world-making.

The lyric passages in *Ceremony* are of two basic types, those which consist of the sociolectic lore and information of traditional healing chantways, and those into which the idiolectic, "story" component of the narrative passages has been interwoven to form a "new" or "revised" chantway. For example, early in the novel, we are told in a lyrical passage the traditional story of Nau'ts'ity'i, who becomes angry with people for neglecting "mother corn altar" and playing around with "Ck'o'yo witchery," a kind of verbal black magic. She punishes them for their disrespect of the "mother" by starving them: "she took / the plants and grass from them. / No baby animals were born. / She took the rainclouds with her" (48–49).

Later, in the narrative, we are told the same story of human disrespect for the female and of the "disgrace of Indian women" (57). In a lyrical passage taking the form of the traditional chantway, but carrying information from the present, narrated time rather than from the mythic past, we learn again about the consequences of offending the "mother." Full of hatred and violence, World War II veterans Emo and Leroy tell Tayo in a profane chantway about exploiting white women whom they picked up in bars in California. The alert reader comprehends the implied parallels between insulting actual women and insulting there prototypes among the spirit entities.

These two kinds of lyrical passages align the universal human problems described in mythico-spiritual terms with immediate problems described in the particular terms of the narrative. Silko suggests that the reader should look for connections between spiritually and experientially acquired knowledge; perhaps her aim is to teach the reader to interpret within a larger frame of reference which includes a "vertical" (mythico-spiritual) dimension, as suggested by the chants, as well as a "horizontal" (temporal-historical) dimension, as suggested by the ongoing story of Tayo's life. Silko's regenerative purpose is apparently to lead the reader, like Tayo, to see that temporal history is a "part of something larger" (125–26); to see "the pattern, the way all the stories fit together . . . to become the story that was still being told" (246).

A third kind of discourse in *Ceremony* is dialogue—the various speeches of characters that, like the lyrical and narrative passages, do not all originate within the same "worlds." Among the many voices in *Ceremony* are those of Josiah, who tells Tayo and Rocky the traditional stories of the Laguna people and so provides them with the Indian worldview; the voices of white people, the doctors, in particular, who insist that Tayo understand himself in terms of Western-European psychology; the voices of the medicine men, Ku'oosh and Betonie; the voices of characters from the spiritual realm, such as Hummingbird, Buzzard, and the "blue shawl" woman. Just as the lyrical chants and the narrative passages pose fundamental questions about origination and legitimation of their content, the dialogue becomes another site of instability by presenting myriad worldviews and corresponding interpretive systems. Once again, the reader's experience mirrors Tayo's, for both must decide how to define the world in terms of the multiple messages they receive before they can understand the role they are to play in this world.

However, just as Tayo is assisted by Ku'oosh and Betonie, so is the reader assisted by the text. Silko includes instructions to the reader about how to participate in *Ceremony*. Like the ceremonial bear tracks which guide Tayo's steps "home [and] back to belonging" (144), parts of Silko's ceremonial narration and dialogue guide the reader through the potential confusion of the text to the place where "the stories fit together . . . to become the story that [is] being told" (246). Silko specifically addresses the role of thought and language in the construction and destruction of reality. Ku'oosh, for example, tells us that "the world is fragile" (35). The narrator explains his meaning:

> The word he chose to express "fragile" was filled with the intricacies of a continuing process, and with a strength inherent in spider webs. . . . It took a long time to explain the fragility and intricacy because no word exists alone, and the reason for choosing each word had to be explained with a story about why it must be said this certain way. That was the responsibility that went with being human, old Ku'oosh said, the story behind each word must be told so there could be no mistake in the meaning of what had been said. (35–36)[18]

Betonie likewise explains the relationship of words and the world. He teaches Tayo that contemporary evil originated in an evil "story" told by "witches" showing off their magic powers through a "contest / in dark things" (132–33). The narrator reinforces the message about story: indeed, the narrator tells us, "the world" is "made of stories" (95).

Ceremony rewrites the rules for reader performance under maximum conditions of semiotic instability in order to reveal the ways in which "story" makes reality or, in the words of Thomas Sebeok, the ways in which "life modifies the universe to meet its needs, and accomplishes this by means of sign action" (1991:128). By heightening our awareness of the ways in which we make and receive meaning—including the ways in which Eurocentric readers, in particular, decide what is "real" and "true" versus what is "imaginary" and "false"—*Ceremony* instructs the reader concerning the logonomic interface between the "world" of the text and the "text" of the world. Made aware of this interface and empowered by such awareness, the reader understands not only that a "story" may lead to a world with atomic weapons, but also that such a world may be "reread" as a "story" and revised. Oppositional logonomic systems, contradictory codifications of space, and other semiotic features of the text are the occasion for the reader's interpretive struggle; they are also the means by which readers (all kinds, including white and Indian) begin to understand how to reinhabit the earth by recognizing and transforming aspects of our linguistic relationship to it.

INSTABILITY CONSTITUTES THE EPISTEME of *Ceremony* and fundamentally defines the crisis of dwelling in this novel. Such instability is also iconized in the overdetermined symbol of the "sandpainting"—the atomic bomb crater—in the heart of the American desert.[19] The atomic "sandpainting" is both a space and a story. More precisely, it is the spatial realization of the evil story begun by the Ck'o'yo magician and carried on by humanity. Atomic energy is the ultimate expression of deliberate unbalancing of natural forces (atomic energy is released when the nucleus of a heavy atom is split—not a naturally occurring phenomenon on earth). Trinity Site thus becomes in *Ceremony* an icon of the humanly created, unstable conditions of existence that threaten not only our ability to dwell peacefully but also our place of dwelling itself—the earth.

Tayo's responsibility as a shamanic storyteller involves revising the story of total destruction before it is too late. He returns to Laguna, where "[i]t took a long time to tell them the story" (257). Though "the old men started crying" and saying "We will be blessed / again" (257), Tayo knows that human beings are always threatened by their own capacity for "witchery"—for telling evil stories that become reality. On his vision quest in the Southwestern desert, Tayo has understood that the cartography of the human spirit and imagination may lead to an actual map of horror or of "spaces [filled] with new dreams" (219). Thus, Silko's story ends hopefully, at "Sunrise," with a plea to "accept this offering" (262), an offering in the form of an alternative story to the one which humanity is currently "thinking." In *Ceremony,* Silko encodes a crisis of dwelling designed to assist the reader in creating a new map through a new, alternative story.

Notes

1. Certainly, a critic must be careful to avoid unwarranted generalizations about "Native American" ways of thinking, writing, etc., since there are over three hundred tribes in the United States that consist of many and diverse individuals with their own points of view. The same is obviously true of "white" or Euro-Americans, whose numbers include many individuals of diverse national origins. In this essay, if I occasionally refer to "Native Americans" or "Indians" in general, I am primarily referring to Silko's (or, where specified, other Indian writers') implied and stated conceptions of what it means to be "Indian," I am not assuming that any particular American Indian writer or group of writers speak monolithically for Indian cultures, any more than I would assume that Hemingway or Wharton speak monolithically for Anglo-Americans, Toni Morrison for African-Americans, etc. Moreover, every writer, no matter what his or her heritage, to some extent "reinvents" her/his cultural milieu; some of these writers' revisions and reinventions, in turn, become culturally inscribed and thus, to some degree, representative. Jorge Luis Borges, for example, is well known for his statement that he "cannot imagine the universe" as if writers such as Shakespeare, Dostoyevsky, and Poe had never written. Thus, whin I occasionally speak generally in this essay of Native Americans, I speak with a full awareness of the fact that I am ultimately referring to the "Native American" who is "invented" and "represented" by Silko and other Indian writers who are currently inscribing American culture with new ideas and images of diverse Indian peoples.

2. For an excellent discussion of some Native American concepts of "home,: see Bevis. He compares and explores the implications of the Western pattern of leaving home versus the Native American pattern of seeking home.

3. My work in progress on the "semiotics of regeneration" in narratives by some contemporary Native Americans includes extensive discussion of the idea of a "semiotic self" as it applies to character development in several of these works. See also my remarks on Louise Erdrich's Native American characters' processes if individuation (Rainwater 1990).

4. In connection with this discussion of reclamation through semiosis, see also Todorov, who provides a fascinating analysis of how (South) American Indians *lost* America partially owing to Western-European sophistication in managing linguistic signs, both written and spoken.

5. Another Native American writer to perceive her culture as "buried" or, more precisely "submerged," is Louise Erdrich (1984). *Love Medicine* ends with Lipsha

looking out over an artificially created body of water that covers his ancestral lands.

6. Umberto Eco and Jean Baudrillard both use the term "hyperrealtiy" to refer to particular traits of mass culture. Eco (1986) refers to theme parks, museums, zoos, etc., which are copies of original places but which somehow seem to promise a richer experience than the original offers. I use "hyperreality" more in Baudrillard's sense, to refer to the breakdown of distinctions between thing and idea. The advertisement in a consumer culture creates a world of its own—a hyperreality. This hyperreality, in turn, orchestrates consumer desire. The idea associated with the thing, and not the thing itself, is the true object of desire: "The flight from one signifier to another is no more than the surface reality of a *desire,* which is insatiable because it is founded on a lack. And this desire, which can never be satisfied, signifies itself locally in a succession of objects and needs" (Baudrillard 1988:45).

7. In her study of Momaday, Scarberry-Garcia also discusses healing and the Native American relationship to land. Frederick Turner's discussion of *Ceremony* (1989) is also valuable on this subject.

8. On Navajo and Pueblo medicine and ceremony, see Reichard (1950), Kunitz (1983), and Hammerschlag (1988).

9. The average or implied "reader" I discuss may or may not be literally "Euro-American." As reader-response theorists have demonstrated repeatedly, there are many actual readers, but the hypothetical "reader" is always a theoretical construct, to some extent. Unless I specify otherwise, the assumed "reader" to whom I refer is someone who has, in general, internalized the dominant culture's conventional strategies of reading and producing meaning from novels, no matter what his or her ethnic identity might be. I believe Silko's text is directed primarily toward such a reader, who may most benefit from acquiring some non-Eurocentric perspectives.

10. Hodge and Kress (1988:3) explain how ideological complexes "constrain behaviour by structuring the versions of reality on which social action is based." The on- and off-reservation versions of Native American social reality impose a wide variety of "constraints" upon their social action, as I hope my discussion of Silko's revisionary efforts suggests.

11. On the nature of Tayo's illness and its relation to his half-blood status, see especially Allen 1986:138–47.

12. Cassell (among a growing number of physicians who are responding to contemporary demands for more humanized medicine) explains the difference between "physiological" and "ontological" theory of disease. The former may be compared to "holistic" medicine with its "ecological" view of persons and maladies; the latter theory, which held sway in the age of "scientific medicine" in the West, emphasizes the disease-causing "entity" (such as a microbe of a structural

malfunction). It focuses therapy on the site of the problem, rather than on the patient as a whole person.

13. On the semiotics of reader-response, theorists whose works are most pertinent to my analysis of Silko's novel are Riffaterre, Scholes, and Silverman.

14. On metatextual features of Native American literature, see Elaine Jahner's fascinating discussion in Vizenor (1989:155–85).

15. I intend Riffaterre's meaning of "given" here. See Riffaterre 1983.

16. I make the now fairly standard structuralist distinction between the events narrated (story) and the narrating voice's way of telling (narration).

17. Hayden White (1987) is especially thought provoking on the subject of the rather paradoxical distinctions we make between what is "true" and what is "imaginary" content in verbal representation. Though he does not employ Hodge and Kress's concept of logonomic systems, his discussion emphasized the fact that different agendas of reception (activated in the reader by the form of a work) to a great extent determine what we think of as "history" versus "myth," even though the two contents are often carried in similar forms. On the subject of how the illusion of truth is semiotically created and sustained in fiction, see also Riffaterre 1990.

18. Krupat (in Swann and Krupat 1987) discusses this passage. He argues that the concern with clear, fixed, and stable meanings of signifiers is not a part of oral tradition but has arisen since Native Americans have shifted to written literature. Oral storytellers, he claims, basically assumed that such meanings were "at least possible" (117). The need to insist or to argue the point, says Krupat, arises when storytellers shift to Western form during the post-structuralist era. Krupat's claim supports my general argument along similar lines, that contemporary Native American writers are beginning to claim new textual "territory" and thus to transform the novel as well as many of their traditional ways of telling stories.

19. On the subject of Silko's treatment of nuclear war in *Ceremony,* see Jaskoski (in Anisfield 1991).

Glossary

LOGONOMIC RULES   Rules that specify who may with credibility say what to whom and in what form; only a qualified physician may make a credible diagnosis; she will state it in technical language for an audience of peers, and in layman's language for the ordinary audience.

LOGONOMIC SYSTEM   A set of rules that prescribe the conditions for the production and reception of meaning in a given act of communication. A simple example might be the rules that govern the production of professional knowledge: only a pathologist with appropriate credentials may credibly analyze biopsied tissue, and only a physician with appropriate credentials may deliver a diagnosis based on this received knowledge. Likewise, we distinguish between the professional and the "arm-chair" historian. Both may know history, but only the former is "qualified" to speak to us with authority about history. We "receive" the words of each type of historian with different levels of confidence.

METONYMIC REFERENCES   Single words that evoke broad, extratextual contexts: for instance, for readers of *Ceremony,* the color blue evokes a variety of Western, romantic associations as well as an array of Navajo and Pueblo meanings.

SOCIOLECT   An extratextual, encyclopedic reservoir of denotative, connotative, cultural, historical, and other meanings that readers bring to bear as they interpret literary texts; in other words, the body of information that readers have prior to reading a text that enables them to interpret it.

SYNTAGMATIC CHAINS OF REFERENCES   Sequences of different but closely associated words in a narrative that evoke particular impressions; for example, words such as "fuel," "fanbelts," "motor oil," "service station," and so on in *Ceremony* are used in ways that create for the reader a general or background impression of the United States as a "highway," and an impression of all of its people as in perpetual motion.

Works Cited

Allen, Paula Gunn. 1983. "Introduction," and "The Sacred Hoop: A Contemporary Perspective," *Studies in American Indian Literature: Critical Essays and Course Designs.* Paula Gunn Allen, ed. New York: MLA.

———. 1986. *The Sacred Hoop: Recovering the Feminine in American Indian Traditions.* Boston: Beacon.

Anisfield, Nancy, ed. 1991. *The Nightmare Considered: Critical Essays on Nuclear War Literature.* Bowling Green: Bowling Green State University Popular Press.

Baudrillard, Jean. 1988. *Jean Baudrillard: Selected Writings.* Mark Poster, ed. Stanford: Stanford University Press.

Bevis, William. 1987. "Native American Novels: Homing In." In Swann and Krupat, 580–620.

Boelhower, William. 1987. *Through a Glass Darkly: Ethnic Semiosis in American Literature.* New York: Oxford University Press.

Cassell, Eric J. 1991. *The Nature of Suffering and the Goals of Medicine.* New York: Oxford University Press.

Eco, Umberto. 1986. *Travels in Hyperreality: Essays.* Trans. William Weaver. San Diego: Harcourt, Brace, Javanovich.

Erdrich, Louise. 1984. *Jacklight: Poems,* New York: Henry Holt.

————. 1984. *Love Medicine.* Toronto: Bantam.

Hammerschlag, Carl A. 1988. *The Dancing Healers: A Doctor's Journey of Healing with Native Americans.* San Francisco: Harper and Row.

Hodge, Robert, and Gunther Kress. 1988. *Social Semiotics.* Ithaca, N.Y.: Cornell University Press.

Jahner, Elaine. 1989. "Metalanguages." In Vizenor, 155–85.

Jaskoski, Helen. 1991. "Thinking Woman's Children and the Bomb." In Anisfield, 159–76.

Krupat, Arnold. 1987. "Post-Structuralism and Oral Literature." In Swann and Krupat, 113–28.

Kunitz, Stephen J. 1983. *Disease, Change, and the Role of Medicine: The Navajo Experience.* Berkeley: University of California Press.

Rainwater, Catherine. 1990. "Reading between Worlds: Narrativity in the Fiction of Louise Erdrich." *American Literature* 62 (September): 14–24.

Reichard, Gladys A. 1950. *Navajo Religion: A Study of Symbolism.* Princeton: Princeton University Press.

Riffaterre, Michael. 1983. *Text Production.* New York: Columbia University Press.

————. 1990. *Fictional Truth.* Baltimore: Johns Hopkins University Press.

Rock Point Community School. 1982. *Between Sacred Mountains: Navajo Stories and Lessons from the Land.* Sam and Janet Bingham, eds. Tucson: Sun Tracks and University of Arizona Press.

Scarberry-Garcia, Susan. 1990. *Landmarks of Healing: A Study* of House Made of Dawn. Albuquerque: University of New Mexico Press.

Scheick, William J. 1979. *The Half-Blood: A Cultural Symbol in 19th-Century American Fiction.* Lexington: University Press of Kentucky.

Scholes, Robert. 1982. *Semiotics and Interpretation.* New Haven: Yale University Press.

————. 1989. *Protocols of Reading.* New Haven: Yale University Press.

Sebeok, Thomas A. 1991. *American Signatures: Semiotic Inquiry and Method.* Iris Smith, ed. Norman: University of Oklahoma Press.

Silko, Leslie Marmon. 1977. *Ceremony.* New York: Viking.

Silverman, Kaja. 1983. *The Subject of Semiotics.* New York: Oxford University Press.

Swann, Brian and Arnold Krupat, eds. 1987. *Recovering the Word: Essays on Native American Literature.* Berkeley: University of California Press.

Tedlock, Dennis, and Barbara Tedlock, eds. 1975. *Teachings from the American Earth: Indian Religion and Philosophy.* New York: Liveright.

Todorov, Tzvetan. 1984. *The Conquest of America: The Question of the Other.* Trans. Richard Howard. New York: Harper Torchbooks.

Turner, Frederick. 1989. *Spirit of Place: The Making of an American Literary Landscape*. San Francisco: Sierra Club.

Turner, Victor. 1988. *The Anthropology of Performance*. New York: Performing Arts Journal.

Vizenor, Gerald, ed. 1989. *Narrative Chance: Postmodern Discourse on Native American Indian Literatures*. Albuquerque: University of New Mexico Press.

White, Hayden. 1987. *The Content of the Form: Narrative Discourse and Historical Representation*. Baltimore: Johns Hopkins University Press.

Woodard, Charles L. 1989. *Ancestral Voice: Conversations with N. Scott Momaday*. Lincoln: University of Nebraska Press.

The Function of the
Landscape of *Ceremony*

ROBERT M. NELSON

❖ ❖ ❖

You pointed out a very important dimension of the
land and the Pueblo people's relation to the land
when you said it was as if the land was telling stories in the novel. That is it exactly, but it is so difficult to convey this relationship without sounding
like Margaret Fuller or some other Transcendental-
ist. When I was writing *Ceremony* I was so terribly
devastated by being away from the Laguna country
that the writing was my way of re-making that
place, the Laguna country, for myself.

—Leslie Marmon Silko,
The Delicacy and Strength of Lace

CRITICS OF SILKO'S NOVEL, like those treating *House Made of Dawn* and *The Death of Jim Loney* (and those who treat regionalist works in general), are quick to show how the special quality of thought—the "vision"—of a "satellite culture"[1] operates to endow certain places with specialness. My contention here is that, in the relationship between vision and place, shaping can and does operate in the reciprocal direction as well: vision can, and in these works demonstrably does, grow *out* of place, so that place, in the sense of a physical landscape, provides a reader a referent that allows verification or confirmation of the accuracy of the vision. This is the sort of verifiability that is, often rather disturbingly, missing or unavailable in other major works of postwar American fiction in which vision seems to be derived solely from "ideal," or philosophical, antecedents.

Whatever else the ceremony in Silko's novel *Ceremony* is about, it is clearly about the process of what Jung calls "constellation." I want to say quickly here that although I'm borrowing this term from Jung to refer to the idea of pattern-formation, I do not wish to claim that the referent of the pattern that evolves in this novel is "archetypal" material in the Jungian sense, nor do I intend a Jungian reading of the novel. Jung's term does, however, draw attention to the prototypal image of pattern-alignment that Silko uses in her novel, an image that gathers together elements of landscape, story, vision, and the world preceding vision. This is the pattern of stars seen first by old Betonie in his vision and then drawn in the dirt for Tayo to memorize (152), the pattern Tayo sees later both in the night sky to the north over Mount Taylor (178) and on the shield hanging on the wall of the hunting lodge at Mount Taylor (214), the pattern contained as well in the pouches hanging on the east and south walls of Kaup'a'ta's house in a traditional Keresan winter story (174–75), the pattern that, seen finally by Tayo in the night sky (247), functions as his signal to begin the final movement in his ceremony of redemption. In both Jung's sense of the term and in Silko's use of star imagery, "constellation" refers not only to a quantity—a certain number of stars or other images all given a singular, categorizing label—but also, and more important, to an emerging event, the event or process of constellation. In the special case that is Tayo's, images of experience need to be ordered, and, further, the ordering process must bring those images into alignment or congruence with certain other patterns: not only "what" Tayo has seen and sees but also "how" Tayo comes to see these things must become constellated within Tayo's vision as well as brought into alignment with the way things ought to be, if the ceremony he participates in is to be completed successfully.

"The way things ought to be": to the postwar critic's ear, that term "ought" may sound suspiciously subjective, and justifiably so. As the novel unfolds, the elements of Tayo's experience that cry out for (re-)patterning, or constellating, become clear; what may not be so clear is just what pattern these elements "ought" to be aligned *with*. Since so much of postwar fiction and theory argues that all order is finally and fundamentally arbitrary,[2] a contemporary reader might be tempted to assume that *any* patterning of these elements would suffice to complete the ceremony and bring order out of the chaos, the perceived fragmentariness, of Tayo's experience and identity.

In this context, the specialness of Silko's creative vision in *Ceremony* is that the process of constellation that is the ceremony of the novel proceeds on three equally important planes, and each plane is aligned finally with each of the other two.[3] On the most obvious level of all, Tayo's personal experience constitutes one of these planes. In addition, much criticism points out and explicates the plane we might call the experience of the "satellite culture," encoded and preserved as it is in the Story of the People, which Story Tayo must re-enact if he is to feel once again culturally "at home." And while the alignment of these two constellated planes yields all by itself a satisfactory fiction by most aesthetic standards, it also leaves a reader with that disquieting sense of "subjectivity" I mentioned earlier, since the referent that validates Tayo's reordering of his personal experience is itself patently a fiction (a consensus vision of how things are or ought to be, to be sure, but still a self-referential product of imagination). The third plane operating in this novel offers the reader—and Tayo—a way to ground these two planes, and the evolving congruence between them, in the world that precedes subjective versions of it, for the constellation of Tayo's consciousness unfolds to conform in pattern not only to the Story that preceeds Tayo's personal quest, but also to the physical terrain, the fundamental geography of the place where this other process unfolds, allowing for a species of validation, or verification, of the process of internal constellation and realignment that most postwar fictions lack. We do not have to know, in advance of reading the novel, the special patterns of thought that characterize Laguna thinking; it is enough to know only how the land itself is configured in order to gain access into the world of the novel. Where Mount Taylor is in relationship to Pa'to'ch Butte, where the sandstone mesas lie in relationship to the red flatlands, where the setting of the opening of the novel lies in relationship to the setting of the ending of the novel: these landmarks in the novel operate to confirm that the subjective-looking pattern of Tayo's vision is constellating with reference to, and in congruence with, the lay of a real landscape. The existence and shape of this landscape, its text and texture, so to speak, is real in the sense that it can be said to exist outside the subjective consciousness of Tayo, outside the collective consciousness of the People his ceremony will finally redeem, outside the creative consciousness even of the author in charge of fabricating the fiction we read.

In sum, then, the novel offers the reader an experience in which three modes of reality come into constellated congruence so that each mode of reality functions as an exact metaphor for each of the others. The pattern, or "interior landscape," of Tayo's consciousness is, at last, accurately tuned not only to the pattern of the culture he needs to reenter, but also—and very importantly, whenever the issue of "validation" comes up—it is congruent, finally, with the pattern and terrain of an external landscape, that relatively objective place in which these other two subjective patterns take form.

GENERALLY SPEAKING, the central ceremony in the novel is Tayo's, who, like the People in general, needs "recentering," regrounding at the center of this new universe he and they find themselves in when the novel opens. Their universe now includes such hitherto invisible (immanent, perhaps, but not yet manifest) elements as fissionable uranium, World War II with its Pacific Theater, long-range potentials for annihilation, and other elements that simply did not exist earlier in human history, either in the world or in the minds of the People, and hence, their traditional ceremonies take no direct account of such specifically postwar phenomena. The need for some ceremony that takes such phenomena directly into account is indicated near the end of the novel, when Ts'eh points out that the sacred elk has not been renewed (repainted) "since the war" (231); and, of course, the seven-year drought, which the people and the land are experiencing as the novel opens, also indicates that the life of the People is out of harmony with the place where they happen to be. It's the same place, and the same People; but the *relationship* between them has fallen out of balance—is, to use the Hopi term, *koyaanisqatsi*. Broadly speaking, what's called for (according to the voice on page 3 of the novel, according to old Ku'oosh, and according to Betonie) is a "ceremony" designed to bring the misguided People back into harmony with the world they happen to be living in, a process that will involve inter alia revisiting (i.e., reaffirming the existence of and the efficacy of) the traditional Spirit Helpers of the People. Just as important, these helpers/healers must be visited *at certain places*—which is to say Tayo must revisit the land itself in order to reestablish contact with the power of healing that he may find there.

Within the context of this larger pattern of redemptive/regenerative rediscovery of the People's Power (when rightly and delicately aligned with the ways of certain spirit helpers) to Make Things Happen, we can see Tayo as functioning as a sort of eponymous representative of the People; his ceremony, if successfully completed, will bring the People, as well as himself as a delegate of the People, back into graceful balance with the external world.

As a delegate of the People, then, Tayo's function is to bring this force back into the lives of the People by bringing it back from the land that the People have, in some special sense, become separated from. To do so, Tayo must go and actively seek out the force, align his own identity with it, and then bring his own renewed identity back to the place that needs it. In the ceremony of this novel, it is not enough for Tayo merely to repattern his own internal landscape; he must also move literally outside and beyond the solipsistic confines of that small room where he lies at the beginning of the novel if he is ever to recover the speckled cattle, or the rain clouds, or any of the other avatars of that spirit of regeneration that has been lost or taken from him.

The question becomes, then, where will he have to go to find, and there recover, the regenerative spirit? That the spirit exists somewhere is implied very clearly in the opening structure of the novel, for even before Tayo appears we are given the figures of Thought-Woman and her sisters, eternally present somewhere, weaving the world out of their collective generative impulse. In the structure of the novel, Tayo will find the spirit he seeks wherever he encounters an avatar of Ts'its'tsi'nako. Thus, another way of phrasing the question "where does Tayo have to go to find the power he seeks" is to ask "where does he have to go to find Ts'[eh]?"

All who study the novel agree that the figure of Ts'eh plays a crucial role in this ceremony. Furthermore, the efficacy of this ceremony depends on the precise relationship that Tayo establishes with the figure Ts'eh. The entity whom Tayo encounters is, clearly, to be understood as a "spirit of place," a more-than-human being who represents the land's own life, who knows How Things Work and who is willing to share this knowledge with the People.[4] The People must acknowledge her existence and find a way to see her for what she is, a way to make a place for her in their conceptual map of the world and the forces at work there.

In the novel itself, the energy that Tayo reencounters in the latter half of the novel in the form of the one who names herself "Ts'eh" is a constant presence. In the opening words of the novel, she takes form as "Ts'its'tsi'-nako, Thought-Woman," who we are told "is sitting in her room / thinking of a story now," which story takes textual form as the novel itself. To a reader unfamiliar with the Keresan language, "Ts'its'tsi'nako" looks like a mouthful, and perhaps this is why, when Tayo later indirectly inquires after her name, she tells him (and us) "You can call me Ts'eh. That's my nickname because my Indian name is so long" (223). Tayo recognizes Ts'eh as the woman he encountered some nine months previously on Tse-pi'na, Mount Taylor; but Tayo also encounters her (or at least the ensemble of generative powers of which she is a part) prior to the postwar chronological setting of the novel, both in the form of a grandmother spider and in the form of the woman people called the Night Swan.[5] The pattern of these four successive encounters is the pattern of Ts'its'tsi'nako's transformation from the realm of traditional story into the Fifth World, from story form to human form, from potentiality into reality.

The Spring: Spider Grandmother

Tayo's first encounter (in the chronological order of the novel) with this regenerative force occurs "the last summer before the war" (93). For this encounter, Tayo has to ride at sunrise from the Pueblo "south to the spring in the narrow canyon" (93); here, perhaps because "the things he did seemed right, as he imagined with his heart the rituals the cloud priests performed during a drought," Tayo receives a provisional answer to his prayer for regeneration as Ts'its'tsi'nako, in her story form, that of a spider ("Thought-Woman, the spider" [1]), appears to him at the spring. As Tayo continues to pray for rain, other life forms associated with water gradually appear—frogs, blue dragonflies, and eventually a hummingbird. At the same time, rainclouds begin to form over Mount Taylor and to move in his direction; later that afternoon, the People receive the blessing of rain.

At this point, Tayo associates the spider he sees at this place only with the figure of Ts'its'tsi'nako of the old stories: "He remembered stories about her. She waited in certain locations for people to come to her for help. She alone had known how to outsmart the malicious mountain Ka't'sina who imprisoned the rain clouds in the northwest room of his magical house" (94). Though Grandmother Spider's appearance (and knowledge) here anticipates the help Tayo will get from her Mount Taylor avatar as he re-enacts the story he is remembering prior to World War II, not until later in the ceremony that is his life will Tayo himself weave the memory of this encounter with Spider Grandmother and his subsequent encounter with the Night Swan into a vision of a single spirit helper—the life of the land itself.

Cubero: The Night Swan

The (re-)generative force Tayo seeks to recover both before and after the War reappears later that day, at Lalo's place in Cubero village, in the form of the woman called the Night Swan—again a grandmother (87), but in human form.

As the Night Swan, working into this world through Josiah but significantly touching Tayo as well, this genetrix figure reveals another one of the places where she can be found. At the end of her story of how she danced into being her desire for a bad man's death, the Night Swan tells Josiah why she left wandering around southern New Mexico:

"One day I got up and walked down the main street of Socorro. The wind was blowing dust down the little side streets and I felt like I was the only one living there any more. . . . . I rode the bus this far. I saw the mountain, and I liked the view from here." she nodded in the direction of the mountain, Tse-pi'na, the woman veiled in clouds. (87)

While the Night Swan claims to remember only her dancing and not the sequence of towns in which she danced prior to her arrival and settlement at Cubero (just off the northwest edge of the main parcel of Laguna Reservation land), the places she does remember having lived in on her way to Cubero (El Paso, Las Cruces, Socorro) align cartographically in a rather straight line running from the border of Mexico north and a little west to Cubero; if this line were extended a little, it would run straight to Mount Taylor. The trajectory of the Night Swan's motion, it seems, has *always* been approaching the site of Mount Taylor, as though that is what she has been becoming as well as where she has been going.

According to the nine-part framing story of the coming of the Ck'o'yo magician Pa'caya'nyi and the subsequent departure and recovery of the Corn Mother, when Nau'ts'ity'i left the people, "she took the / rainclouds with her" (49); the next time we hear about the rainclouds in the form of traditional story, they are being held captive by Kaup'a'ta, another Ck'o'yo magician, who lives "up North" (170). All this makes little sense at the time to Tayo: he is too young to carry the burden of a regenerative ceremony yet, and he has yet to participate in World War II and so has not yet experienced the need for this ceremony. Even so, the lady tells him (and us) that she, along with the "woman veiled in clouds" (87), understood as the place where her vision takes form and will later take form for Tayo, are integral elements of the ceremony that Josiah's purchase of the speckled cattle has already set in motion at Laguna: "You don't have to understand [yet] what is happening. But remember this day. You will recognize it later. You are part of it now" (100). In this sense, Tayo's prewar encounter with the Night Swan prefigures his re-encounter ("You will recognize it later"[6]) with another avatar of the genetrix force, one shaped more clearly to the exigencies of Tayo's individual ceremony, on Mount Taylor.

North or South?: Returns to Cubero

Once Tayo has received from old Betonie an outline of a cognitive map of the ceremony that awaits his participation, a map that includes four important elements awaiting constellation (stars, cattle, mountain, woman [152]), and once Tayo himself has confirmed Betonie's vision in his own dream (145), which incorporates three of the four elements Betonie says need constellating, Tayo is ready to go to seek out whatever it is he, and the People, have become separated from.

Again the question "*Where* should he seek?" becomes crucial to an understanding of how the novel's ceremony works. When Tayo dreams of the speckled cattle immediately following Betonie's rutual, the cattle are moving south and southwest from the general site of Laguna village, where Tayo locates his dreaming point of view: "They were gone, running southwest again, toward the high, lone-standing mesa the people called Pa'to'ch"; Tayo's immediate response to his dream is to want to be at the place he has dreamed: "He wanted to leave that night to find the cattle; there would be no peace until he did" (145). Following Betonie's story about his grandparents and their role in the continuing ceremony (145–52), we find Tayo moving toward the place in his dream where he last saw the speckled cattle, having hitchhiked from Gallup to San Fidel (at the western edge of Laguna land) and about to be picked up by Harley and Leroy, who are returning from Gallup with Helen Jean in tow (155). Apparently, then, Tayo is thinking of bringing himself to the place near Pa'-to'ch Butte, as though to align himself in Fifth World time and space with the cattle he has seen in his dream moving in that direction. He goes along for the ride with Harley, Leroy, and Helen Jean, a ride that brings him to chaos at the Y Bar (at Los Lunas, just off the eastern edge of the Laguna Reservation) and ends with Tayo in the driver's seat; the return ride ends at Mesita, where Tayo leaves Harley and Leroy passed out in the truck, and continues on foot toward Laguna, "going by memory and the edges of old ruts" (169).

To explain how Tayo ends up, seven pages later, north of Laguna village rather than south near Pa'to'ch, we need to interpolate a memory of Tayo's at this point, one associated with the last time in the chronological pattern of the novel Tayo was at this place, into the pattern of the broader regenerative ceremony. At that time, after his encounter with old man Ku'oosh and before encountering old Betonie, Tayo is returning home from the drinking spree with Harley that takes him north from the sheep shack to the highway and west along the string of bars running from Budville through San Fidel and ending up at McCartys. There, at sunset, the bar closed and Harley gone somewhere, Tayo finds himself alone, tugged in one direction by reason and in another by "feeling": "He stood outside facing the south, but all his feelings were focused behind him, northeast, in the direction of Cubero" (102), where earlier in his life he once encountered the Night Swan. Tayo then walks to Cubero, following a natural path already laid out ("The yellow sandstone outcrop ran parallel to the big arroyo behind the bar. All he had to do was follow it" [102]), only to find Lalo's closed and the place deserted. He sits, then, and stares at the adobe walls of the place where the Night Swan had lived and notices how the exposed adobe squares are "beginning to lose their square shape, taking on the softer contours of the mesas and hills" (108); as the things he looks at begin to take on the contours of the land itself, Tayo finds himself feeling more peaceful and at rest: "In a world of crickets and wind and cotton-wood trees he was almost alive again; he was visible. . . . The place felt good; he leaned back against the wall until its surface pushed against his backbone solidly" (104). The experience of feeling part of the land itself is thus constellated, in this episode, with the significance of the Night Swan in Tayo's consciousness; though she is not physically present, she seems to have left a trail of association for Tayo to experience and remember, and to follow, later. With the memory of the Night Swan in the forefront of his consciousness, Tayo stripes the backs of his hands with some of the white plaster dust from the place she once occupied, a gesture that ties Tayo at once to this place (and the pattern of the broader redemptive ceremony it figures in), to the image of the speckled cattle (as the dust makes a "spot-ted pattern" on his "light brown skin" [104]), and to the rituals of the cere-monial dancers of Laguna: "then he knew why it was done by the dancers: it connected them to the earth. He became aware of the place then, of where he was" (104). When he then gets up to explore that place, he finds what he knew would be the case all along: "The room was empty. His steps inside sounded hollow, like a sandstone cave in the cliffs" (104). The pat-tern of revelation that here becomes part of Tayo's constellated internal landscape both confirms the efficacy of the path he has taken so far and predicts the course that he must follow, in the external landscape, to re-cover fully the spirit he seeks. The experience suggests that, while some-thing to the south certainly awaits Tayo's coming (and awaits him at a "sandstone cave in the cliffs"), the proper approach to it is through a route that will first carry him north of where he happens to be in time and space, more specifically north in the direction of Mount Taylor. This is how place is configured, prior to World War II, in the pattern of the redemptive cere-mony encoded in the old Stories; it is also how place is configured in the most efficacious moments of Tayo's motion between the time he returns from the War and the time he returns to Laguna land with Betonie's coun-sel added to his awareness of what he seeks and where it must be sought.

The pattern, then, if it is to continue to unfold in fractal fashion, invites Tayo to turn north, rather than south, at the moment he finds himself reentering Laguna from his encounter with old Betonie. And that is where we find him, on the other side of what otherwise looks formally to be a leap of surprisingly arbitrary suddenness, on page 176 of his ceremony.[7]

Mount Taylor: The Woman of Tse-pi'na

In this next phase of the healing ceremony, the reconstellation of powerful feelings, powerful memories, and imagery to which those feelings and memories are bonded in Tayo's consciousness moves once more toward its completion. Here in the northwest corner of the world as seen from Laguna village, Tayo moves an important step forward in the process through which the shape and pattern of his conscious identity move into congruence with the shape and pattern of the land itself.

That Tayo is on the right track seems confirmed, formally, by his two encounters with the same generative spirit that has manifested earlier in the forms of the Spider Grandmother and the Night Swan. These two encounters are best understood as a sort of single encounter that brackets and blesses Tayo's otherwise solo encounter with the Ck'o'yo medicine, or counterforce, of the overall ceremony. Within the context of his quest to recover the speckled cattle, this counterforce manifests itself as the spirit of possession (and hence deprivation), as a spirit that in turn informs both the figure of the Ck'o'yo gambler Kaup'a'ta of the frame story and the figures of the two fence riders, agents of the white outsider Floyd Lee, who has separated the land from itself with his "high fence of heavy-gauge steel mesh with three strands of barbed wire across the top . . . a thousand dollars a mile to lock the mountain in steel wire, to make the land his" (187–88).

In the chronological sequence of her manifestations to Tayo, the genetrix figure appears to get "younger" with each successive appearance; in the avatar he encounters at the immediate onset of the Mount Taylor phase of the ceremony, "She wasn't much older than he was," though "she wore her hair long, like the old women did, pinned back in a knot" (177). Perhaps we are to understand, then, that the spirit Tayo seeks is increasingly tailoring herself physically to Tayo's form, just as, reciprocally, Tayo's vision of his own role in the greater ceremony of life is increasingly becoming tailored to suit the physical place of which she is the life-giving spirit. At any rate, this lady, who stands figuratively at both the entrance and the

exit to the spirit mountain Tse-pi'na, is clearly at home here where she is:
the challenge in her voice ("What are you doing here?" "Who sent you?")
and the suggestion of Ka't'sina identity in the description we're given of
her ("Her eyes slanted up with her cheekbones like the face of an antelope
dancer's mask" [176–77]) both imply that she functions, here in the evolving ceremony, as a spirit belonging to this place in ways that Tayo does not
yet belong. Because she is encountered where she is, and because she seems
so "at home" in this place, she should probably be taken as the mountain
avatar of the genetrix spirit—a version of Tse-pi'na, "the woman veiled in
clouds," as well as a more youthful version of both Spider Grandmother
and the Night Swan. Furthermore, since she is assigned no name in this
episode, and since physiognomically she appears, in retrospect, to be identified with the one who calls herself "Ts'eh" later in the novel, and since
"Ts'eh" as a nickname could be taken to be a shortened form of either
"Ts'its'tsi'nako" *or* "Tse-pi'na," we can hear at this stage of the ceremony of
the novel a significant coming-together of heretofore uncomfortably separated aspects or avatars of the regenerative force Tayo seeks—and seeks to
integrate into his own vision and experience.

The connection between the woman and the land becomes manifest in
the account (filtered through Tayo's evolving awareness) of his lovemaking with her, an event during which her body takes shape in Tayo's consciousness as a landscape, while his sense of his own relationship to her
takes shape in the language of geographical awareness: "He was afraid of
being lost, so he repeated trail marks to himself. . . . He eased himself
deeper within her and felt the warmth close around him like river sand,
softly giving way under foot, then closing firmly around the ankle in
cloudy warm water. But he did not get lost . . . when it came, it was the
edge of a steep riverbank crumbling under the downpour" (180–81). While
these lines can, of course, be understood as sexual metaphor, they can also,
very importantly, be taken to represent a gift of vision from the spirit
whom Tayo is beginning to identify more and more correctly: these lines
describe not only the body of the one he encounters on Mount Taylor but
also prefigure the place in the external world of the novel (as well as the
external world in which the novel is set and which it replicates so precisely) where Tayo will receive his final spiritual briefing from her (221–22).

As though to confirm that Tayo's identification of the woman with the
land itself is crucial to the efficacy of the broader ceremony, their lovemaking leads to a "continuous," "uninterrupted" dream about those cattle
that Tayo takes, at this point in the pattern of his own motion, to be his
immediate reason for coming to this particular place; just as, prior to their

lovemaking, her words seem both to anticipate and to confirm his own thoughts,[8] her voice here adds recognizable geographical contour to Tayo's otherwise spatially nonspecific dream: "and when he heard her whisper, he saw them scatter over the crest of a round bare hill" (181; compare 196–97). In the morning, in this state of heightened awareness of the messages the land holds for him, "He stood on the steps and looked at the morning stars in the west," but what he breathes in is "a distinct smell of snow from the north, of ponderosa pine on the rimrock above" (181). He will be guided northward toward the cattle by this smell and also by the directions communicated to him wordlessly by the woman in the pattern of the stones she lays out on the table for him to see: first "an ocher yellow sandstone with a powdery fine texture he had never seen before," then a "pinkish gray stone," and finally a "powder blue stone" (183)—trail markers, for Tayo, to help keep him from getting lost on the body of Tse-pi'na.[9]

Thus prepared by his reencounter with a form of the spirit he seeks to reestablish within himself, Tayo finds himself, following the trail marked out for him by the convergent patterns of the woman's stones and the physical terrain he moves through on Mount Taylor, entering not only a special place but also a special quality of time. It is presented to us as a sort of Sacred Time, the kind of time the kurena, kashare, and ka't'sinas live in:

> The silence was inside, in his belly; there was no longer any hurry. The ride into the mountain had branched into all directions of time. He knew then why the oldtimers could only speak of yesterday and tomorrow in terms of the present moment: the only certainty; and this present sense of being was qualified with bare hints of yesterday or tomorrow, by saying, "I go up to the mountain yesterday or I go up to the mountain tomorrow." The ck'o'yo Kaup'a'ta somewhere is stacking his gambling sticks and waiting for a visitor; Rocky and I are walking across the ridge in the moonlight; Josiah and Robert are waiting for us. This night is a single night; and there never has been any other. (192)

Just as we are to understand Ts'its'tsi'nako, the Night Swan, Tse-pi'na, and Ts'eh as avatars of some ultimately single entity, so Tayo here begins to re-experience remembered moments of his existence as manifestations of a single moment.[10] To complete this phase of the process of constellation, Tayo must anchor this unified moment of consciousness in the land, thus identifying time with place as but two aspects of this event. For this to happen, his special sense of time must align with an equally special, qualitatively analogous sense of place.

Tayo experiences such a sense of place during his first night out on

Mount Taylor. It comes to him in the wake of a "strange paralysis," an "overwhelming fatigue" (195) that accompanies some thoughts of failure that in turn derive from a reasonably "realistic" assessment of his chances of returning the cattle to his family's ranch: in a world where time can run out and where meaning and purpose are mere subjective fictions, the Power To Make Things Happen is by definition an illusion, and a dangerous one at that. Lost in his own ratiocinations and thus oblivious to the external world pe se, Tayo is overwhelmed momentarily by the sense of alienation, futility, and "existential despair" so familiar to readers of most postwar fiction:

> His stomach tensed up again. Whatever night this was, he still had a big hole cut in their fence, and he had to find the cattle and get them out before the fence riders found the break. They would be after him then, hunting him down as they had hunted the last few bears on the mountain. His chest was aching with anger. What ever made him think he could do this? The woman under the apricot tree meant nothing at all; it was all in his own head. When they caught him, they'd send him back to the crazy house for sure. . . . As the Army doctors had told him: it was all superstition, seeing Josiah when they shot those goddamn Japs; it was all superstition, believing that the rain had stopped coming because he had cursed it. (194–95)

Once again, as was the case during his stay at the Army hospital, Tayo's response to the enormous possibility of his life's irrelevance is to dissociate his felt self from the consciousness that threatens him, to become once again white smoke drifting into the walls of some abandoned white house. However, lacking at this moment and in this place a closed white room to hide in, he retreats into the only place available: the mountain itself or at least the part of the mountain he finds himself on:

> His face was in the pine needles where he could smell all the tree, from roots deep in the damp earth to the moonlight blue branches, the highest tips swaying in the wind. The odors wrapped around him in a clear layer that sucked away the substance of his muscle and bone; his body became insubstantial, so that even if the fence riders came looking for him with their .30-30s loaded and cocked, they would see him only as a shadow under the tree. (195)

While clearly Tayo's motion here is born of his sense of fear and despair, his motion also brings him into touch, intimate contact, with the land.

By blending into place and surrendering himself to the land in this way, Tayo in effect achieves the state of identity with Mount Taylor that is, in the larger measures of the ceremony, the whole point of being at this place, at this time. As though to confirm that some such transformed vision of relationship to the land is the proper step to be taking here, the shadow-self that Tayo has become is visited by "Mountain lion, the hunter. Mountain lion, the hunter's helper" (196).

Within the framework of Laguna story (and, by extension, the framework of Laguna cultural literacy), the figure of the mountain lion is already constellated with the figure of Mount Taylor (185), and it is certainly important to recognize that Tayo's redemption and future efficacy as a delegate of the People depend, in part, on his ability and willingness to integrate his own identity with the energy attributed by the People to the mountain lion. Here, as elsewhere in the novel, however, Tayo's encounter with the land proves to be his access to cultural tradition: as Tayo moves into a state of relatively undifferentiated harmony with the place he is in, wherever that place happens to be, he moves also into relatively undifferentiated congruence with the life to be found there, whatever form it takes, and these representatives of life function in turn to confirm the value of such self-identification with place.

Specifically, the mountain lion functions in this part of the novel (and, it would seem, in Tayo's vision) as a shadow-self in this shadow-place, an animal "helper" figure with which Tayo can be identified but which is also naturally at home in the special quality of time and place in the way that the woman of Tse-pi'na is.[11] In recognizing and confirming the sacredness of the mountain lion (by sprinkling yellow pollen in its footprints), Tayo, by extension, then, recognizes and confirms the sacredness of his own existence: since they are, in this special time and place, two avatars or "shadows" of the life of Mount Taylor, to confirm the reality of the one is to confirm the reality of both.

Refreshed by his encounter with this animal spirit form of Mount Taylor, and having reframed his vision to allow the place itself to serve as the locus where all elements of constellating reality gather here and now, Tayo locates the speckled cattle. They, too, are functioning in this ceremony as images of what must be found and returned to the heart of the place where the People dwell. Every time the cattle have previously appeared in the novel, as remembered or dreamed by Tayo, they have been heading south, a direction that takes them out of the landscape that lies in the field of the People's lives and vision. From Mount Taylor, however, Tayo can count on their "instinct," as yet unchanged, to move them in the direction of re-entry into everyday life (197). What may not be obvious is that the direction of eventual recovery here is also the direction in which the mountain lion must have been moving for it to meet and then pass by Tayo: to get his first glimpse of the cattle, we are told, Tayo "rode the mare west again, in the direction the mountain lion had come from" (196), also aligning him once again with the "sound of the wind in the pine branches and the smell of snow from the mountain" (196). Such sounds and smells have been associated with Tayo's "goal" since the beginning of this phase of the ceremony: as Tayo arrives at the cabin at the base of Mount Taylor, "A cool wind blew down from the northwest rim of the mountain plateau above them and rattled the apricot leaves" (176); the next morning, when he follows the lady outside, "He breathed deeply, and each breath had a distinct smell of snow from the north, of ponderosa pine on the rimrock above" (181).

Just as Tayo cannot literally move Mount Taylor from where it is relative in space to Laguna village or any other place in space, so he cannot literally follow the path of the mountain lion beyond its point of re-entry into the Fifth World, the world in which humans are always living, wherever else they might also simultaneously exist during extended moments such as Tayo's on Mount Taylor. Re-entering the part of the world he has ventured out from and following the recovered speckled cattle to get there require that Tayo *choose* to re-enter, a choice tantamount to choosing to leave the state of absolute certainty and control that characterized his existence in the spirit world for the uncertainties and shakier possibilities of control that characterize his, and any human being's, existence in the Fifth World. This choice is presented to Tayo when he is forced to choose his way out of the shadow-state he entered just prior to his encounter with mountain lion. (Compare this shadow-state with the state he remembers being in during his hospital stay immediately after World War II, a state he can exit either by turning into white smoke and dissipating into the white walls or else by getting better and going on living as a human being [14–15, 32–33].) It comes down to a choice of two possible "directions" with which he will now align his life: the direction of finality (=certainty), "sinking into the elemental arms of mountain silence," a state he knows would be "a returning rather than a separation" (201), to become absolutely undifferentiated from this place; or the direction of possibilities (=uncertainty), a direction that in passing will require him to discover or invent ways to order "the noise and pain in his head" and to settle for embraces less complete and final than the one he feels awaiting him, should he choose, on Tse-pi'na. As Silko puts it, and as we are to understand Tayo recognizes is the case, "It was up to him" (202).

Tayo's choice, to continue as a human being, sets the plot (and, seemingly, the world) back into motion. Immediately, the figure of the mountain lion splits off from the figure of Tayo, its path to be picked up some miles away by men more interested in hunting a trophy puma than in shepherding a wounded Indian off to the Grants jail. With the fence riders off chasing Tayo's spirit doppelganger,[12] Tayo is left to make his way, painfully, back into the part of the world that lies below.

Tayo's route from the shadow world back to the base of the mountain replicates, in several of its particulars, the path old Betonie laid out in the earlier recovery ceremony in the Chuska Mountains (see 128–45, and especially 141–44), a ceremony itself designed to bring human beings back from the shadow world of animal identity into the Fifth World and thence into identity with the People. Read one way, this earlier ceremony, in conjunction with the story and songs accompanying it, constitutes a teleological map of Tayo's Mount Taylor experience.[13] Just as importantly, it provides a set of specific trail markers that function in two important ways: to assure us that Tayo's literal journey is congruent with his culture's Way and to assure us in turn that his culture's Way is, still, aligned with the landscape that it must map accurately if it is to be efficacious in the first place. In this second respect, the "map" provided by the ceremony is accurate enough: to exit the shadow world of Mount Taylor and re-enter the Fifth World, Tayo moves sequentially through the pattern of vegetation laid out in Betonie's ceremony, from the scrub oak trees (which provide shelter from the snowstorm) (203) down through piñon trees (which provide food, as well as trail markers) (205) back to the cabin, where the cattle are penned in an arroyo behind a barricade made of "unskinned juniper poles" (211).

Presumably, then, the final hoop predicted in Betonie's ceremony through which Tayo must pass in order to return rehumanized to the People, the one made of "wild rose," is represented in Tayo's experiential version of the ceremony by the woman of Tse-pi'na herself, whom he finds awaiting his return just where he last encountered her. On this side of the Mount Taylor part of Tayo's ceremony, the woman continues to function as a more-than-human figure, possessing the sort of knowledge about how the pattern will take shape that makes Tayo uneasy:

> "I wonder if they'll come looking for the cattle?"
> She shrugged her shoulders, unconcerned.
> "They won't come down here," she said.
> "Why not?"
> She gave him a look that chilled him. She must have seen his fear because she smiled and said, "Because of the snow up there. What else?" She was teasing him again. He shook his head. (213)

Leaving Mount Taylor behind him also involves leaving the particular form of the genetrix spirit that is part of that place, too. Once Tayo says "Good-bye" to the woman and turns his attention south again, only the sound of her voice remains in the place: "'I'll be seeing you,' she said. When he turned to wave at her, she was gone" (213).

What Tayo has recovered from Mount Taylor, and what he "takes away from" that place, is a fragile but powerful webwork of vision. In this vision, his revitalized relationship to the land on the one hand and to the spirit *of* that land on the other are constellated to function as metaphors for one another without distortion of either the natural shape of the land or the necessary patterns of the ceremonial stories attached to it by the People. Structurally, the pattern of Tayo's thinking replicates the pattern of the land as well as the teleological pattern of regenerative spirit abiding there. The virtual identification of these three constellated patterns makes it possible in the subsequent stages of his ceremony for Tayo to care for, and express his care for, the life he sees in all three patterns—makes it possible again for him to "love."

Pa'to'ch: Ts'eh

After returning to the foot of Mount Taylor with Robert to pick up the recovered cattle, Tayo returns to his family's home at Old Laguna village, where he stays until the end of May. During this period, he dreams. Perhaps dreams are always about unfinished business, about what remains to be integrated into one's constellated vision of the relationship between self and the world; at any rate, Tayo's dreams no longer seem to need to account for that ensemble of disconnected past voices that preoccupied him at the outset of the novel, let alone the speckled cattle that occupied him on the way up Mount Taylor. All of those elements have been reconstellated during the process of the ceremony, so that part of the business of this healing ceremony is complete, resolved by and in Tayo's experience and vision of Mount Taylor:

> The dreams had been terror at loss, at something lost forever; but nothing was lost; all was retained between the sky and the earth, and within himself. He had lost nothing. The snow-covered mountain remained, without regard to titles of ownership or the white ranchers who thought they possessed it. They logged the trees, they killed the deer, bear, and mountain lions, they built their fences high; but the mountain was greater than any or

all of these things. The mountain outdistanced their destruction, just as love had outdistanced death. The mountain could not be lost to them, because it was in their bones; Josiah and Rocky were not far away. They were close; they had always been close. And he loved them then as he had always loved them, the feeling pulsing over him as strong as it had ever been. . . . The damage that had been done had never reached this feeling. This feeling was their life, vitality locked deep in blood memory, and the people were strong, and the fifth world endured, and nothing was ever lost as long as the love remained. (219–20)

At the same time that Tayo's vision here functions to confirm that much of the ceremony of regeneration is now completed, it functions also to identify and bracket the as-yet unfinished business still awaiting constellation. On Mount Taylor, the "unfinished business" in Tayo's mind was his memory of the speckled cattle and how to recover them; now Tayo has in mind to recover that "feeling which was their life," and Tayo's, too. Tayo dreams now of holding, and of being held by, that regenerative spirit embodied most fully thus far in the evanescent figures of Spider Grandmother, the Night Swan, and the woman of Tse-pi'na. Hence, at the beginning of the penultimate movement of his quest to bring this spirit back to the land for all the People, "He was dreaming of her arms around him strong" (217); waking from this dream to "the smell of wet earth" and propelled by "the feeling he had, the love he felt from her," as well as by "the love he felt for her," Tayo "ran down the hill to the river, through the light rain until the pain faded like fog mist. He stood and watched the rainy dawn, and he knew he would find her again" (218).

To find her this time, Tayo will have to move approximately the same cartographical distance to the south of Laguna village as previously he moved north to find her. The move takes Tayo once again to the very edge of Laguna land, out into the "red clay flats" lying southeast of Acoma village, to the sheep ranch that lies practically in the shadow of Pa'to'ch Butte. There, as removed from the village as he was at the base of Mount Taylor, Tayo is closer, apparently, to the source of what he dreams of: "The terror of the dreaming he had done on the bed [earlier in the novel] was gone, uprooted from his belly; and the woman had filled the hollow spaces with new dreams" (219). In the process of reconstellating all of his life's possibilities, Tayo comes to this place at the south corner of his life's space to test his own reacquired capacity to love life into being.

Significantly, the image of Tayo as he gets up and goes outside on the morning of his re-encounter with the spirit he seeks is enclosed formally by the image of Mount Taylor on the one side and the image of Pa'to'ch on the other. The dream and thought about the dream quoted at length above precedes this movement, while the movement itself is described this way:

> He got up [from these thoughts] and went outside. The sun was behind the clouds, and the air was cool. There were blue-bellied clouds hanging low over the mountain peaks, and he could hear thunder faintly in the distance. He walked north along the road. A year before he had ridden the blind mule, and Harley rode the burro. Pa'to'ch was standing high and clear; months and years had no relation to the colors of gray slate and yellow sandstone circling it. (220)

The color imagery in the passage recalls the stones (blue, gray, yellow) shown to Tayo earlier by the woman he seeks; where previously those stones functioned limitedly to encode the geology of the landscape that at once separated Tayo from and connected him to the cattle, here they encode a much broader geography, as well as the vastly expanded range of Tayo's own vision, which now encompasses all of the Laguna land (and presumably by extension all the life emerging from it) lying between Mount Taylor to the north and Pa'to'ch to the south. Furthermore, if indeed we assume that the woman's stones (rather like Pilate's in *Song of Solomon*) represent places that are homes to her spirit, then we have the suggestion (in the form of the yellow sandstone) that the woman is tied to this place, at the foot of Pa'to'ch, in much the same way she is tied by the blue stone to Mount Taylor. Here, the ceremony finally begins clearly to spiral inward on itself: what Tayo seeks turns out to lie not at the sequential end of this pattern of blue, gray, and yellow rock, but rather *within* the pattern. This motional direction is analogous to the psychological "direction" Tayo must sooner or later take if he is to become a source of what he seeks: if Tayo is to live in the Fifth World with love, he must find a "source" of that love within the land defined and bounded by the two spirit mountains, as well as within himself. Perhaps this helps to explain why Tayo's path, then, moves north, relative to Pa'to'ch, back toward the heart of the world bracketed by those two mountains.

Tayo's path in this part of his ceremony should, if this reading is correct, lead him to some point between Mount Taylor to the north and Pa'to'ch to the south, and within that pattern to a point somewhere in between his isolated room at the edge of Laguna land and the village at its humanized heart. In fact, the route Tayo seems to be taking toward his last encounter with the lady of his dream does have its counterpart in the

physical landscape lying outside the novel (as well as in it): to get to Marmon Ranch (as it is labeled on Geological Survey (GS) maps[14]) from Old
Laguna, one would do best to go west from Laguna about eight miles to
Rt. 23, the Acoma Road, which runs generally south from Casa Blanca (at
the western edge of Laguna land), following that road six or seven miles to
Country Road 49, which branches off Rt. 23 east into the mesas near a formation called Engine Rock (cf. 236); the road quickly bears south again,
running for about seven miles through mesa country and ending at the
northern edge of the flat red clay country used by the Laguna people for
sheep and cattle ranching. At that point, dirt paths run off in three directions ranging from southwest to east; the middle one runs about four
miles south to the Marmon Ranch. We are told in the novel that Tayo
"walked north along the road" from the sheep ranchhouse; curiously
enough, the perspective along this section of the road is such that one's
field of frontal vision is quite literally framed by the view of Pa'to'ch Butte
on the left and the view of Mount Taylor, clearly (and bluely) visible on the
right; the road itself, until it joins up with Country Road 49, appears to
lead one along a line running almost exactly in between these two landmarks. Along this stretch of road, we are told, Tayo pauses to gather "yellow pollen gently with a small blue feather from Josiah's pouch" (220),
thus bringing together in one act the color associated with the Night Swan
and Mount Taylor on the one hand and the color associated with Pa'to'ch
and the one he seeks near there on the other. Tayo then "continued north,
looking to the yellows and the orange of the sandrock cliffs ahead, and to
the narrow sandrock canyons that cut deep into the mesas, exposing the
springs" (220); such a view is precisely the view one would have at a point
about halfway along Country Road 49, heading toward the Acoma Road
juncture. At this point on that road today, a trail has been laid down by the
Marmon family trucks to the place called "Dripping Springs" on GS maps;
the springs themselves, perhaps half a mile from the road, seep from the
face of the mesa there into two parallel arroyos running off the southeast
face of the mesa. In the novel, Tayo

> left the road and took a trail that cut directly to the cliffs, winding up the
> chalky gray hill where the mesa plateau ended in crumbling shale above the
> red clay flats. The sun felt good; he could smell the juniper and piñon still
> damp from the rain. . . . The trail dipped into a shallow wash. The sand
> was washed pale and smooth by rainwater and wind. He knelt and touched
> it. He pulled off his boots and socks and dug his toes deep into the damp
> sand; then he started walking again. (220–21)

Earlier in the ceremony, we should recall, the image of feet sinking into sand functioned to give a form to the feeling of entering the woman on Tse-pi'na and to foreshadow the critical experience of feeling physically one with the mountain itself; here, Tayo's gesture not only recalls those events but also foreshadows his physical re-encounter with the spirit of the Laguna land, this time in its southern avatar. Just as his merging into the place on Mount Taylor was preceded by his encounter with mountain lion, a sort of test to see whether Tayo was prepared to love rather than destroy this representative spirit of the place, so here Tayo's path is crossed by "a light yellow snake, covered with bright copper spots" (221), and his ceremonial response ("He knelt over the arching tracks the snake left in the sand and filled the delicate imprints with yellow pollen": cf. 196) is once again rewarded with a suffusion of the spirit he seeks ("As far as he could see, in all directions, the world was alive. He could feel the motion pushing out of the damp earth into the sunshine—the yellow spotted snake the first to emerge, carrying his message on his back to the people" [221]) as well as a physically human avatar of that spirit, who "emerges"[15] in the next line of the novel to greet his coming. Like her pre-figuration on Mount Taylor, the lady springs very suddenly into Tayo's (and our) field of vision, almost as though she is realized by Tayo's mind moving into alignment with the life message of the earth all around him—the yellow flowers, the yellow snake, and of course the presence of Pa'to'ch, to whose existence "months and years had no relation" (220). As though to confirm that this stretch of land between the Marmon Ranch and Laguna village is as completely a part of Tayo's experience as the woman is a manifestation of its life-sustaining spirit, she offers this time no challenge to Tayo's coming; rather, "she turned to him as soon as he saw her, as if she had been waiting" (221; see also 224), and her first words offer welcome not challenge ("'I'm camped up by the spring,' she said, pointing at the canyon ahead of them. "Here, this way. I'll show you'" [221]). *Y volveré.*

Ts'eh's identification with the spring she points to,[16] and thus with both water and the motif of emergence (this is, after all, a "spring" rather than a river or a lake), has been much discussed. This identification, in con-juction with Tayo's need to reconfirm his own ability to merge with the land and thus with the regenerative spirit immanent in the land, is enough to explain the apparent synesthesia Tayo next experiences. He "lay down beside the pool, across from her, and closed his eyes," and immediately "dreamed he made love with her there. He felt the warm sand on his toes and knees; he felt her body, and it was as warm as the sand, and he couldn't feel where her body ended and the sand began" (222). Again we see and hear in these lines the echo of Tayo's dreamlike experience of his encounter with the lady at the base of Tse-pi'na; but whereas on Tse-pi'na such a description must be read as a metaphor (if only because Mount Taylor's terrain is rock and lava, not sand), at *this* place the textures of geology and feeling finally move into exact congruence (the ground around these springs is, both in the novel and in fact, quite literally sandy). When Tayo later, having awakened to find himself lying in this sand alone, is momentarily gripped by the fear that this spirit is only a creature of his imagination, the land itself again confirms and validates the accuracy of his vision: "The imprints were there; he traced his finger lightly along them. He had not [only] dreamed her; she was there as certainly as the sparrows were there, leaving spindly scratches in the sand" (222).

Tayo then follows her to the top of the mesa, up where "the canyon and the rock of the cliff seemed suddenly gone as if he had stepped from the earth into the sky; where they were, the sky was more than half the world; it enclosed the mesa top where they stood" (223). Here in a place of special, broader perspective on the land,[17] and in response to Tayo's implied questions, the woman provides Tayo with the sound ("Ts'eh") that serves to name her and at the same time to link this form of her with other avatars Tayo has encountered in story form, in place name, and in person. Here also Ts'eh maps with names her relationship to the land "enclosed" by the sky at this place: "I'm a Montaño," she says, and, although the capitalization of the word in the text of the novel denotes this as a surname, the word (Spanish for "mountain") confirms also her identification with both Mount Taylor and Pa'to'ch. Furthermore, the word labels the family she identifies herself with: "We are all very close, a very close family" (223). Pointing to the south, she tells Tayo she has "a sister who lives way down that way" (who is "married to a Navajo man from Red Lake" [Arizona, far to the west]); she tells him that another sister "lives near Flagstaff," way to the west, and that "my brother's in Jemez" off to the east. Presumably, we have already been introduced to her kinsman of the here-unmentioned fourth direction;[18] at any rate we have already seen how "at home" Ts'eh seems to be in such places. More important, I think, about this revelation of her "family" relationship to some (perhaps all) other mountain spirits of the Southwest is that she is also as much at home in the place Tayo calls home as she is in the places the Hopi, the Jemez, the Apache, and the Navajo call home—at home and waiting to be recognized and loved, in any or all of her forms.

As fall approaches, Tayo continues to heal, a process that depends on reanchoring his own spirit in the land and in the love he brings to, and receives from, Ts'eh: "Their days together had a gravity emanating from the mesas and arroyos, and it replaced the rhythm that had been interrupted so long ago" (227). That this "gravity" derives not so much from the temporary form of Ts'eh as from Pa'to'ch Butte, the source of her power to heal Tayo, is finally made clear: "She was looking at Pa'to'ch, and the hair was blowing around her face. He could feel where she had come from, and he understood where she would always be" (230). Tayo's recognition of Ts'eh's identification with Pa'to'ch echoes Josiah's earlier recognition of the Night Swan's affinity with Mount Taylor: " 'I saw the mountains, and I liked the view from here.' She nodded in the direction of the mountain, Tse-pi'na, the woman veiled in clouds. . . . Josiah pulled her close, promising himself he would never ask her what it was about the mountain that caused her to stop here" (87).

This healing process, during which Tayo becomes almost as much a part of the "Montaño family" as Ts'eh, is not an end in itself. Like all his previous encounters with the spirit forms of the land, this one, too, is preparation for the next phase of the ceremony. The signals that Tayo is ready to participate in this next phase include not only his recovered ability to locate the She-Elk petroglyph (230–31: cf., earlier, the significance of his being able to locate the speckled cattle) but also his recovered ability to feel enough a part of the land, even without Ts'eh's corporeal presence to sustain him, to act on the land's (and, by extension, his own and Ts'eh's) behalf. By the end of the summer, Tayo's "connection with the ground [is] solid" (231) enough to enable him to see what moves on the land besides the spirit Ts'eh embodies, to imagine clearly which of those presences are only apparent threats to the generative spirit of the land and which are truly bent on bringing about "the end of the story" (231). In concert with Ts'eh, Tayo comes to understand how the ceremony is moving him toward an encounter with the spirit that drove her into exile in the first place, the manipulative spirit of the Gunnadeyahs, the followers of the Ck'o'yo Way last encountered in the form of the fence riders on Mount Taylor and waiting, now, to be confronted in the form of Emo, Tayo's contemporary counterpart and old antagonist. Here, the issue becomes reduced to which of two versions of the single story of life, lived out on the land, will take form in the Fifth World history of this place: the version in which life goes on, growing out of the land and itself the way it always heretofore has, or the version in which life "ends here, the way all their stories end, . . . right here, with you fighting to your death alone in these hills" (231–32).

Jackpile Mine: Emo

Up to this point, ceremony functions to bring Tayo into identity with the land and thereby into intimate relationship with the spirit that awaits rediscovery and reintegration into Tayo's consciously felt self and into the vision that expresses that self. By the time he parts ways with Ts'eh in the vicinity of Pa'to'ch, Tayo has acquired such vision. It remains for him now to test his vision, to sustain it even in the context of all that remains in the world once this regenerative force has been factored out; it remains for Tayo to come to terms with the powerful forces of "manipulation" and "witchery" at work in the universe of the novel, forces that threaten to annihilate the fragile web of Ts'its'tsi'nako's weaving.[19]

This is a post–World War II fiction, and so it makes sense that in this renovated ceremony the spirit of the Destroyers should be invested in the fact of the atomic bomb.[20] Just as the land contains within itself the stuff of potential regeneration (including Ts'its'tsi'nako and her avatars), so it also contains the potential for annihilation (along with people willing to use it that way). The test of the regenerative spirit, and of the spirit of Tayo who carries it now, is whether it can continue to exist (or even coexist) in the presence of its antithesis, or even in the place where that potential can be seen clearly for what it is.

To get to the place where the ceremony will realize its potential for either annihilation or regeneration, Tayo moves out in the direction that Ts'eh seems to point out to him as she leaves him, at the juncture of the trail to the springs and the road she takes back to Acoma Road: "The road curved through the red clay and junipers to the northeast" (234). To get to the place he must be in order to complete the ceremony, Tayo moves from the cave at the spring up to the mesa top, then due north to "the ridge south of Engine Rock" (236), and from there down the west face of the ridge to a culvert under the Acoma Road where he sleeps that night. Walking north along the Acoma Road the next morning, he is picked up by Harley and Leroy and transported with them up "into the hills northwest of Cañoncito" (241), presumably off Laguna land.[21] From this place, Tayo must walk west, back onto Laguna land (as well as back into the direction of his own disturbing history of life lived in the wake of World War II's destruction) to the Jackpile Mine, which is located on the north-central edge of Laguna land. To the east lies a barren saltweed wasteland of lava hills, ranging to a point just northwest of Cañoncito (on a pocket of Navajo Reservation land), and to the west lies Mount Taylor (whose peak is just off the northwest corner of Laguna land), while the mine itself lies about halfway between these two places. Thus situated geographically, things could indeed go either way here.

The way things have been going here, since around 1940 (about the time of the onset of drought in the novel; about the time World War II became inevitable; about the time the Manhattan Project was authorized, this bringing even this remote patch of land into the pattern of nuclear holocaust), is unequivocally in the direction of annihilation. The uranium mined here during the early years of the Manhattan Project[22] was fed into the stream of uranium supplied to scientists at Chicago, Oak Ridge, and (later) Hanford for conversion into enough fissionable uranium to fashion into an artificial New Mexico sun, one designed to blind rather than illuminate (245), to destroy rather than to nurture: "He knelt and found an ore rock. The gray stone was streaked with powdery yellow uranium, bright and alive as pollen; veins of sooty black formed lines with the yellow, making mountain ranges and rivers across the stone" (246). "Bright and alive as pollen," "mountain ranges and rivers": one can harness the power of the land to the ends of regeneration *or* final annihilation. With this insight, Tayo's vision of the pattern of the ceremony takes a quantum leap of perspective, from Pan-Indian to Pan-human:

> There was no end to it; it knew no boundaries; and he had arrived at the point of convergence where the fate of all living things, and even the earth, had been laid. From the jungles of his dreaming he recognized why the Japanese voices had merged with Laguna voices, with Josiah's voice and Rocky's voice; the lines of culture and worlds were drawn in flat dark lines on fine light sand, converging in the middle of witchery's final ceremonial sand painting. From that time on, human beings were one clan again, united by the fate the destroyers had planned for all of them, for all living things; united by a circle of death that devoured people in cities twelve thousand miles away, victims who had never known these mesas, who had never seen the delicate colors of the rocks which boiled up their slaughter. (246)

The easier course to take, we are told, is the course of annihilation. Even bolstered by his recent encounter and quarter-year stay with Ts'eh, Tayo's own commitment to regenerative action is strained almost to breaking by witnessing Emo and the others work their Ck'o'yo medicine in the night: "This ceremony was draining his endurance. He could not feel anything, then, not for Josiah or Rocky and not for the woman" (250). The power he draws from his relationship to the land itself is vitiated in this place; here, where even the water tastes bitter (244–45), Tayo is on ground that has too long been held in the service of the Gunnadeyahs and their design, scarred so completely and violated so thoroughly that the land itself seems irredeemable, irrecoverable, lost forever: "He knew why he had felt weak and sick; he knew why he had lost the feeling Ts'eh had given him, and why he had doubted the ceremony: this was their place, and he was vulnerable"(242–43).

Clearly, the source of Tayo's powerful feeling of loss is this particular part of the body of Laguna, where the land has been most deeply and visibly wounded by the mining operation. Within the larger context of the ceremony he understands himself to be involved in, however, this is but one of many sites that need to be brought into realignment—not changed, but only reconstellated:

> But he saw the constellation in the north sky, and the fourth star was directly above him; the pattern of the ceremony was in the stars, and the constellation formed a map of the mountains in the directions he had gone for the ceremony. For each star there was a night and a place; this was the last night and the last place. . . . He had only to complete this night, to keep the story out of the reach of the destroyers for a few more hours, and their witchery would turn, upon itself, upon them. (247)

Insofar as the emerging pattern of the ceremony is also the emerging pattern of Tayo's own "internal landscape," Tayo's reconfrontation here with the figure of Emo can be understood to be at the same time Tayo's confrontation with his own heart's capacity for violence. In this place, Tayo is perfectly capable of acting out his own life into a destructive form—perfectly capable of "jamm[ing] the screwdriver into Emo's skull the way the witchery had wanted, savoring the yielding bone and membrane as the steel ruptured the brain" (253). In such a place, Tayo's only nondestructive course of action is to learn how to rely on the love he has drawn from the land, how to use this love to control his own powerfully felt impulse to bury the screwdriver in Emo's skull. In order to remain regenerative, the power to live must not be used to destroy, ever; the question is (and was always) only whether it can survive the reality of the destructive potential invested here in the form of Emo and in the form of the ruined landscape where Emo feels so at home.

At the Jackpile Mine, then, Tayo completes his ceremony of self-regeneration. The capacity for love that he has drawn from the land outlives his reconfrontation with the capacity for annihilation that also inheres there. The last words Ts'eh speaks, as she turns to head in the direction of Tayo's final encounter with the land, are "I'll see you" (235); moving in the direction her spirit steers for him, Tayo acts in accord with the spirit she represents. All that remains is for Tayo to make his way back to the Pueblo and report his story to the People, thus completing the process of transforming the life he has recovered from the landscape into renewed cultural energy.

Laguna: The People

The path Tayo takes to return from his showdown with Emo to the Pueblo is apparently designed to accommodate the further transformation of Tayo's individual life into a fuller representation of the life of the People. As he moves south in the night, "his body . . . lost in exhaustion, his bones and skin staggering behind him" (254), Tayo is sustained in motion by the spirit of love in several recollected forms. We are told that he "dream[s] with his eyes open," first of his relationship to the genetrix figure whose shared powers have helped him survive the night, which power he foresees himself translating back to the land itself ("He would gather the seeds for her and plant them with great care in places near sandy hills" [254]). He then dreams of his spirit relation to some of those mortals—literally relatives—he has loved and still loves (Josiah, old Grandmother, Rocky) and whom he knows have loved and still love him; he dreams "They were taking him home" (254).

The consciousness that returns to the Pueblo, then, is a shared one: not only Tayo but also Ts'eh, Josiah, Rocky, and others are in a sense coming "home," and it is precisely the shared quality of this consciousness that sustains Tayo's movement across the "sandy flat below Paguate Hill" and on south to the railroad tracks running east and west parallel to the river below the village, where "the creosote and tar smell of the railroad tracks woke him from his dreaming" just before sunrise. We are told that "when he felt the dampness of the river, he started running" through the "broken shadows of tamaric and river willow" (255), presumably to position himself near the "big cottonwood tree" that, I suspect, marks the river crossing southeast of the village where the Ka't'sinas traditionally come into the Pueblo in late November (182). There, as the sun rises, Tayo finds himself knowing, as he has been coming throughout his ceremony to know, that "They had always been loved. He thought of her then; she had always loved him, she had never left him; she had always been there: (255).[23] The "she" Tayo has in mind, I believe, is the genetrix figure in any and all of her several avatars: Ts'its'tsi'nako, the Night Swan, the Lady Tse-pi'na, Ts'eh, and, finally, becoming part of that constellation at this moment, Tayo's own biological mother. Earlier, we may recall, Aunt Thelma tells Tayo the single story he has been given about his mother, Laura, typically referred to as Little Sister or Sis (Ts'its"? [33–34]), whom Auntie encountered one morning at sunrise, standing naked save for her high-heeled shoes, at precisely this place (70). At least one new Ka't'sina, it seems, has been in the process of joining the ranks of the Old Ones; and while it is perhaps ironic that Catholicized Auntie should have been the first to witness her emergence, it is not surprising that Auntie would not welcome her to the village, that this spirit has waited years for one who has acquired the quality of vision that is a prerequisite to bringing her back to the heart of the People and making a place for her there. On this first morning following the Fall equinox, finally, "the transition [is] completed": as Tayo "crosse[s] the river at sunrise" (255), he brings them all, loved and loving extensions of himself, into the village and into the kiva at the spiritual heart of the village.

There in the kiva, Tayo tells to old Ku'oosh and to other Pueblo elders the story of the genetrix spirit he has encountered in the land. "It took a long time to tell the story" (257), in part because the old men understand the necessity of grounding such stories realistically in the land if they are to work ("they stopped him frequently with questions about the location and the time of day; they asked about the direction she had come from . . . [257]), and in part because Tayo's story of his encounter must be woven carefully into the webwork of all the other kiva lore that the old men take to be its proper context:

> They started crying
> the old men started crying
> "A'moo'ooh! A'moo'ooh!"
> You have seen her
> We will be blessed
> again.

Part of the appeal of Tayo's story to the kiva elders is that it reestablishes the Pueblo as the geographical (and hence spiritual) center of a visible world, a particular landscape that contains, within itself, the power to heal and make whole and sustain life in the face of those destructive forces (both internal and external to human consciousness) that cohabit the universe. The world Tayo has probed in all directions relative to the Pueblo is a world of places, places that offer up and confirm their power to revitalize the human spirit and the life of the People. To be sure, cultural identity, for the individual as well as for the People, depends on keeping the stories alive—by retelling them, by reliving them, and even by revising or adding to their ensemble to accommodate the new realities and "shape" of the world as it changes. To be equally sure, though, such revitalization depends intimately on those stories' being constellated, and if necessary *re*-constellated, to the shape and pattern of the landscape itself, "because, after all, the stories grow out of this land as much as we see ourselves as having emerged from the land there" (Silko and Wright, *Delicacy* 24).

Notes

1. For a fuller discussion of this term (coined originally by T. S. Eliot) as it is used in the context of literary regionalism, see Watkins, esp. 8–11.

2. I have in mind here, for instance, Todd Andrews' dictum in the "piano-tuning" section of *The Floating Opera* about "versions of the case," or Borges's "games with infinity," or Robbee-Grillet's amusement in *The Voyeur* with Mathias's absurdly futile programs for selling his watches and his equally futile attempts to fix a "point of reference" outside his own imagination, or Skipper's several versions of his heart's experience in Hawkes's *Second Skin.* The proposition that all pattern is a figment of imagination is, I think, the essential proposition underlying postwar "postmodernist" thinking and literary creative vision.

3. Several critics have noted the three-level structure of this novel. Allen's analysis of the novel as a healing ceremony ("The Psychological Landscape of *Ceremony*") talks of "sickness in individuals, societies and landscapes" (10); however, her analysis of how those three elements of the novel are brought into healing alignment treats "landscape" as a feminizing spirit *of* place rather than treating place in any specificity. Sands also alludes to the three-level structure of the ceremony of this novel ("untangling painful memories, understanding ancient rituals, and participating in the present must merge the ongoing myth of the people" ["Preface" 3]) and further suggests that this "participation in the present," which in this novel she sees as healing "the breach between Tayo and the land and its creatures," may constitute a characteristic of Native American literature: "Land and nature, myth and ritual, cyclic patterns and continuum, ceremony and the sacredness of storytelling are all basic elements that distinguish the Indian mode of literature from any other" (4). Mitchell, too, says the novel "can be viewed as three simultaneous planes that interweave throughout" (27), though her three planes ("human plane," Socio/cultural plane," and "myth/ritual plane") make so special place for the function of the landscape in the novel.

4. Wiget, for instance, groups Ts'eh with the Night Swan and Descheeny's wife as "Earth Woman/Yellow Woman figures" and later says of the Ts'eh of Mount Taylor that "she may in fact be a mountain spirit" (*Native American Literature* 88); Copeland (who makes no distinction between the Ts'eh of Mount Taylor and the Ts'eh of

Dripping Springs) speaks of Tayo's "sense of her identity as a nature spirit, a mountain spirit or ka'tsina" (*"Black Elk Speaks* and Leslie Silko's *Ceremony"* 166). Allen sees
Ts'eh as a version of "Reed Woman, Spider Woman, Yellow Woman, on and on"
(Sands and Ruoff 67), and Mitchell seems to concur (33). Lincoln identifies the Ts'eh
Tayo encounters at "the novel's center" as a "spirit sister of Yellow Woman [Kotsinin-
inako], whom the Laguna call 'the mother of all of us,'" and further identifies this
figure with the kurena spirits who are associated with sunrise, said to live in the
northeast (*Native American Renaissance* 234). I think Lincoln's identification is *too* precise,
though: Tayo's Ts'eh never once in the novel enters Tayo's vision from the northeast, nor is he ever moving northeast when he meets her; and the only time Tayo's
ceremony takes him northeast of Laguna village is when he moves that way at the
end of the novel to witness Emo's witchery up in "the hills northwest of Cañoncito"
(241); there, "The headlights appeared suddenly from the northeast" (248).

5. The relationship of the figure of the Night Swan to the figure of Ts'eh, and
of both to Ts'its'tsi'nako of the frame story, is treated very convincingly by both
Allen (*The Sacred Hoop* 121–22) and Lincoln (*Native American Renaissance* 240–41). Both
Allen and Lincoln point out the recurrence of blue imagery in the depictions of
both figures. To their lines of argument I would add that we have at least one other
formal reason to connect the figures of Ts'eh and the Night Swan to the figures of
the generative sisters in the frame story: their names. I have already suggested that
"Ts'eh" can be read (and heard) as a shortened form of "Ts'its'tsi'nako"; perhaps we
can hear, in the "Night Swan," an Anglicized version of Thought-Woman's sister,
"Nau'ts'ity'i." (In the version of the "Laguna Thought Woman Story" Allen cites,
these two names are spelled, respectively, "Tse che nako" and "Naotsete.")

6. One of the elements that floats unconnected in Tayo's fevered consciousness
as the novel opens is "the singing, . . . two words again and again, *Y volveré'*" (6).
This memory fragment presumably derives from the time Tayo visits the Night
Swan on Josiah's behalf: as he ascends the staircase to her room, he hears "A
scratchy Victrola . . . playing guitars and trumpets; a man sang sad Spanish
words. *"Y volveré'* were the only words Tayo could understand" (97). The words are
a promise ("and I will return") delivered upon leaving. That the power of regeneration lying behind the figure of the Night Swan does keep this promise is, in part,
the contention of this study.

7. Arguably, the sequence of Tayo's motion is also predicated by the pattern of
Betonie's ceremony, because the route of recovery (as Silko paints it on pages
141–42) involves moving successively from the "dark mountain" to the blue, yellow, and finally white mountains. In the novel, the Chuska Mountains (where
Betonie performs his ceremony) are characterized as "a thick powdery black" (145),
while Mount Taylor is characteristically blue (100, 128); the yellow mountain of the
ceremony then has its Fifth World analog in the form of Pa'to'ch Butte, a formation

of primarily yellow sandstone (220), while the white mountain would seem to be the villages of Laguna (both Cubero and Old Laguna), constructed out of white gypsum sandstone (104, 256). The traditional Keres name for where the People live (and have lived) is Kush Kutret, "the white village," and one of the seven present-day Laguna settlements, the one located closest to Acoma land to the west, is called Casa Blanca, "white house."

8. For instance, on page 178: "'The sky is clear. You can see the stars tonight.' She spoke without turning around. He felt a chill bristle across his neck, and it was difficult to swallow the mouthful of stew. He had watched the sky every night, looking for the pattern of stars the old man drew on the ground that night. Late in September he saw them in the north." Here, the lady's ability to speak Tayo's own mind spooks him because it implies that she is somehow in league with Betonie.

9. To get to the cattle, it turns out, Tayo follows "the trail [that] was parallel to the top of the orange sandrock mesa" (184), a trail that becomes so narrow that his mare cannot possibly turn around, much less stray off the configured path; at the place where this trail debouches, Tayo proceeds "west . . . toward the *cerros,* gently rounded hills of dark lava rock which were covered with a thin crust of topsoil and grass" (185), finally gaining direct access to the "blue" summitry of Mount Taylor as he moves onto "the land [that] ascended into a solid pine forest" (185), the place referred to as "North Top." Whatever other significance Ts'eh's stones have, they also help to orient Tayo in, and on, the land itself.

10. One way to account for this special sense of time that Tayo experiences in these lines is to call his experience a moment of deconstructive awareness, during which the consciously held fiction that differentiates subject from object, self from other, is suspended, allowing him a holistic rather than sequential vision of the relationship between moments of experience (or more precisely between the separable memories *of* those experiences). In effect, this new quality of vision reframes all of Tayo's experience, both remembered and immediate, as a single event rather than as a sequence of (time-differentiated) events.

11. Understanding how mountain lion and the woman of Tse-pi'na are *both,* in this sense, avatars of the spirit of this mountain can do much to refresh, by reframing, one's rereading of that loveliest of Silko's poems, "Survival: Indian Song" (*Story-teller* 35–37)—the last line of which, "Running on the edge of the rainbow," provides the title for a videotape of Silko's readings ("Running on the Edge of the Rainbow: Laguna Stories and Poems. With Leslie Marmon Silko," a videotape in the series *Words and Place: Native Literature from the American Southwest,* Larry Evers, Project Director [New York: Clearwater, 1978]).

12. The fence riders will catch up with neither the lion nor, once they have lost sight of him, the lion's human doppel. Mount Taylor, in the form of the lady Tse-pi'na working her storm blanket medicine, has taken care of all that:

The snow was covering everything, burying the mountain lion's tracks and obliterating his scent. The white men and their lion hounds could never track the lion now. . . . He smiled. Inside, his belly was smooth and soft, following the contours of the hills and holding the silence of the snow. He looked back at the way he had come: the snowflakes were swirling in tall chimneys of wind, filling this tracks like pollen sprinkled in the mountain lion's footprints. (205)

13. Bell, I think, provides the best single analysis of Betonie's ceremony, both in terms of its ritual antecedent (identified as the Navajo Coyote Transformation rite from "The Myth of Red Antway, Male Evilway") and in terms of its relationship to Tayo's experience on Mount Taylor. An excellent study of how individual consciousness and mythic patterning come into constellated congruence, Bell's essay (see this volume) takes no particular account, however, of the geographical realism that, I contend, is crucial to the *healing* efficacy of Tayo's Mount Taylor experience.

14. For maps detailed enough to locate the specific geological and topographical details mentioned in this paragraph and in other parts of this chapter, see the U.S. Department of the Interior Geographical Survey's quadrangle (7.5 minute) series of topographical maps for Valencia County, New Mexico. The plats "Acoma Pueblo Quadrangle," "Marmon Ranch Quadrangle," and "South Butte Quadrangle" cover the area treated in this paragraph.

15. Emergence motifs are, of course, vital elements of the cultural myths of many people. However (and unlike, say, the Eden of the Judeo-Christian origin myth), people in most of the Pueblo cultures can point exactly to the spot where the People are said to have emerged from the Fourth World into this one. Given the structure of *Ceremony,* one may be tempted to assume that in Laguna tradition the Emerging Place would fall either on Mount Taylor (as, for instance, Lincoln does [*Native American Renaissance* 234]) or in the immediate vicinity of Pa'to'ch, where Tayo comes "closest" to Ts'eh. Silko states that in Laguna tradition the Emergence Place (*sipapu*) is "located slightly north of the Paguate village" ("Landscape, History, and the Pueblo Imagination" 91)—i.e., in the vicinity of the village of Seboyeta (where, incidentally, state highway 237 simply ends in the front yard of the "Cebolleta" Post Office building), a site a good 30 miles from the Mount Taylor (northwest) corner of Laguna land and at nearly the dead center of the northern boundary of the Laguna Reservation lands. She also adds a caution about identifying Emergence Places too rigidly:

> . . . the Pueblo stories about the Emergence and Migration are not to be taken as literally as the anthropologists might wish. Prominent geographical features and landmarks which are mentioned in the narratives exist for ritual purposes, not because the Laguana people actually journeyed south

for hundreds of years from Chaco Canyon or Mesa Verde, as the archaeolo-
gists say, or eight miles from the site of the natural springs at Paguate to the
sandstone hilltop at Laguna. (91)

Consistent with Silko's words about the function of Emergence motifs, and Lincoln's claim notwithstanding, I think it is best to read the novel as a post–World
War II version of an older ceremony and to concede that, in *this* version of the Story,
the "Emerging Place" of what Tayo seeks—the place where the form of the regeneration calling itself "Ts'eh" appears to him—is to be found precisely where Tayo
finds it, and her, at the place called Dripping Springs.

16. For what it's worth, the place Silko has selected to be the setting of this part
of the novel, designated "Dripping Springs" on GS maps, features not just one but
four "springs." It is a doubled canyon running off the south face of the mesa; the
west-side canyon contains one very active spring, while the east-side canyon contains three, one of which is particularly active. Silko seems to have had in mind the
spring of the west-side canyon as the "Emerging Place" of Tayo's ceremony: no willow grows immediately beside any of the east-side springs, and "swallows inside
their round mud nests, making high pitched noises" (221) are to be found only
around the cliff face of the west-side spring.

17. Compare the analogous moments of panoramic vision Tayo experiences
twice previously: in the Chuska Mountains just prior to Betonie's ceremony (139),
and then on the "blue" mountain when he is situated geographically right above
the spot where he encounters the humanized avatar of Mount Taylor (184–85).
Both of these moments, in turn, recall the special pre–World War II feeling of limit-
less identity with the land and its possibilities that Tayo remembers having experienced "when he and Rocky had climbed Bone Mesa, high above the valley
southwest of Mesita" (19). This feeling, which can be acquired only from such a
panoramic view of the land, is one of the crucial components of *healing* vision—not
only in *Ceremony* but also in *House Made of Dawn* and *The Death of Jim Loney.*

18. I have in mind, of course, the hunter (who is identified with the spirit of the
mountain lion by the hat he wears) Tayo meets on his way back down Mount Taylor. Like Ts'eh, he has that Pan-Indian, or at least a Pan-Southwest Indian, cast of
character: Tayo recognizes the chant he sings on page 206 as a Laguna deer song,
like the hunter's rifle an "old one" that "works real good. That's the main thing";
his second song, though, "sounded like a Jemez song, or maybe one from Zuni"
[207] (or maybe one so fundamentally "good" it would work at Jemez *and* Zuni, and
anywhere in between).

19. In a 1976 *Sun Tracks* interview, Silko characterized these forces this way:

In the novel, I've tried to go beyond any specific kind of Laguna witchery or
Navajo witchery. . . . I try to begin to see witchery as a sort of metaphor

for the destroyers or the counter force, that force which counters vitality and birth. That counter force is destruction and death. . . . Another name for the counter forces are the manipulators. (Copeland and Carr 32)

20. In a 1980 interview published in the University of Arizona's student literary magazine *Persona,* Silko reiterates the sense of the bomb's significance that she attributes to Tayo in the novel:

> SILKO: The day after the first bomb was detonated, if you want to try to look for a single instance, seems to me the big dividing point for human beings.
>
> PERSONA: Is that why you chose the post–World War II era as the setting for *Ceremony* and not, say, the Korean War, or Viet Nam?
>
> SILKO: Right. Because after that day all human beings, whether you were a Hopi who believed in traditional ways or whether you were a Madison Avenue Lutheran, all human beings faced the same possible destruction. . . . When you can destroy the entire planet and make it uninhabitable for life for thousands and thousands of years, that's a big change. That's a change like never ever before. (Fitzgerald 34–35)

21. We are told that Tayo wakes up "at the foot of a rocky little hill covered with cholla" and that all around "the hills were covered the dark lava rock" (241)—terrain that recalls the setting of Betonie's story of witchery's origins, "up in the lava rock hills / north of Cañoncito" (133). Such a formation, labeled Mesa del Lobo ("wolf mesa") on GS maps, lies about 10 miles both east of Paguate village and north of the Jackpile fence.

22. This is how Silko tells it in the novel. In fact, Jackpile mining operations didn't commence until after World War II had ended: see Silko, "The Fourth World."

23. Compare the passage, already cited, on pages 219–20, as well as Ts'eh's words on page 231. I take the "they" in this passage to refer specifically to those relatives we have just seen co-occupying Tayo's mind (Josiah, Grandmother, and Rocky) and to refer more generally, by this moment in the evolution of Tayo's sense of his identity, to the People collectively; I take the true subject of this passive voice construction (that is, the "agent" of the love referred to) to be Tayo, as well as Josiah/Grandmother/Rocky, as well as the People, as well as the "she" of the second sentence of the passage.

Works Cited

Allen, Paula Gunn. "The Psychological Landscape of *Ceremony*." *American Indian Quarterly* 5.1 (February 1979): 7–12.

_____. *The Sacred Hoop: Recovering the Feminine in American Indian Traditions.* Boston: Beacon, 1986.

Barth, John. *The Floating Opera.* 1956. New York: Doubleday, 1967.

Bell, Robert C. "Circular Design in *Ceremony.*" *American Indian Quarterly* 5.1 (February 1979): 47–62.

Copeland, Marion W. "*Black Elk Speaks* and Leslie Silko's *Ceremony*: Two Visions of Horses." *Critique* 24.3 (Spring 1983): 158–72.

Copeland, Marion W., and Denny Carr. "A Conversation with Leslie Marmon Silko." *Sun Tracks* 3.1 (Fall 1976): 28–33.

Fitzgerald, James. "Interview: Leslie Silko, Storyteller." *Persona* (1980): 21–39.

Hawkes, John. *Second Skin.* New York: New Directions, 1964.

Lincoln, Kenneth. *Native American Renaissance.* Berkeley: University of California Press, 1983.

Mitchell, Carol. "*Ceremony* as Ritual." *American Indian Quarterly* (February 1979): 27–36.

Momaday, N. Scott. *House Made of Dawn.* New York: Harper, 1968.

Robbe-Grillet, Alain. *The Voyeur.* 1955. Tr. Richard Howard. New York: Grove, 1958.

Sands, Kathleen M. "Preface: A Symposium Issue." *American Indian Quarterly* 5.1 (February 1979): 1–6.

Sands, Kathleen M, and A. LaVonne Ruoff, eds. "A Discussion of *Ceremony.*" *American Indian Quarterly* 5.1 (February 1979): 63–70.

Silko, Leslie. *Ceremony.* New York: Viking, 1977.

_____. "The Fourth World." *Artforum* 27.10 (Summer 1989): 125–26.

_____. "Landscape, History, and the Pueblo Imagination." *Antaeus* 57 (Autumn 1986). 83–94.

_____. *Storyteller.* New York: Seaver, 1981.

Silko, Leslie, and James Wright. *The Delicacy and Strength of Lace.* Ed. Anne Wright. Saint Paul: Graywolf, 1985.

U.S. Department of the Interior Geological Survey. "Acoma Pueblo Quadrangle: New Mexico-Valencia Co./7.5 Minute Series (Topographic)." Denver and Washington, D.C.: U.S. Geological Survey, 1961.

_____. "Marmon Ranch Quadrangle: New Mexico-Valencia Co./7.5 Minute Series (Topographic)." Denver and Washington, D.C.: U.S. Geological Survey, 1961.

_____. "South Butte Quadrangle: New Mexico-Valencia Co./7.5 Minute Series (Topographic)." Denver and Washington, D.C.: U.S. Geological Survey, 1961.

Watkins, Floyd C. *In Time and Place: Some Origins of American Fiction.* Athens: U of Georgia P, 1977.

Welch, James. *The Death of Jim Loney.* 1979. New York: Penguin, 1982.

Wiget, Andrew. *Native American Literature.* Twayne's United States Authors. Series 467. Boston: Hall, 1985.

No Boundaries, Only Transitions

Ceremony

JAMES RUPPERT

◆　◆　◆

CEREMONY HAS RECEIVED wide praise from almost the first day of publication. Presently, it is still the mainstay of many courses in Native American literature. It is increasingly read in Contemporary American literature classes. The novel remains popular among Native students and among sophisticated critics of contemporary literature. The wide cross-cultural attention is testimony to the novel's richly textured and mediational character; Silko's various audiences are challenged, satisfied, and challenged again.

Silko's novel circles around critical, personal, and cultural decisions about what to fuse from the old and the new. However, the novel expresses these decisions in terms of the various discourse fields it engages and then modifies. Silko's oral influences emphasize the way her utterance will define identity and mesh with other discourse: "One of the things I was taught to do from the time I was a little child was to listen to the story about you personally right now. To take all of that in for what it means right now. To take all of that in for what it means right now, and for what it means for the future. But at the same time to appreciate how it fits in with what you did yesterday, last week, maybe ironically, you know drastically different" (quoted in Coltelli 141). With a similar dialogic orientation, implied reades are alerted at the very start of the novel to the fact that everything they will read is actually Thought Woman's narrative. She contends that the evolving stories in the novel are the only defense against evil. The stories alone will replenish the life of the people. As in the narratives Silko heard while growing up, the stories in the novel will define and continue life, allowing readers to appreciate "the idea that one story is only the beginning of many stories, and the sense that stories never truly end" ("Language" 56).

Throughout the novel, Silko's goals are truly mediational as she seeks to translate the languages of the Other, but for both Native and non-Native fields of discourse, she must answer what has been asked before, acknowledge previous discourse, and advance cultural conversations. Yet she must also open up a field of access where Native implied reader can mediate their experiences just as the non-Native implied reader must. Ultimately, the text leads the reader to validate Native epistemology—a central goal in the mediation of contemporary Native American literature—and to appreciate the new structures of meaning that mediation creates.

Clearly, Silko's discourse fields come from arenas as widely separate as ancient stories of the Pueblo peoples, which we tend to call "myths," and World War II soldiers-on-leave stories that come from mainstream culture. Mary Slowik notes the adventure and detective story elements in Silko's novel. Dasenbrock (see this volume) identifies the novel as having "generic affiliations with this naturalistic Tradition of American literature" in its use of the themes of the postwar novel (315). Ruoff writes about how Silko's work incorporates Keres traditional narratives, and Robert Nelson (see this volume) ties the novel to an ongoing discourse about Laguna place and landscape, exploring how the stories grow out of the land.[1] He reveals how the intersection of myth and place anchor Tayo's story into the webwork of all other kiva stories. Silko observes, "The structure of Pueblo expression resembles something like a spider's web—with many threads radiating from a center, criss-crossing each other. . . . Words are always with other words, and the other words are almost always in a story of some sort" ("Language" 54–55).

But since her text draws from even larger fields of contemporary American discourse and traditional Laguna and Navajo discourse, the critical decisions center on how to embed her artistic choices in the continuing multicultural conversations. Her new textual structure must be a new ceremony, one growing and evolving, a contribution to Laguna ceremonial discourse, and an enactment of the goals of the novel itself. Allen notes: "Two of *Ceremony*'s major themes are the centrality of environmental integrity and the pacifism that is its necessary partner, common motifs in

American literature in the last quarter of the twentieth century. Silko develops them entirely out of a Laguna/Keres perspective, for both themes are fundamental to the fabric of Keres pueblo life and thought" (*Sacred* 96). Allen perceives these discourses as played out through the introduction of the ideas and values "of ecology, antiracist, and antinuclear movements," which advance the plot and major themes in the novel (*Sacred* 145). These contemporary discourses contribute to the cultural conversation on modern American life, but Silko engages them not only to have her say but also to redirect the way they articulate these values. Her method is subversive in the best sense. Per Seyersted misunderstands the introduction of this level of the text when he complains, "Occasionally there are passages or scenes which seem contrived, and in certain descriptions of what the whites have done, Silko's expression comes closer to that of the activist than we would expect" (34) Actually most non-Native readers expect a great deal more activist discourse from any Native American writer. Silko gives just enough to establish a historical and sociological perspective, then uses that basis to alter Western epistemology.

The experienced reader of Western fiction can readily identify in *Ceremony* the outlines of a protest novel. As a result of his participation in the American army in World War II, the main character appears to be the victim of social forces. His people have been oppressed by an indifferent and often hostile dominant culture. They have been beaten, robbed, and victimized. His traditional beliefs are under seige by an intolerant worldview. Silko even brings in the atomic bomb as the ultimate act of cultural and global violation. Obviously, in this discourse context, books and stories about World War II, minority rights, poverty, and prejudice create a field upon which *Ceremony* builds, answers, and extends. Reference to this field encourages implied readers to exercise their liberal conscience. They search for a sociological analysis of events in the text and come up with insights that Silko encourages. For instance, she describes the white doctors' attitudes toward Tayo's communal orientation. They want him to think only of himself and to stop using words like "we" and "us" (125). Similarly, when Tayo cuts the wire on the mountain, he cuts away the social lie of brown-skinned inferiority.

However, while these passages fit neatly into a tradition of social analysis in Western literature, they are not so familiar to implied Native readers. Silko's use of social analysis may lead them to new insight into how this lie, embedded in American discriminatory discourse, has become internalized. While the use of Western discourse might also respond to previous Western discourse, Silko's goal is mediational since Tayo cuts through that social lie so that he can get to a deeper truth about a mythic relationship between whites and Indians.

An excellent example of how mediation shifts perception and discourse can be seen when the text shifts toward the middle of the novel. After a long, relatively straightforward discussion of displaced people like Helen Jean and Gallup, and subjects like Indian drinking and war veterans, Tayo tries to vomit out everything, "all the past, all his life" (168). After this purging, the text shifts to a Native perspective on the sociological narrative, developing an Indian parable about the land and spiritual destruction. Then, Tayo voices his belief in the necessity of transitions, and Silko give us the story of how Sun, with the help of Spiderwoman, beats the evil Gambler and releases the rain clouds. These Native and mythic perspectives on the events described balance and challenge the previous sociological perspective. Both implied readers become primarily involved with maneuvering through the transitions in the text. However, the mechanism of mediation here also works to validate each perspective, revealing their strengths and limitations. Both implied readers are led to question which perspective is more complete, which explains more, and which leads to healing and unity. The dialogism of the text leads implied readers to seek ways to merge and understand both perspectives.[2] At this point in the novel, Silko does not provide any clear path to produce this healing. Tayo and the implied readers must make their own transitions. Such action prepares them for the time later in the novel when the transitions are supplied.

Iser sees this process of the creation and reevaluation of meaning not as a jumble of dizzying switches between perspectives, but as the very essence of a dynamic process of self-correction that is reading itself. He concludes: "In the literary text, not only is the background unformulated and variable, but its significance will also change in accordance with the new perspectives brought about by the foregrounded elements; the familiar facilitates our comprehension of the unfamiliar, but the unfamiliar in turn restructures our comprehension of the familiar" (94). To satisfy the discourse expectations of both audiences, Silko must restructure how each audience values truth, reality, and knowledge. The result is not only an increased appreciation of Native worldview by non-Native audiences, but also an evolution of Native worldview through the constant interaction between meanings as Holquist characterizes Bakhtinian dialogism.[3]

Just as the social discourse is transformed into myth, so must the psychological discourse. The novel begins with a Laguna discourse frame and then swiftly moves to a fragmented narrative that mirrors Tayo's mental state. As the text progresses, the narrative structure becomes more linear, though not necessarily more chronological. When Tayo is healed, the text becomes more coherent, until by the end it does not foreground fragmentation. This pattern of healing and growth, familiar from Western psychological novels, is translated into Laguna mythic terms: as Tayo heals and the fragmentation of his life and of the text retreat, he emerges fully into the world of myth and ceremony, seeing the web of stories.

In discussing what originally caused Tayo's illness, Allen argues that Tayo's illness stems from his acceptance of the witchery's mistaken perception that humans and other creatures are not part of a larger oneness: "The cure for that misunderstanding, for Tayo, was a reorientation of perception so that he could know directly that the true nature of being is magical and that the proper duty of the creatures, the land, and human beings is to live in harmony with what is" (*Sacred* 125). Betonie informs Tayo that his sickness is part of something larger than himself and his cure would be found "in something great and inclusive of everything" (125). Tayo's ultimate realization is that he has never been crazy, that he was simply always perceiving the timeless way things truly are, without the artificial boundaries imposed by Western thought, especially psychology (192, 246). Past and present, and all levels of identity, are one.

Indeed, the whole question of identity, which is at the heart of psychological discourse, is mediated in *Ceremony*. At the start, Tayo feels bereft of identity, and non-Native readers tend to follow the information presented about his mother, his upbringing, and the death of his brother to try to piece together a conventional image of self; however, he comes to realize that his identity is bound up with Laguna's identity, with something larger than his own psyche. It is this insight that leads him to the revelation of who he is, and not an acceptance of repressed unconscious material— which psychoanalytic theory would have us believe is the path to integration and identity.[4]

As we shift our discussion from the goals of mediation to the form of mediation in *Ceremony*, we could explore how changes in typeface and text formats in the novel indicate shifts to new fields of utterance and new context. A study of the spacial breaks as opposed to chapter breaks might reveal how Silko expresses the flow of one unified field of mediational experience existing in the novel. This field is designed to thwart linear chronological development by allowing events, since they are not locked into chapters, to resonate and return later in the text. The end result is to dismantle Western notions of narrative structure and time so as to allow Native and mediative perception to create meaning.

Much of Silko's method can be revealed by an analysis of the juxtaposition of poetry and prose in the text. The lines in the text that look like poetry indicate a self-reflexive and consciously Western form, yet they serve to carry across the traditional communal and mythic discourse of Laguna.[5] These lines, which are referred to as Thought Woman's cognition taking the shape of reality, establish a Native discourse context linked to past conversations as well as an interpretive frame. It is this frame that will ultimately shift the implied reader's perception to create an experience that achieves one of Silko's major goals. Ideally, Silko would like both implied readers to hear the poetry lines, for she feels they are closer to oral discourse contexts.[6] In contrast to the poetic sections of the text, the familiar Western sociological and psychological account of a shattered war veteran is presented in prose, disjointed and disrupted from its expected discourse context. The prose presents a reality, but a contorted reality. Initially, the oral, mythic text is the most coherent, though its context is unfamiliar to non-Native readers, while the fragmented psychological narrative has context but no coherence. Dreams, a traditional Native source for meaning, are scrambled. The Native audience must search for the context of the psychological narrative. Tayo, who does not appear in the poetry at the beginning of the book, feels in the prose sections as if he has no name, a verbal sign that could tie him equally to either the Native or the non-Native discourse spheres.

The poetry is at first thematically separate from the prose, just as Tayo's past is cut off from his present. For the non-Native implied reader, the familiar war story discourse is cut off from the exotic discourse in the poetry, a discourse that expresses another level of the life and experience of Laguna Pueblo. An ideological and epistemological translation must take place to create meaning form the various discourse elements in the poetry and prose sections. Both audiences must begin a mediational process to appreciate a new discourse field, to change their sense of what is real and what is meaningful.

As the novel continues, the text teases both audiences by pretending to slip smoothly into the familiar Western discourse about returned veterans or even returned native sons; however, in the middle of the novel, the Laguna war stories are suddenly expressed in poetry rather than prose. As the reality-based stories are raised to myth, Silko emphasizes how myths grow, complement, and structure reality—how mythic discourse and practical discourse are built out of the same components.[7] In doing this, Silko contends that she is "trying to affect the old, old, old way of looking at the world" ("Conversation" 32).

Progressively, the form of Silko's text reveals one further goal—the merging of those categories Western discourse has termed myth and reality. The myth or poetry sections pace the progress of the prose (the section of the text that we read as describing reality). As Eliade reminds us, "myth is always exemplary, providing paradigms for all significant human acts" (*Myth and Reality* 18). The Laguna paradigms lead the reader to new events, and comment on action, but always lend a sense of order to the fragmented prose just as myth often does to reality. For example, the story of Sun who defeats the Gambler and releases the rain clouds (170) is a precursor of the myth in which hummingbird, fly, and buzzard purify the town. This purification story also foreshadows the return of the "clouds with round heavy bellies" (255) at the end of the novel, though now they are in the prose section. What is important here is not so much that poetic sections parallel prose sections, but that they are different expressions of the same phenomena.

One could further say that the poetic sections create meaning in the prose or more precisely that the interfacing between the two creates meaning for the implied readers as they initiate the ideological translation of the language of the Other. Facilitating this process is Silko's method of creating mediation. Silko, of course, never separates the two perceptual fields; instead, in the novel, she refers to them both as "story." Ts'eh reminds Tayo that the whites have stories about them as much as do the Indians—one person's story of reality is as real as the next person's. What is important is whether the stories end correctly and whether they create identity while holding off illness and death (232). Tayo must end the story in the terms of mediative mythic discourse and not in the sociological discourse of maladjusted war veterans and psychotic murderers.

To do this both Tayo and the readers must employ a mythic way of knowing. They must be able to appreciate, in addition to other modes of knowing, this manner of giving meaning to events. Elaine Jahner (see this volume) reasons:

> Through the narrative events of the novel, protagonist and reader gradually learn to relate myth to immediate action, cause to effect; and both reader and protagonist learn more about the power of story itself. The reader seeks to learn not only what happens to Tayo but how and why it happens. The whole pattern of cause and effect is different from most novels written from a perspective outside the mythic mode of knowledge. ("Act" 44)

The prose becomes increasingly more coherent as both readers develop greater context for both spheres of discourse and various modes of perception. Though the chronology continues to move between past and present, the shifts are less jarring. Those distinctions that could be made between psychological, mythic, sociological, and communal narratives are conflated as all levels of narrative become one story. Tayo's personal story is presented first in the lines of poetry that follow the description of Betonie's ceremony (153) and then later in poetic form when the old men of the Pueblo recognize his role in the mythic level of reality (257). They acknowledge him as part of the ongoing life of the community; the discourse of the Pueblo has been elaborated to include him. Tayo's story has been tied in to the many stories that comprise Laguna discourse. Silko comments on the nature of such discourse when she describes old Ku'oosh's highly self-reflexive language, a discourse intricately tied with discussions of its own origin and all that has been said before. Each word is fragile, each has a story (34). Indeed, she contends, "language *is* story" ("Language" 56).

The text of *Ceremony* generates its own highly contextualized discourse in order to help non-Native implied readers see the relevancy of this discourse to Native worldview and to help them ideologically translate and mediate their perceptions. The Native implied readers learn how to incorporate Western sociological and psychological discourse into their unified and *growing* worldview. Betonie serves as a model here since he is able to translate Western and Native discourse spheres into new ceremonies and ceremonial visions. His phone books, newspapers, bear stories, and medicine pouches objectify mediation and cross-cultural discourse. Situated as he is physically between Native and non-Native, town and mountain, Betonie is, of course, the ideal person to affect the cure of Tayo and to help him mediate the discourses.

By the end of the novel, when Tayo has realized that there are no boundaries either in space or time, *Ceremony's* form reflects this illumination. Tayo and the reader have begun to live the myth and, as Eliade concludes, "by 'living' the myths one emerges from profane, chronological time and enters a time that is of a different quality, a 'Sacred' Time at once primordial and indefinitely recoverable" (*Myth and Reality* 18). Tayo's dreams and his reality are acknowledged to be the same (222). As clouds gather, the spirits of the dead are present in much the same way that the dead return with the rain clouds as katchinas. The transition is complete when Josiah and Rocky wrap Tayo up and take him home—he is at last dreaming with his eyes open. Myth and reality have merged in the story still being told, the mediative discourse developing in both spheres. We must remember that the mythic story of the Destroyers is not a traditional

Laguna narrative, but a translation, a mediation that both addresses and furthers Native discourse. And the external and illusory distinctions between prose and poetry are forced to reveal an underlying larger epistemological unity—a unity that not only mirrors Laguna epistemology but also enlarges it by enabling an appreciation of how the cross-cultural discourse context has generated new ceremonies, new mythic discourse. The oral tradition that nurtured Laguna narrative has been enriched and complemented.

In the final sections of the novel, the reading of the text turns into a dynamic interaction with the extratextual world. Tayo's view of himself has become highly self-reflexive, but so has the reader's. Jahner concludes that the text brings readers face to face with their own way of understanding: "The ebb and flow of narrative rhythm in the novel creates an event in the process of telling about event. The entire process is ceremonial, and one learns how to experience it ceremonially by achieving various kinds of knowledge attained not through logical analysis but through narrative processes that have their own epistemological basis" ("Act" 39). The self-reflexive ability to perceive an event as the process of telling about event guides the reader into a ceremonial epistemology. As readers read and misread the nature of Tayo's sickness and the significance of events like the vision of Josiah during the War, they initiate a dynamic interaction with the text. They participate in creating meaning and change their perspective on events in the text. However, their changing expectations and experiences are outside the text. Iser believes that it is this kind of communication that makes literary texts successful:

> The text must therefore *bring about* a standpoint from which the reader will be able to view things that would never have come into focus as long as his own habitual dispositions were determining his orientation, and what is more, this standpoint must be able to accommodate all kinds of different readers. . . . Thus the standpoint and the convergence of textual perspectives are closely interrelated, although neither of them is actually represented in the text, let alone set out in words. Rather they emerge during the reading process, in the course of which the reader's role is to occupy shifting vantage points that are geared to a prestructured activity and to fit the diverse perspectives into a gradually evolving pattern. (35)

Readers then grasp the different starting points of textual perspectives and their ultimate coalescence as the readers are moved through an evolving pattern to a concluding standpoint, where meaning is both fixed and fluid. In the case of *Ceremony*, it is to a point where implied readers have an insight into how the Destroyers work in the world around them. They are given the perception to prepare them for future action and to initiate appropriate ceremonial responses.

The ceremonial process to which Jahner refers transforms the telling of the myth into the action of ritual. The act of reading becomes a ceremonial experience for both audiences because ceremonial language and event are performative. *Ceremony* draws on mythic narrative prototypes for its efficacy and authority. The mythic discourse of the novel prepares implied readers for the ceremony in which they will participate.[8]

To help us appreciate how the experience of reading the novel as a whole finally shifts the standpoint of both audiences out of the text and to a position where they both can create new meaning, I want to turn briefly to Todorov's analysis of ancient texts, which straddle oral and written traditions. He identifies two modes of speech that seem to structure such intermediary texts: *speech-as-action* and *speech-as-narrative*. It is clear that one of *Ceremony*'s goals is to shift the function of the written text from just incorporating various discourse contexts to evoking novel perceptual experiences where the reading of the novel becomes a new ceremony in itself. Todorov outlines these modes of discourse:

> First, in the case of speech-as-action, we react to the referential aspect of what is said [it is concerned with the act performed, which is not simply the utterance of the words.] . . . Speech-as-action is perceived as information, speech-as-narrative as a discourse. Second, and this seems contradictory, speech-as-narrative derives from the constantive mode of discourse, whereas speech-as-action is always performative. It is in the case of speech-as-action that the whole process of speaking assumes a primordial importance and becomes the essential factor of the message; speech-as-narrative deals with something else and evokes the presence of an action other than that of speech itself. (*Poetics* 59)

To create a written literature that will enhance the oral tradition and provoke changes in the reader's epistemological structures, Silko must shift the mode of textual discourse. She must take speech-as-narrative, which underlines the contextual frame at the heart of Bakhtin's view of literature, and encourage the reader to perceive the way it ultimately functions as speech-as-action. As Thought Woman believes, the story comes into being when it is told. When readers are able to merge myth and reality, they are able to see the novel as a ceremony and as a prayer. And this is new meaning, information to both audiences. The act of utterance encoded in the text and emulated by the participant/reader takes on "primordial importance" while the reading of the novel becomes a ceremony and a prayer.

On Mount Taylor, Tayo prays in the form of a song that the Dawn people sang. The novel begins, centers, and ends with the same word with which the song/prayer begins—*sunrise*. Consequently, the reading of the text becomes a prayer, becomes itself a new ceremony, yet this is a ceremony with roots in traditional religious discourse. Implied readers are placed in the position of Dawn priests. As Tayo's words and actions become completely integrated into a fused discourse, drawing upon sources as divergent as traditional Native ceremonies and the rhetoric of nuclear disarmament, the otherness of unfamiliar discourse spheres is overcome and at the same time revitalized. The text's effect shifts from speech-as-narrative to speech-as-action. Mediation is complete.

This analysis of one element of the form of the novel, the use of poetry and prose, has returned us to a discussion of the larger goals of the text. Certainly, Silko leads all readers to an expanded appreciation of the multiple meaning of events and a new understanding of narrative. Indeed, a new reality is created for implied readers as they find meaning in that which previously held only fictional meaning, hence, no reality, no meaning. In *Ceremony,* myth becomes reality. Eliade identifies the ontological function of mythic epistemology when he writes "an object or act becomes real only insofar as it imitates or repeats an archetype. Thus, reality is acquired solely through repetition or participation; everything which lacks an exemplary model is 'meaningless,' i.e., it lacks reality" (*Myth of the Eternal* 34). Tayo is in the middle of an epistemological struggle similar to that of many Native and non-Native readers as they attempt to endow the text with meaning. He may, however, be ahead of the game because deep down, he still believes in the old ways, that everything has a story and that mythic discourse *is* reality. As the novel moves to order his turmoil about what is real, it teaches its implied readers how to understand not only text, but also the events and forces in the world around us outside of the text. Humanity must unite to act against the work of the Destroyers.

However, to do this the reader must change, and most people are afraid of change. Tayo and Betonie know that those who are different often are scorned and become outcasts. Both audiences must acknowledge the growth of new myths and the renewal and evolution of the ceremonies. They must examine their attitudes toward different people, positions, and types of discourse. Their acts of mediation constitute Bakhtin's "ideological translation of the language of the other" and lead to a perspective on the text that merges the different spheres of discourse while continuing each of them. Readers must gain "the ear for the story and the eye for the pattern" (255), as Tayo did, before their perception can be transformed.

When readers reach this level of perception, a number of elements take on multiple significance. Silko would have both implied readers develop a "mind holding all thoughts together in a single moment" (237). The drought that has plagued Laguna can be seen as more than a phenomenon of the climate. It can be seen as the result of Laguna misbehavior and inattentiveness to the mythic/communal well-being (45). The people have followed the Destroyers who want them to think only of the loss and forget to renew and re-create the ceremonies (249). However, the drought is Tayo's drought as well. He is as barren of love as he is of identity. The drought is physical, communal, and mythic, and thus it must have a physical, communal, and mythic solution in the creation of a new ceremony. The rain clouds come to him and to Laguna when he has made his peace with the dead. The myths offer a path back to well-being not only for Tayo and Laguna but also for the modern world which has not realized the extent of the drought of meaning in which it dwells. Implied readers must realize that the mixed-blood cattle can survive in the drought because they have the best qualities of both worlds. They can follow their instinct and become contemporary survivors. Readers must follow the cattle, Tayo, and Betonie and become epistemological mixed-blood survivors.

It is important for both Tayo and the implied readers to understand that there are no boundaries enclosing events into one-dimensional notions of reality. Tayo believes he has seen Josiah while looking at the Japanese, and the novel insists that we believe he has. Tayo talks with the hunter and Ts'eh in the mountains, and readers must know that they are indeed mythic beings with the same ability to be both human and animal that beings possessed in the age of myth. When Ts'eh folds her storm blanket, the snows stop.

These insights into the multiple significance of events help prepare the implied readers for the final fusion when Tayo sees the mountains around him and all the peoples of the world becoming part of Betonie's sand painting—the object that centers and orders the ceremony (246–47). Time boundaries, discourse boundaries, and racial boundaries all fall away. Everyone is included and harmonized in the struggle against the Destroyers who threaten the false sunrise of worldwide nuclear destruction. Defeating the Destroyers will require power from everywhere, even from the whites (150, 204). The novel's conclusion is set during the autumnal equinox when there is perfect order and balance between summer and winter, between night and day, as all the people of the world become one clan again.[9]

Tayo remarked earlier that Betonie's vision was a story he could feel happening. Reality, story, and myth are thus one, but one question remains. Ts'eh tells Tayo that the old men have been asking after him. They want to know who he is. Tayo's identity on all levels of meaning finally becomes clarified at the end of the novel when he established identity on each narrative level.

On the level of the psychological narrative, Tayo emerges from invisible, inarticulate white smoke to become a lover. His gutted emotions are healed by Ts'eh. He loves her, but he also loves all those important to him in his life. Tayo now knows that "nothing was ever lost as long as the love remained" (220). He is restored to his family almost as a son. Auntie now talks with him in the same way she talks to Robert and Grandma. He sees his own strength and knows he is healed. He has found power in the core of his being so that he can return to being a sane, balanced personality. He acknowledges his responsibility in a fragile world and demonstrates confidence in his ability to be whole and right. His psychological identity is solidly constituted.

In the end, Tayo's social identity centers around his position as a partial outsider, accepted now into the social structure but rejecting the imposed social definition of the drunk, shell-shocked veteran; as a result, his story does not have the ending of a tragic sociological narrative. He is a survivor just like the cattle are that he now cares for. No longer a scapegoat, he now feels responsible for those around him, a contributor to his Laguna society. Since he is a successful returned veteran, a warrior turned cattleman, the people now want to send to him veterans who are still troubled and other dysfunctional individuals for help in blending the two social worlds.

The communal narrative of identity concludes with Tayo assuming the role of a kiva priest. When he returns from the mountains, the old men come to inquire as to what he has to tell them. Perhaps they recognize that Tayo's trip into the mountains is the same trip that the elders make when they want to pray for rain. He now is an elder, a messenger, and a bringer of blessings since he has seen A'moo'ooh, carrier of life. The people will now be blessed, healed, purified. He crosses the river, returning to the village like a katchina (182) or religious initiate. He is now a protector of Laguna, a caretaker of the rain plants. He can tell the people of the new ceremony and they will listen.

The mythic narrative creates an identity for Tayo by depicting his role as one who struggles against the Destroyers. He knows who he is in the myth, as well as in the world around him. He knows what he must do; however, he also is a culture hero and as such, he functions like Arrowboy or Sun. Perhaps it is even more accurate to say that he acts like Hummingbird and Fly, who restored the people and the world. In Tayo's story, there is an echo of the old stories of orphans who bring new insights and of Arrowboy (247). Wiget's analysis of the novel underscores the importance of Tayo's identity as a culture hero: "A ceremony is required to reintegrate Tayo's self by reimpressing upon his fragmented psyche the whole mythic pattern of the culture hero and his quest, thus restoring the shape of his personal and communal history and reestablishing his identity" (*Native* 87).

As Wiget points out, it is important to see that all of these levels of identity support each other. Moreover, the identities are conflated in such a way that the mythic and psychological, and the social and communal, are all perceived by both audiences as unified. Silko's sense of character identity extends beyond simple metaphors of continuity and survival to the complex processes Clifford refers to as utilizing "appropriation, compromise, subversion, masking, invention, and revival" (338). On the mountain, these processes combine Betonie's vision and the reality of the cows; the she-elk and the woman, Ts'eh; the hunter and the mountain lion; the hunter whom Coyote bewitched in the myth/poetry passages and the bewitched Tayo in the prose. Mythic and psychological levels of identity must be invented and revived by Ts'eh and Tayo's love. The identity given by the ceremony must appropriate and subvert the social role of the drunken ex-soldier. Tayo's new communal identity as bringer of blessings to the community must combine with his personal love for Ts'eh, Josiah, and Rocky. And the mask must be uncovered as Tayo realizes what Grandma always knew: the stories are all the same; only the names change.

Notes

1. See Ruoff, "Ritual and Renewal," and Nelson, "Place and Vision."

2. Velie, seeing the dialogism and mediation in the text, attempts to explain them psychologically. He perceives a conflict between a contemporary acculturated mixed-blood Silko and the Indian values of her novel that imply that Natives are best off when they remain in their tradition. To solve the conflict, he refers to Wayne Booth's concept of the implied author, suggesting that Silko can say these things without personally believing in them (*Four* 113–15). However, perhaps Silko's intent here is just to suggest that mixing contemporary and traditional values will create evolving Native worldviews that will prove more humane and ecologically sound.

Lincoln suggests that there is a determining level of the text that goes beyond anthropological antecedents: "The narrator *is* the story, positioning, interweaving, toning, speaking for the characters . . . listening to them speak, following their struggles to pattern their lives, according to the old, never-ending Indian balances and harmonies: (*Native* 238). However, Lincoln does not define qualities of an individual narrator, nor does he explore the perspective on the text such a narrator would need to take.

3. Appreciating the dialogic nature of Silko's writings can prove useful for many critics. For example, Krupat has applied an appreciation of dialogism and polyvocality in his analysis of Silko's *Storyteller* and in his discussion of Native American autobiography (*Voice* 132–70; "Dialogic" 55–68).

4. Drawing upon Lacan, Gretchen Ronnow argues that the novel chronicles Tayo's quest across the possibilities of language for a lost mother and a sense of Otherness. This interpretation has value for Silko scholarship because it bridges the gap between the psychological individual inside Tayo and the "something larger" outside him. However, this bridging of the gap is ultimately not the locus of healing prescribed by Betonie.

5. This discourse field is introduced into the text in enough detail to bring the non-Laguna reader into a mediative posture that will evoke a mythic path for validating experience. A complete analysis of how the novel continues the discourse of Laguna narratives in their own field is outside the scope of this chapter. The contours of Silko's Laguna responses have been outlined by Ruoff ("Ritual"), Hoilman, and Swan ("Laguna"). These authors draw on the ethnographical work of Franz Boas, John Gunn, Hamilton Tyler, and Elsie Crews Parsons.

6. See Kim Barnes, "A Leslie Marmon Silko Interview" (98).

7. Mary Slowik discusses extensively the relation between the poetry and prose sections in the novel and their influence on the reader. While her analysis is hindered by her lack of understanding of the structure and function of Native American oral tradition, she does point to some ways the two narrative modes interrelate. She discusses the way the mythic stories displace and focus the prose narrative and thus create an ironic perspective for the reader. Since the novel reveals that "narrative is ontology" (113), "we now read contrapuntally; that is, as the weave of one story crosses the weave of another" (115). Unfortunately, when she decides that the reader reads the sections concerning the cattle and the Witchery pragmatically, she seems to be ignoring the nature of mythic epistemology.

8. The ceremonial analogues to the novel's process have been extensively explored by Carol Mitchell in "*Ceremony* as Ritual," Robert Bell in "Circular Design in *Ceremony,*" and Edith Swan in "Healing via the Sunrise Cycle in Silko's *Ceremony.*"

9. Many scholars have commented on this shift of vision at the end of the novel. Robert Nelson observes, "Tayo's vision of the pattern of the ceremony takes a quantum leap of perspective, from Pan-Indian to Pan-Human" (310). Nelson does

not follow the implications for the reader of this change. Dasenbrock notes, "Silko relies upon Western forms only to finally have her protagonist break free of them and perceive them as Anglo forms: his perceptions are hers and should be ours" (317). Slowik agrees with some points of my analysis when she writes that in the end, "by allowing us to read two distinct narrative modes, sometimes contradictory narrative modes simultaneously, *Ceremony* ultimately educates us, its readers, to accept the marvelous as readily and as easily as Marquez" (106). Silko's perception is that "storytelling always includes the audience and the listeners, and, in fact, a great deal of the story is believed to be inside the listener, and the storyteller's role is to draw the story out of the listeners" ("Language" 57). The shift of vision at the end would then correspond to the reader's increasing realization the the story is inside him or her.

Works Cited

Allen, Paula Gunn. *The Sacred Hoop: Recovering the Feminine in American Indian Traditions.* Boston: Beacon Press, 1986.

Bakhtin, Mikhail. *The Dialogic Imagination: Four Essays by M. M. Bakhtin.* Ed. Michael Holquist. Austin and London: University of Texas Press, 1981.

Barnes, Kim. "A Leslie Marmon Silko Interview with Kim Barnes." *Journal of Ethnic Studies* 13.4 (1986): 83–105.

Bell, Robert C. "Circular Design in *Ceremony*." *American Indian Quarterly* 5 (1979): 47–62.

Booth, Wayne. *Rhetoric of Fiction.* Chicago: University of Chicago Press, 1961.

Clifford, James. *The Predicament of Culture: Twentieth-Century Ethnography, Literature, and Art.* Cambridge: Harvard University Press, 1988.

Coltelli, Laura, ed. *Winged Words: American Indian Writers Speak.* Lincoln: University of Nebraska Press, 1990.

Dasenbrock, Reed Way. "Forms of Biculturalism in Southwestern Literature: The Work of Rudolfo Anaya and Leslie Marmon Silko" *Genre* 21 (1988): 307–20.

Eliade, Mircea. *Myth and Reality.* Trans. Willard Trask. New York: Harper & Row, 1963.
————. *The Myth of the Eternal Return.* Trans. Willard Trans. New York: Pantheon Books, 1954.

Hoilman, Dennis. "A World Made of Stories: An Interpretation of Leslie Silko's *Ceremony*." *South Dakota Review* 17 (1979–80): 54–66.

Iser, Wolfgang. *The Act of Reading.* Baltimore: Johns Hopkins University Press, 1978.

Jahner, Elaine. "An Act of Attention: Event Structure in *Ceremony*." *American Indian Quarterly* 5.1 (1979): 37–46.

Krupat, Arnold. "The Dialogic of Silko's *Storyteller*." *Narrative Chance: Postmodern Discourse on Native American Indian Literatures.* Ed. Gerald Vizenor. Albuquerque: University of New Mexico Press, 1989.

————. *The Voice in the Margin: Native American Literature and the Canon*. Berkeley: University of California Press, 1989.

Lincoln, Kenneth. *Native American Renaissance*. Berkeley: University of California Press, 1983.

Mitchell, Carol. "*Ceremony* as Ritual." *American Indian Quarterly* 5 (1979): 27–35.

Nelson, Robert. "Place and Vision: The Function of Landscape in *Ceremony*." *Journal of the Southwest* 30.3 (1988): 281–316.

Ronnow, Gretchen. "Tayo, Death, and Desire: A Lacanian Reading of *Ceremony*." *Narrative Chance: Postmodern Discourse on Native American Indian Literatures*. Ed. Gerald Vizenor. Albuquerque: University of New Mexico Press, 1989.

Ruoff, A. LaVonne. "Ritual and Renewal: Keres Traditions in the Short Fiction of Leslie Silko." *Multi-Ethnic Literatures of the United States* 5 (1978): 2–17.

Seyersted, Per. *Leslie Marmon Silko*. Western Writers Series. Boise: Boise State University Press, 1980.

Silko, Leslie. *Ceremony*. New York: New American Library, 1978.

————. "A Conversation with Leslie Marmon Silko." Larry Evers and Denny Carr, Eds. *Suntracks* 3 (1976): 28–33.

————. "Language and Literature from a Pueblo Indian Perspective." *English Literature: Opening Up the Canon*. Eds. Leslie Fiedler and Houston Baker. Baltimore: Johns Hopkins University Press, 1981. 54–72.

Slowik, Mary. "Henry James, Meet Spider Woman: A Study of Narrative Form in Leslie Silko's *Ceremony*." *North Dakota Quarterly* 57.2 (1989): 104–20.

Swan, Edith, "Healing via the Sunrise Cycle in Silko's *Ceremony*." *American Indian Quarterly* 12.3 (1988): 229–49.

————. "Laguna Symbolic Geography and Silko's *Ceremony*." *American Indian Quarterly* 12.4 (1988): 313–28.

Todorov, Tzvetan. *The Poetics of Prose*. Trans. Richard Howard. Ithaca: Cornell University Press, 1977.

Velie, Alan. *Four American Indian Literary Masters: N. Scott Momaday, James Welch, Leslie Marmon Silko and Gerald Vizenor*. Norman: University of Oklahoma Press, 1982.

Wiget, Andrew. *Native American Literature*. Boston: Twayne, 1985.

Contested Ground

Nature, Narrative, and Native American Identity in Leslie Marmon Silko's Ceremony

RACHEL STEIN

◆ ◆ ◆

IN *CEREMONY*, LESLIE MARMON SILKO revisits the American mythos of the conquest of the continent from a Native American vantage point. While *Ceremony* is set in the recent past, Silko's characters come to realize that both the desperate ills of reservation life and the corruptions poisoning mainstream American society result from the way in which American national development has been predicated over and against Indian inhabitation of the land.[1] Her characters must unravel the polarizing mechanism that historian Richard Slotkin calls that "fatal opposition" through which Europeans justified the displacement of Native Americans from their homelands: "Even at the source of the American myth (of conquest) there lies the fatal opposition, the hostility between two worlds, two races, two realms of thought and feeling."[2]

Silko argues that this fatal opposition is not, as the settlers believed, an essential and irresolvable racial enmity, but rather a struggle between irreconcilable notions of land use and land tenure, a struggle between different cultural orientations toward the natural world. She utilizes Laguna story-tradition to reframe the fatal opposition as a story war; when Europeans arrived in America, two conflicting stories about the human relationship to nature were thrown into confrontation, and the European story of human dominion over nature authorized white settlers' ruthless subjugation of the Indian peoples, who viewed themselves as kin to the spirits of the land. Furthermore, Silko asserts that the European story of conquest was itself a fatal opposition—an ideology through which settlers alienated themselves from the American landscape, posing themselves as separate and superior to the natural world and native peoples whom they took as lifeless objects of their expansionist desires. In Silko's novel, then, the social relation to nature is contested ground, the ground of conflict between these embattled cultures.

Silko's *Ceremony* addresses the violent history of this fatal opposition between the aboriginal stories of partnership and reciprocity with nature and the Euro-American stories of detachment and dominion. By focusing upon the productive and destructive effects of the contrasting stories, Silko argues that the historic white/Indian confrontation is not an essential racial enmity but a conflict of opposing paradigms that could be renegotiated and rectified. The protagonists of this novel must construct new stories that redress the fundamental disagreements between native and white cultures.

As Tayo realizes in *Ceremony,* contact with Euro-Americans has irrevocably entered into Laguna traditions: "The fifth world had become entangled with European names: the names of the rivers, the hills, the names of the animals and plants—all of creation suddenly had two names: an Indian name and a white name. . . . Now the feelings were twisted, tangled roots, and all the names for the source of this growth were buried under English words, out of reach. And there would be no peace and the people would have no rest until the entanglement had been unwound to the source" (68–69).[3] Paradoxically, this painful "entanglement' of cultures will offer the very means of undoing the fatal opposition between white and native America. In Silko's fiction it is often people at the margins of tribal/dominant culture—people of mixed descent, or of mixed acculturation, those who bear the conflict between cultures in their own persons and who must inevitably negotiate the entanglement of competing cultures—who are driven to create new stories that reframe the relations of native culture and dominant white culture by reaffirming the reciprocal relation of humans to nature. Paula Gunn Allen notes that mixed-blood, or half-breed, protagonists are a recurrent feature of contemporary Native American literature, as these characters, lost between two opposing cultures, embody the alienation endemic to living as a Native American in the midst of a hostile white society. These characters realize that "there is no way to be acceptably Indian (with all the pain that implies) and acceptable to whites at the same time."[4] While Silko's characters of mixed descent certainly struggle with alienation, they also serve the additional purpose of finding ways to negotiate between the warring native and white cultures, utilizing their painfully gained knowledge of the white worlds in order to reformulate Indian stories and practices that can counter the destructive practices of the dominant culture.

These characters of mixed descent and acculturation inhabit Gloria Anzaldua's *Borderlands,* a place of unsettling contradiction that challenges the false boundaries the dominant culture has imposed between itself and all other cultures: " A borderland is a vague and undetermined place created by the emotional residue of an unnatural boundary. It is in a state of constant transition. The prohibited and the forbidden are its inhabitants. *Los atravesados* live here: the squint-eyed, the perverse, the queer, the troublesome, the mongrel, the mulatto, the half-breed, the half dead; in short all those who cross over, pass over, or go through the confines of the 'normal'. . . . Tension grips the inhabitants of the borderlands like a virus. Ambivalence and unrest reside there."[5] Those mixed-breed characters who reside in this borderland between native and white call into question the belief in essential white/Indian racial identities because, for them, originary racial identity is an impossibility. Therefore, as these characters illustrate, identity becomes a fabrication or an amalgamation, a construction of self through the choice of positions and perspectives choice of the stories that one will live by.[6] Through these characters, Silko shifts the historic polarity of white/native so that it becomes an adoption of one or the other contrasting relations to nature, instead of an opposition between biologically determined identities. It becomes a matter of competing paradigms, conflicting stories, rather than of blood. Through this shift, change and movement beyond the fatal opposition become a possibility.

Silko's first novel, *Ceremony,* employs and affirms the Laguna view of the restorative power of American Indian stories to challenge the dominant society's ethos of detachment from nature that has decimated the Laguna tribe and the natural and social worlds. *Ceremony* is a multilayered novel, constructed of frame poems surrounding a contemporary plot. Interspersed through the body of the novel are a number of tribal story-poems containing traditional legends about threats to the natural world and to Laguna people. The stories in these poems correspond to the central plot of Tayo's quest to save his tribe and end the drought. The reverberations between the layers of story-poems and main narrative in this novel enact the Laguna belief that stories produce the tribe by articulating relations between human, spirit, and nature. The contemporary plot echoes the story-poems, the poems offer an interpretive framework for the plot, divine entities from stories appear in the plot, and the protagonist learns how to construct and enact new stories that will produce new relations. In this vein, Silko introduces *Ceremony* with a poem that presents the novel as a manifestation of Thought Woman's stories: "Thought-Woman, / is sitting in her room / and whatever she thinks about / appears. / . . . She is sitting in her room / thinking of a story now / I'm telling you the story / . . . she is thinking" (1).

Ceremony addresses the embattled uncertainties of contemporary Laguna reservation existence in the face of the ever-present loss of native lands and in the midst of an actively hostile dominant culture that constantly works to undermine tribal traditions and native people's cultural identities. Tayo, the protagonist of the novel, returns home to the reservation in a state of severe shell shock and cultural confusion. Tayo suffers waves of physical illness and disturbing visions in which the Japanese enemies whom the Allies killed in the Philippines appear to be Tayo's uncle Josiah, who died on the reservation while Tayo was away at war. Similarly, Tayo believes that the drought that is decimating the Laguna Reservation has been caused by his cursing the incessant Philippine jungle rain that he blamed for his wounded cousin Rocky's being put to death by Japanese soldiers. Tayo is disturbed by the irrational associations of his visions in which the normal logical boundaries of the modern Western World—such as between family and enemy, home and foreign territory, mental curses and external conditions—fail to hold. During the course of the novel he will come to use his madness as a vision from the borderlands, a vision in which the unbounded, traditional Indian vision of the collective nature of events has run up against the wall of Euro-American conceptual oppositions. Tayo's cure will lie in untangling this conflict of paradigms.

The usual power imbalance of white / native relations has also been aggravated by the war, and the ambiguity of Tayo's half-breed status continues to haunt him upon his return to the reservation. Tayo continues to be denied complete acceptance within the tribe, yet he has always been excluded from the white world off the reservation, which only temporarily deemed Indians real Americans while they were in military uniform, fighting Asians for the good of the nation. The other full-blooded Laguna veterans enjoyed this fleeting taste of white power, white acceptance, and white women, and now that they are once again second-class citizens confined to the reservation, they drown their sense of the white world's betrayal through drinking, fighting among themselves, and feeling gnawing envy of white entitlement, which they direct against Tayo because of his mixed descent. The drought that is killing the tribespeople's livestock and crops only adds to the veterans' scorn for tribal ways. Tribal elders are at a loss for an effective means of curing the veterans and the drought-struck land.[7]

Ceremony describes the process of Tayo's healing as he comes to use his cultural confusion and ambiguous social position in order to renegotiate the relations between Indian and white cultures through a ceremonial reconstruction of the traditional Laguna relationship to the land. Tayo's exposure to the brutal hostilities of World War II that culminated in the atomic bombings of Japan have taught him the extreme devastation inherent within the Euro-American model of division and dominion. His ensuing shell shock and madness force him to comprehend the unbearable contradiction between the Indian belief in reciprocal relatedness and the white mode of destructive detachment. During Tayo's ceremonial healing under the direction of the unorthodox half-breed medicine man Betonie, he discovers and enacts new, empowering stories that alter the power imbalance between whites and natives and restore the partnership between tribe and nature. Much as *Meridian's* civil rights activism demonstrated the political application of African-American animistic tradition, the process of Tayo's healing reaffirms the viability of traditional Indian animistic culture as a means of rectifying the ravages wrought by the white world. During the ceremony that Tayo performs throughout the course of the novel, he comes to perceive potentiality and renewed life, where the white world has wrought only sterility, drought, and death.

Tayo's cure begins with his growing comprehension of the way that the white conquest of tribal lands underlies Indian social subordination and the threatened dissolution of tribal culture. The seizure of native lands—which, as I have argued above, was justified by white claims of cultural superiority and divine mandate to people the wilderness—has come to be interpreted by whites and certain Indians as a sign of the superiority of the Euro-American model of private property and progress over the Indian model of nonexploitative partnership with nature. In a twist of circular logic, as whites violently usurp more and more land, fulfilling their vision of productive progress, their conquest becomes self-endorsing: white predominance upon the land comes to signify white superiority. Whites and even many Indians interpret the hardships of reservation life that are actually directly related to the loss of prime farming and hunting grounds—such as economic impoverishment, lack of higher education and professional positions, overwhelming unemployment, "backwards" subsistence farming methods, as well as the accompanying emotional hardships, such as drunkenness and depression—as a sign of Indian racial inferiority and inability to survive the rigors of the white world. For many of the tribespeople of *Ceremony,* the loss of land leads to bitter cultural self-doubt and growing accession to white ways. Tayo realizes that Auntie's Christianity, Rocky's emulation of the white mainstream image of success, and even the veterans' self-destructive envy of white entitlement all stem from the omnipresent loss of ancestral lands: "They were never the same after that: they had seen what the white people had made from the stolen land. . . . Every day they had to look at the land, from horizon to horizon, and every day the loss was with them; it was the dead unburied, and the mourning of the lost going on forever. So they tried to sink the loss in booze, and silence their grief with war stories about their courage, defending the land already lost" (169).

Worse yet, white encroachment upon native ancestral lands threatens the reciprocity between humans and nature. Tayo describes the tribespeople's painful realization that they cannot protect the natural entities whom they regard as spiritual kin from abuses at the hands of whites. When former tribal lands that have been seized by the government are sold to ranchers and loggers, the land is stripped for profit and the animals are exterminated for sport: "The loggers had come, and they stripped the canyons below the rim and cut great clearings on the plateau slopes. . . . The loggers shot the bears and mountain lions for sport. And it was then the Laguna people understood that the land had been taken, because they couldn't stop these white people from coming to destroy the animals and the land" (186). The inability of the tribe to prevent this wanton desecration leads to terrible sorrow and guilt.

Tayo's illness accentuates the necessity for the Laguna people to redress this omnipresent loss of land and reciprocity so that the tribe might heal from crippling guilt and self-hatred. Central to Tayo's ceremonial healing and to Silko's unsettling of the fatal opposition is a story-poem that the healer Betonie recounts to Tayo about Indian sorcerers' creation of white people as implements of destruction who believe themselves to be separate from nature and who thus ravage everything and everyone associated with the natural world. Not only does this poem reinterpret the European disjunction from nature from a Laguna point of view, but the poem also reframes the European conquest of America as the product of an Indian witchery story, since "white skin people" are conjured into existence when the witch speaks this poem. In this story-poem the conflict between Indian and European paradigms is reframed within a larger conflict between beneficent Indians who claim kinship with nature, and maleficent Indian sorcerers, or witches, bent on fomenting death and destruction, who employ "white skin people" as tools for their diabolical work. Within this poem, the social and political power that the Indians have lost during the white conquest of America is effectively restored, as Betonie tells Tayo: "We can deal with white people, with their machines and their beliefs. We can because we invented white people" (132).

This story-poem tells of a witchery contest during which a witch conjures the white-skin destroyers by recounting a story-poem about their decimation of the natural and native worlds. The witch introduces the poem with the warning, "as I tell the story / it will begin to happen" (134), demonstrating the power of stories to set things in motion, for good or ill. Thus, the witchery poem is testament to the Indian belief in the productivity of stories, even as it recounts the decimation of the Indian world through the advent of the white settlers' dangerous new story of detachment from and destruction of nature and native peoples. The witch tells the following story of witchery, white people, and ultimate destruction:

> Caves across the ocean
> in caves of dark hills
> white skin people
> like the belly of a fish
> covered with hair.

> Then they grow away from the earth
> then they grow away from the sun
> then they grow away from the plants and animals.
> They see no life. . . .

> They fear
> They fear the world.
> They destroy what they fear.
> They fear themselves.

> The wind will blow them across, the ocean
> thousands of them in giant boats
> swarming like larva
> out of a crushed ant hill.

> They will carry objects
> which can shoot death
> faster than the eye can see.

> They will kill the things they fear
> all the animals
> the people will starve.

They will poison the water
they will spin the water away
and there will be drought
the people will starve

They will fear what they find
They will fear the people
They kill what they fear.

Entire villages will be wiped out
They will slaughter whole tribes

Corpses for us
Blood for us
Killing killing killing killing.

And those they do not kill
will die anyway
at the destruction they see
at the loss
at the loss of the children
the loss will destroy the rest.

Stolen rivers and mountains
the stolen land will eat their hearts
and jerk their mouths from the Mother
The people will starve.

They will bring terrible diseases
the people have never known.
Entire tribes will die out
covered with festered sores
shitting blood
vomiting blood
corpses for our work.

Set in motion now
set in motion by our witchery
set in motion
to work for us.

They will take this world from ocean to ocean
they will turn on each other
they will destroy each other

Up here in these hills
they will find the rocks,
rocks with veins of green and yellow and black.
They will lay the final pattern with these rocks
they will lay it across the world
and explode everything.

Set in motion now
set in motion
to destroy
to kill
objects of work for us
objects to act for us
Performing the witchery.
(134–36)

In effect, the witchery poem realigns the historic-American antagonism between the Indian mode of relationality of human to nature and
the supposedly superior Euro-American mode of detachment and dominion. While white and Indian modes are still shown to be dichotomous in
this poem, whites are described as agents of destruction and puppets of
witchery rather than as divinely ordained bearers of enlightened progress,
as their historic self-descriptions would have it. In this poem, white-skin
peoples' detachment from nature causes all their violent actions. When
the white-skin people "grow away" from the earth and the sun and all
other beings, and when they come to regard natural entities as dead things
with no life, their alienation leads to fear and enmity toward nature and
those peoples still associated with the natural world. The poem describes
the white objectification of nature as inherently destructive: because
whites believe that natural entities and native peoples are dead things, they
deaden them through violent assault, thus enforcing their story about the
lifelessness of the surrounding world. Each act of violence leads to greater
and greater destruction, and, as the world is made ever more dead and
alien, the devastation eventually circles back upon the white destroyers as
enmity toward fellow whites and, ultimately, as a final, all-encompassing
debacle of nuclear immolation. Thus, the witchery poem reframes the historic fatal opposition as truly fatal to all involved, since the white mode of
thought and behavior is based upon a fatal denial of life to anything perceived as Other. In the poem, the white mode of objectification and domination is itself shown to be a fatal opposition between subject and object
that produces alienation, fear, and death.

The deadly divisiveness at the core of the white-skin paradigm corresponds to the radical separation of subject and object that feminist analysts of science find responsible for the objectification of nature within the Western model of scientific objectivity. Keller notes: "Having divided the world into two parts—the knower (mind), and the knowable (nature)—scientific ideology goes on to prescribe a very specific relation between the two . . . one of distance and separation. It is that between a subject and an object radically divided. . . . Nature is objectified."[8] Keller explains that this radical division is the basis of the traditional scientific stance of dominant mastery, in which nature and people identified with nature—such as women and people of color—are to be forcibly appropriated in the service of Western development. Haraway further analyzes the appropriative dynamic between omnipotent knower and passive, inert object within the Western analytic tradition:

> The analytic tradition, deeply indebted to Aristotle and to the transformative history of "White Capitalist Patriarchy" . . . turns everything into a resource for appropriation, in which an object of knowledge is finally itself only matter for the seminal power, the act of the knower. Here, the object both guarantees and refreshes the power of the knower, but any status as *agent* in the production of knowledge must be denied the object. It—the world—must, in short, be objectified as thing, not as an agent; it must be matter for the self-formulation of the only social being in the productions of knowledge, the human knower. . . . Nature is only the raw material of culture, appropriated, preserved, enslaved, exalted or otherwise made flexible for disposal by culture in the logic of capitalist colonialism.[9]

Haraway notes the power imbalance through which the object of analytic knowledge becomes only "matter," or as Silko puts it, "dead thing," that shores up the all-consuming subjectivity of the knower. In this epistemological model, nature is "objectified," "enslaved," and "disposed of," in a manner analogous to the white-skin "deadening" of the natural world and native peoples in Silko's witchery poem. This critique of the exploitative dynamic within traditional models of objectivity, which is crucial to feminist scientists' efforts to theorize more egalitarian, accountable, and mutually interactive subject / object relations for the sciences, corresponds to the exposure of the whites' fatal opposition to nature in the witchery poem, which is similarly crucial to Tayo's struggle to reconstruct less exploitative and hostile relations between the two races and between the tribe and the natural world.

Through the witchery poem, Tayo comes to understand that the hos-

tilities and divisions that he sees everywhere—the enmity of white and Indian, of rich and poor, of Japanese and American, the division of the natural world into exclusive tracts of private property, and the growing separation of humans from an increasingly plundered and degraded natural
environment—are all the result of this fatal opposition between alienated
subject and objectified world. Through the poem, Tayo comes to attribute
polarization to the witchery rather than to the white-skin invaders and to
regard whites as tools of a greater evil, rather than as evil in themselves.
After hearing this poem, Tayo understands that Indians, too, may fall prey
to this divisiveness, and he will perceive Emo and other veterans as menac-
ing agents of the witchery. He realizes that polarization itself, rather than
any group of people, is the core problem. But before any widespread resolution can occur, whites, too, must face the racial polarity inhering in the
foundational American mythos that assumes that Euro-Americans are the
innocent civilizers of a land lost to Indian savagery—a mythos that serves
the witchery by keeping both peoples divided and turned against each
other. The "lie" of white manifest destiny and Indian savagery now threatens to destroy everyone: "If white people never looked beyond the lie, to
see that theirs was a nation built on stolen land, then they would never be
able to understand how they had been used by the witchery; they would
never know that they were still being manipulated by those who knew
how to stir the ingredients together: white thievery and injustice boiling
up the anger and hatred that would finally destroy the world: the starving
against the fat, the colored against the white" (191).

The witchery poem and the plot of the novel, which links the uranium
mines on the reservation to the nuclear bombing of Japan, assert the very
real threat that the destroyers' paradigm will come to final fruition
through nuclear annihilation; yet this final threat of nuclear destruction
reforms humans into a new collectivity that subsumes social differences
into a new clan, united by shared danger:

> Trinity Site, where they exploded the first atomic bomb, was only three
> hundred miles to the southeast. . . . And the top-secret laboratories
> where the bomb had been created were deep in the Jemez Mountains, on
> land the Government took from Cochiti Pueblo. . . . There was no end
> to it; it knew no boundaries; and he had arrived at the point of convergence
> where the fate of all living things, and even the earth, had been laid. From
> the jungles of his dreaming he recognized why the Japanese voices had
> merged with Laguna voices, with Josiah's voice and Rocky's voice; the lines
> of cultures and worlds were drawn in flat dark lines on fine light sand, con-

verging in the middle of witchery's final ceremonial sand painting. From that time on, human beings were one clan again, united by the fate the destroyers had planned for all of them, for all living things; united by a circle of death that devoured people in cities twelve thousand miles away, victims who had never known these mesas, who had never seen the delicate colors of the rocks which boiled up their slaughter. (245–46)

The magnitude of the witchery's final pattern of nuclear holocaust confounds divisions between races, nations, species, and geographical distances, reuniting all earthly entities into a global "circle of death." The witchery story comes full circle when the final pattern of destruction reencompasses all within its deadly plot. Paradoxically, the very scope of the destroyers' deadly power has made human beings "one clan again," decreating the boundaries that the witchery story had originally set in motion and thus opening a space for the alternative Laguna story of collectivity and interconnection.[10]

In light of this revelation, Tayo can reinterpret his madness and confusion, in which the Japanese and Laguna people are identical and his curse against the Philippine jungle rain has led to the Southwestern drought, as an alternative vision of genuine interconnections available outside the false boundaries of the witchery. Tayo realizes that the uranium used for the bombing of Japan has been mined on the Laguna Reservation, and so the fate of the Laguna and the fate of the Japanese are truly intertwined.[11] Upon recognizing this, Tayo can reassert the Laguna faith in the interconnectedness of all life within the ordering vision of the stories: "He cried with relief at finally seeing the pattern, the way all the stories fit together—the old stories, the war stories, their stories—to become the story that was still being told. He was not crazy; he had never been crazy; he had only seen and heard the world as it always was; no boundaries, only transitions through all distances and times" (246).

It devolves upon the mixed-breed characters such as Tayo, Betonie, and Uncle Josiah's mysterious lover, the Night Swan, those who have dwelt in the painful borderlands produced by racial polarization and who have personally borne the negative consequences of these divisive boundaries, to move beyond the fatal opposition toward less polarized stories of merging boundaries, fluid transitions in culture, and transracial social adaptation. Appropriately, Tayo's ceremonial healing takes the form of a quest to find his uncle Josiah's lost herd of hybrid Mexican wild cattle, interbred to survive desert conditions. Josiah's experimental herd, which might bring the Laguna tribe a means of farming the arid land during years of drought, symbolizes the way that Tayo might reenvision the borderlands as a promising site of productive intermixing and flexible adaptation to the shifting realities of an always-evolving American landscape composed of many interacting creatures and cultures. Tayo's ceremonial quest is, in essence, an act of recovery of all that has been "stolen" by the witchery. In tracking the Mexican cattle, which have been taken by a rich white rancher, Tayo will find the mountain and woman that Betonie has envisioned, and through them he will recuperate the power of traditional stories to renew the collectivity of tribe and land.

Tayo's cure is fulfilled through his relationship with the mysterious woman named Ts'eh, who helps him to recover Josiah's cattle and whose love and guidance teach Tayo how to regain his health and protect himself from Emo's violent witchery. Ts'eh, whose storm-cloud patterned blanket has the power to conjure storms and whose medicine work with plants and stones renews the drought-struck landscape, appears to be human being, natural entity, and supernatural being at once—a mountain goddess incarnate in a woman's form. Allen notes that the name Ts'eh echoes the Laguna name for Mount Taylor, which is a tribal sacred site known as Tse-pi'na, or Woman Veiled in Clouds.[12] Ts'eh is a sacred shapeshifter, in the tradition of spirit beings such as Buffalo Man and Sun Man, who appear in the traditional Laguna stories that Silko collected in *Storyteller* and that she discussed in the essay "Landscape." Such shapeshifters convey spiritual knowledge to the tribe by momentarily assuming human shape in order to form unions with tribespeople. The nature gods and goddesses act as lovers and teachers, offering their human partners sacred knowledge and sacred items that aid the entire tribe.[13] Thus, these relationships epitomize the Laguna belief in the reciprocal spiritual kinship of human and nature, the belief, discussed above, that the Laguna *became* a people when they articulated a partnership relationship to the surrounding landscape.

As Tayo's lover, protector, and teacher, Ts'eh restores Tayo's faith in the veracity and viability of the old stories of the loving union between tribe and natural world, even in the face of white antagonism to this mode of relation.[14] For Tayo, Ts'eh is living proof of the spiritual animation of nature, of the living presence of the sacred beings of the tribal stories. Through the love of Ts'eh, Tayo is able to renew the bond that tribal stories had articulated between human and nature: "The ear for the story and the eye for the pattern were theirs: the feeling was theirs; we came out of this land and we are hers. . . . They had always been loved. He thought of her then; she had always loved him, she had never left him, she had always been there" (255). Through Ts'eh, Tayo realizes that despite the tribe's displacement from the land and its inability to prevent white encroachments upon nature, even despite the omnipresent sense of loss that the tribe has suffered, the tribe has always retained its compact of reciprocity with nature: "They had always been loved." The "she" who loves in this passage is clearly Ts'eh, yet this omnipresent "she" is also Old Spider Woman or Thought Woman—the primordial Laguna female deity whose thoughts produce the natural world. Through love of Ts'eh, then, Tayo reconstructs and recovers a living relationship to the Laguna sacred principles incarnate in nature, and his rekindled animistic belief absolves the loss and guilt that has plagued the tribe.[15]

Furthermore, the tender, egalitarian, sexual, and spiritual relation between the lovers offers Tayo a healing antidote to the witchery's mode of antagonistic objectification that has sickened him. Tayo's relationship to the shapeshifter Ts'eh defies the diseased disjunctions at the heart of the white-skin mode. Within herself Ts'eh intermingles much that the whites deem to be essentially opposed; she is what Haraway would call a cyborgian entity, at once goddess and woman, mountain and human, supernatural and natural, sacred and sexual, timeless and momentary. Tayo's union with Ts'eh teaches him the falsity of the many sorts of boundaries that the white world has imposed across the American continent—the fences dividing the landscape into private plots, the reservations quarantining the Indians into their allotted place, the indiscriminate plundering of nature. But the lovers reconstruct the Indian mode of animistic relation as potent medicine against the deadening witchery that the whites have unwittingly wrought. As Ts'eh teaches Tayo, the struggle for an ending to the story of the fatal encounter between whites and Indians is not yet settled, and it is vitally necessary to counter the witchery story with an alternative story of kinship, life, love, connection, and renewal. Ts'eh teaches Tayo that the way to end the witchery is not to engage the agents of witchery, such as Emo, in fruitless physical battle, but to refuse to participate in the violent antagonisms the witchery has fomented.[16] While the witchery "can't be called back" and while the Indian mode of relation cannot be returned to some precontact purity, Ts'eh insists that the outcome of the Laguna/white encounter can be rewritten if Tayo adheres to the alternative story of loving collectivity.

The function of the animistic story as antidote to the witchery is analogous to the articulation by feminist analysts of science of alternative, more positive relations between human and nature, subject and object, as antidote to the polarizations that they see still predominating in the sciences. While neither Keller nor Haraway makes claims for the spiritual animation of nature that Silko describes, the feminist analysts do articulate alternative models of constructive interactions between knower and nonhuman actors that closely correspond to Silko's representation of the egalitarian mutuality between Tayo and Ts'eh. Keller describes the transformative possibility of such a paradigm of interdependent subject / object relations by arguing, as I mentioned in my discussion of Dickinson's nature poetry, that if one claims kinship with a complex and resourceful natural world, rather than viewing it as inferior and alien, one's questions and conclusions will shift accordingly.[17] This model of kinship between human knower and resourceful nature echoes the Laguna belief in reciprocity between tribe and surrounding natural world.

Similarly, Haraway argues that the existing paradigms of science that promote Western domination of nature and of native peoples might be contested through the articulation of alternative models of collectivities of human and nonhuman actors. Haraway suggests that "perhaps our hopes for accountability for techno-biopolitics in the belly of the monster turn on revisioning the world as coding trickster with whom we must learn to converse." haraway's notion of a "conversation" with the world as coding trickster who acts with some form of agency and intelligence is reminiscent of the Laguna view of nature spirits as loving teachers who offer the tribe vital knowledge, as Ts'eh "converses" with Tayo. In fact, Haraway often refers to nature specifically as "coyote," in reference to the Indian trickster god of that name, citing the Indian view of the natural world in her own articulation of nature "as witty actor and agent." Haraway finds in Indian animistic beliefs a useful model of nature as "active" "partner" and "coconstructor" of the complex human and nonhuman collectivities within which we live. Like Silko, Haraway finds the borderlands to be a region of hopeful disturbance of false polarities. She proclaims: "We *are all* in chiasmatic borderlands, liminal areas where new shapes, new kinds of action and responsibility, are gestating in the world."[18]

The relationship of Tayo and Ts'eh is an articulation of this gestation of new shapes and new kinds of actions and responsibilities spawned by traditional Laguna animistic beliefs and incubated during the centuries of white siege and seizure. For the image of the mountain/goddess/woman in loving relation with the half-breed Indian man is not a simple, naive, and innocent recapitulation of the precontact Laguna stories. It is instead a canny, conscious redeployment of the Laguna image of sacred female presence in nature—the very image that the whites had early on appropriated in order to justify white settlement of the virgin land. Silko's reappropriation turns this image of the land-as-native-woman back against the white-skin conquerors' commodification of native peoples and nature. Silko's land-as-native-woman entrusts herself only to those who acknowledge her as living presence, rather than as passive object of their desires, and to those who will care for her, rather than ravage her for profit and the perverse pleasures of wanton destruction. Significantly, she entrusts herself to a mixed-breed inhabitant of the borderlands. Rather than being a sentimental metaphor, Silko's Ts'eh is a contestatory recuperation of Laguna story tradition as that which might aid us—as a nation—to escape our continued entrapment within a deadly national mythology.

The relationship between Tayo and Ts'eh is an instance of Keller's and Haraway's calls to us to articulate collectivities composed of human and nonhuman agents in order to counter the deadly traditional "God View" of white master disjunct from the passive world that he has forcibly overpowered. Furthermore, Silko's image insists that in the complex, long-embattled American context, there is no essential innocent position from which we might assume what Haraway calls "new actions and responsibilities."[19] There is truly no way to "untangle" the snarl of white/native relations, nor to disown the witchery. Tayo's union with Ts'eh is historically contextualized against the realities of Indian participation in World War II and Indian complicity in nuclear weaponry through concession to uranium mining on reservation lands. Only by claiming his responsibility for participating in the witchery can Tayo resituate himself within the alternative paradigm embodied in his union with Ts'eh.

At the conclusion of the novel, Tayo assumes his own place in the living web of the Laguna oral tradition. He relates the story of his encounter with the mountain/woman to the tribal council, who receive his words as a sign of divine blessing of the tribe. The old men cry: " 'A'moo'oo!' / You have seen her / We will be blessed / again" (257). Tribal life will be reinvigorated by Tayo's reconstruction and enactment of this new yet perennial story that renews tribal relations to land and sends the witchery back upon itself. Through Ts'eh, Tayo has brought the tribe the sacred knowledge that the witchery story is its own trick; if one sees "no life" in the natural world, the witchery will ascend, but if one proclaims the spiritual life animating the natural world, then the witchery is defeated. The concluding poem of *Ceremony* confirms: "Whirling darkness / started its journey / with its witchery / and / its witchery / has returned upon it / . . . It is dead for now. / It is dead for now. / It is dead for now. / it is dead for now" (261). *Ceremony* insists that, for better or worse, we will re-create the world in the image of our stories.

Notes

1. While there are debates about the use of the word *Indian* versus the more recent title *Native American*, I have chosen to use the former term throughout most of
this chapter because Silko uses it in much of her writing and because the term pre-
dominates in the works of many contemporary Indian writers. Both terms are also
debatable because they erase the cultural specificity of the numerous, greatly diverse tribes that they encompass. I will use *Indian* in contrast with *Euro-American*, but
I will also specify Silko's particular Laguna Pueblo tribal identity when she is referring to that people. See Dorris, "Native American Literature" for a discussion of
these terms.

2. Slotkin, *Regeneration*, 17.

3. See, for example, Silko's writings in *Storyteller* about her Aunt Susie who transcribed the oral stories into written form in order to save them from disappearing
when children were forced by government policy to attend Indian schools far from
the reservation, thus breaking the chain of oral transmission of Indian culture. At
the schools, the children were acculturated in Western ways and taught to despise
their native heritage as false superstition

4. Allen, *Sacred Hoop*, 136.

5. Anzaldua, *Borderlands*, 3–4.

6. See Owens, *Other Destinies*, for discussion of mixed-blood identities. He cites
Silko as the first novelist to write a character able to create a positive, syncretic,
mixed-blood identification based on choice of positions rather than bloodlines. He
also argues that all Native Americans, no matter their descent, are in the position
of negotiating between Euro-American and Native American cultures.

7. Silko, *Ceremony*, 38, refers to the "scalp ceremony" that is a purification ritual
performed to cleanse the taint of death from those who have killed in battle. This
ritual has failed to reintegrate the veterans back into the tribe. Old Ku'oosh, the
healer, is at a loss for how to cure these men, but Tayo believes that the medicine
fails because the veterans have witnessed destruction on a scale unimaginable to
the tribe.

8. Keller, *Reflections*, 79.

9. Haraway, *Simians*, 197–98.

10. Buell, *Environmental Imagination*, 280–96, argues that apocalyptic visions, such
as this moment in *Ceremony*, are actually founded in the ecological notion of life as
an interconnected web within which destruction of one strand will have repercussions upon the rest of the system. Interestingly, in this section of *Ceremony*, the apocalyptic vision of total destruction produces the possibility of a renewed ecological
sense of interconnection among humans across divisions and enmities.

11. The mine itself is also the crux of confrontation between the Indian and white-skin stories of nature, as Indian reluctance to tamper with the "body" of the earth gives way before Euro-American determination to mine the ore that can produce nuclear power and nuclear annihilation. See Merchant, *Death of Nature*, 2–5, for discussion of these contrasting views of mining. See Matthiessen, *Indian Country*, 293–306, for discussion of internal tribal debates over the sale of mineral rights, and the hazards and consequences of the lack of regulation of radioactive mining practices on sovereign reservation lands.

12. Allen, *Sacred Hoop*, 121. Swan, "Laguna Symbolic Geography," also provides detailed explanations of Laguna religious interpretations of the geographic features of the novel, including Ts'ch's connections to Mount Taylor.

13. Smith and Allen, "Earthy Relations," 174–96, traces such instructive sexual liaisons between Indian women and spirit entities within the works of a number of writers, including Silko. They argue that, in contrast to white views, sexual relations are posed as a convergence of spirituality and carnality, and a convergence of animal, human, and supernatural entities, similar to my interpretation of Haraway's cyborg myth.

14. Allen, *Sacred Hoop*, 118–26, views the relationship between Tayo and Ts'eh as a restoration of balance between the masculine and feminine elements of the Laguna world. She sees Tayo's illness as the result of his alienation from the feminine landscape and his recovery as following upon the restoration of connection that he gains through Ts'eh. She traces traditional Laguna patterns of feminine imagery throughout the novel.

15. Tayo's relationship to Ts'eh is evocative of the relationship between speaker and "sweet mountains" in Emily Dickinson's "Sweet Mountains—Ye tell Me no lie—." In Dickinson's poem, the fluid identification between speaker and constant, yet moving mountains counters the exclusive polarities of Calvinist doctrines. In both instances, reciprocity between human and natural entity contests dominant oppositional policies.

16. Betonie had expressed a similar opinion of the folly of trying to withstand the superior brutal force of the whites: "We have done as much fighting as we can with the destroyers and thieves: as much as we could do and still survive" (*Ceremony*, 128).

17. Keller, *Reflections*, 117.

18. Haraway, "Promises," 298, 314.

19. Ibid., 303–15.

Works Cited

Allen, Paula Gunn. *The Sacred Hoop: Recovering the Feminine in American Indian Traditions.* Boston: Beacon Press, 1986.

Anzaldua, Gloria. *Borderlands: The New Mestiza.* San Francisco: Spinsters, 1987.

Buell, Lawrence. *The Environmental Imagination: Thoreau, Nature Writing, and the Formation of American Culture.* Cambridge: Belknap Press of Harvard University Press, 1995.

Dickinson, Emily. *The Complete Poems of Emily Dickinson.* Thomas Johnson, ed. Boston: Little, Brown, 1960.

Dorris, Michael. "Native American Literature in an Ethnohistorical Context." *College English* 41 (October 1979): 147–62.

Haraway, Donna. "The Promises of Monsters: A Regenerative Politics for Inappropriated Others." In *Cultural Studies,* ed. Lawrence Grossberg, Cary Nelson, and Paula Treichler, pp. 295–337. New York: Routledge, 1992.

————. *Simians, Cyborgs and Women: The Reinvention of Nature.* New York: Routledge, 1991.

Keller, Evelyn Fox. *Reflections on Gender and Science.* New Haven: Yale University Press, 1985.

Matthiessen, Peter. *Indian Country.* New York: Viking, 1984.

Merchant, Carolyn. *The Death of Nature: Women, Ecology and the Scientific Revolution.* San Francisco: Harper and Row, 1980.

Owens, Louis. *Other Destinies: Understanding the American Indian Novel.* Tulsa: University of Oklahoma Press, 1992.

Silko, Leslie Marmon. *Ceremony.* New York: Viking, 1977.

————. *Storyteller.* New York: Arcade, 1981.

Slotkin, Richard. *Regeneration through Violence: The Myth of the American Frontier, 1600–1800.* Middletown: Wesleyan University Press, 1973.

Smith, Clark, and Paula Gunn Allen. "Earthy Relations, Carnal Knowledge: Southwestern American Indian Women Writers and Landscape." In *The Desert Is No Lady,* ed. Vera Norwood, pp. 174–96. New Haven: Yale University Press, 1987.

Swan, Edith. "Laguna Symbolic Geography and Silko's *Ceremony.*" *American Indian Quarterly* 12 (1988): 229–49.

Walker, Alice. *Meridian.* New York: Washington Square Press, 1976.

Leslie Marmon Silko

JACE WEAVER

◆　◆　◆

M ANY OF THE SAME THEMES that run through the work of
Vine Deloria propel the writing of Leslie Silko. Sovereignty, community, and the vitality and power of a tradition that is constantly evolving are fundamental categories for the Laguna author. Rejecting racially
based essentializing, she stated in a 1980 interview, "Community is tremen-
dously important. That's where a person's identity has to come from, not
from racial blood quantum levels."[1] Applying such a criteria to herself in
an autobiographical statement six years earlier, she wrote, "I grew up at Laguna Pueblo. I am of mixed-breed ancestry, but what I know is Laguna.
This place I am from is everything I am as a writer and human being."[2] Like
Scott Momaday, she is a writer who sees herself as a writer (and not as a
"representative Indian"), "in whom a concern with memory and the past
operates as a constitutive element in both writing and personal/cultural
survival and growth."[3] And like Momaday (and Mourning Dove before
him), she artfully weaves traditional orature and the sacred/ceremonial
into Western literary forms.[4]

Born in Albuquerque on March 5, 1948, she was raised at Laguna. Describing her cross-blood heritage, she states, "The white men who came to
the Laguna Pueblo Reservation and married Laguna women were the beginning of the half-breed Laguna people like my family, the Marmon

family. I suppose at the core of my writing is the attempt to identify what it is to be a half-breed or mixed blooded person; what it is to grow up neither white nor fully traditional Indian."⁵ At Laguna she learned the Pueblo orature from her grandmothers.

While in college at the University of New Mexico, she wrote a short story, "The Man to Send Rain Clouds," based on an actual incident at Laguna, dealing with respect for the dead and religious syncretism and dimorphism. It was published in 1969, the same year she graduated from college. Five years later, it became the title piece (published with six more of her stories) in an early anthology of native fiction edited by Kenneth Rosen.⁶ She published her first book, a collection of poetry titled *Laguna Woman*, in 1974.⁷ She taught at Navajo Community College in Tsaile, Arizona, and then moved to Ketchikan, Alaska, where she completed her first novel, *Ceremony*, but returned to Laguna. She has taught at the University of New Mexico and the University of Arizona and currently resides in Tucson.

She attended the University of New Mexico's American Indian Law Program for three semesters but turned away from a legal career in favor of writing, believing, that the "most effective political statement I could make is in my art work."⁸ Though she began writing during the most active years of AIM protests, and though she understands the tactics the group employed, she rejects its politics of confrontation. In a 1985 interview, she stated, "I believe in subversion rather than straight-out confrontation. I believe in the sands of time, so to speak. Especially in America, when you confront the so-called mainstream, it's very inefficient, and in every way possible destroys you and disarm you. I'm still a believer in subversion. I don't think we're numerous enough, whoever 'we' are, to take them by storm."⁹ She sees her writing as an act of subversion, dealing with difficult issues like injustice, land expropriation, racism, and discrimination, in subtle and often humorous ways in order to gain a hearing among the dominant culture while still addressing a Native audience.¹⁰

Central to Silko's poetry and fiction is the role of orature, of the power of the story itself to heal the people. In a poetic epigram to *Ceremony*, she writes of the power of story to combat evil, its importance to the People, and its role in the ceremonial.¹¹

Describing this claim to power for story in the novel, Richard Sax writes:

> The problems that have obsessed Tayo [the novel's protagonist] were real events, but the means of coping are linguistically and ritualistically centered. Kenneth Lincoln suggests, "Silko's novel is a word ceremony. It tells

Tayo's story as a curative act." Just as the (re)telling of the tale begins again the cycle of the story, so the solutions to Tayo's dilemmas reside somewhere in the verbal, oral traditions of Laguna culture. When Tayo has grasped or recovered enough of the word to understand that he shares responsibility, though not necessarily guilt, in the deaths of Rocky, Josiah, and the nameless Japanese, then he is ready to make the physical, plaintive effort to recover the spotted cattle which is at once an acknowledgement to the memory and dreams of Josiah at the same time it is reaffirmation of American property law.[12]

When the medicine man, Ku'oosh, is summoned to heal Tayo, the power and importance of language and story is reinforced. Speaking of Ku'oosh's talk with Tayo, Silko writes:

> The world he chose to express "fragile" was filled with the intricacies of a continuing process, and with it a strength inherent in spider webs woven across paths through sand hills where early in the morning the sun becomes entangled in each filament of web. It took a long time to explain the fragility and intricacy because no word exists alone, and the reason for choosing each word had to be explained with a story why it must be said this certain way. That was the responsibility that went with being human, old Ku'oosh said, the story behind each word must be told there could be no mistake in the meaning of what had been said; and this demanded great patience and love.

Such is the centrality of story to Silko that she entitles her autobiographical meditation *Storyteller*.

Tayo at the beginning of *Ceremony* is undefined as a person. The narrative skips back and forth in time and place, reflecting the confused state of Tayo's mind. Only after Tayo meets Betonie and begins his process of reintegration both psychologically and as a member of the community does the novel take on something resembling a straight-line narrative structure. David Murray sees *Ceremony* and James Welch's *Death of Jim Loney* as "representing alternative attitudes to modern Indian identity—the one [*Death of Jim Loney*] pessimistic and emphasizing rootlessness, the other [*Ceremony*] optimistic and emphasizing a continuity and tradition which can be salvaged and retrieved."[13] This dichotomy, however, is a false one. Both works speak to the necessity of community. Jim Loney dies because he cannot reconnect to community, whereas Tayo survives because he does. In contrast to Tayo, Rocky is thoroughly deracinated and does not care what the village people think and is thus destroyed. Tayo is almost seduced by the same impulses. The Amer-European doctors at the VA hospital "had yelled at him—that he had to think only of himself, and not about the others, that he would never get well as long he used words like 'we' and 'us,'" but Tayo knows all along that his "sickness was only part of something larger, and his cure would be found only in something great and inclusive of everything." Ultimately, Tayo is able to achieve wholeness only by re-membering himself in the collective.

This power of community and story is underlined in highly material terms in Silko's latest novel, *Almanac of the Dead*. The ancient notebooks of the title, molded on Mayan codices, are both a symbol and a tool of Native survivance. Their potency as a weapon if resistance is understood by the fact that their Native custodian keeps them in a wooden ammunition box. When the southern tribe that composed the almanac is dying out from the impact of the European invasion, tribal members argue themselves as to what should be done with the book: "Because they were the very last of their tribe, strong cases were made for their dying together and allowing the almanac to die with them. After all, the almanac was what told them who they were and where they had come from in the stories. Since their kind would no longer be, they argued the manuscript should rightly die with them." Finally, however, it is decided to divide the text into parts and send it north with four children, knowing that in that way at least a part of the story would survive. "The people knew that if even a part of their almanac survived, they as a people would return someday." The power of the almanac stories to sustain the people is attested to when the children are forced to eat pages of the notebook as food. They not only survive but thrive. Otherwise, they would have starved. The pages of the book have many properties, both physical and spiritual, to feed the people and make them strong.

This emphasis on tradition does not mean, however, that Silko sees that tradition as static. She notes the rapid change she has seen in her own culture during her lifetime, and, like Vine Deloria, she sees tradition as a process. She believes that if a story has relevance for the People, they will remember it and retell it. If it does not feed the People or ceases to have that relevance, however, it will disappear and die.[14] In her autobiographical *Storyteller*, she recalls having her aunts tell her stories, but always with changes in detail and description. Such change was part of the story. In the process, new stories were created—"a new story with an integrity of its own, an offering, a part of the continuing which storytelling must be."[15] In *Ceremony*, there is an acknowledgment that the old ceremonies cannot cleanse those who fought in World War II. Instead, Tayo's grief is healed by the new ceremony devised by Betonie, whose tools include telephone books, coke bottles, and Santa Fe Railroad calendars. In *Almanac*, an old woman uses a spell to make the "white man's gadgets"—airplanes—crash. Even the ancient almanac itself changes. Pages have been lost and must be reconstructed. The current lives of the people become part of the story. Though the past determines the present, and though past wrongs must be redressed, one must not get stuck in it. Grief is that depression brought on by dwelling on the injustices of the past.

Almanac is a wildly improbable, tragicomic tale involving arms merchants, strippers, drug mules, and television psychics. Its often elliptical structure demonstrates Silko's storytelling method, borrowed from oral tradition. There are numerous complicated digressions and narratives within narratives. Almost 800 pages in print, the manuscript was reportedly cut by half prior to publication.[16] Author and critic Thomas King states, "By the time you get to the judge who abuses bassett hounds, you're saying to yourself, 'Wait a minute! What's Indian about this?' But it's a *very* Indian piece" in its storytelling style. Comparing it to the craft of the traditional storyteller, King continues, "This story is going down the highway at 150 miles an hour. You're following close behind. Then suddenly the storyteller makes a right angle turn at full speed. If you're not careful, you just run right off the road."[17] As Silko herself describes the traditional storytelling process itself in *Almanac*, "The story they told did not run in a line from the horizon but circled and spiraled instead like the red-tailed hawk."

Silko's work reveals a Native worldview in which chronological time means little: "Sacred time is always in the Present." An incident that took place seventy years before *Almanac of the Dead* begins still has ramifications because "seventy years was nothing—a mere heartbeat at Laguna." Amer-Europeans assumed that because the Ghost Dance had not produced immediate, tangible events, it lacked efficacy. In reality, avers Silko, it began a process that still continues and will achieve its goal at the appointed time. Eventually, as the ancient prophecies foretell and as Wovoka predicted, all things European will disappear from the Americas.

Community is central to her vision. Tayo must reconnect to community in order to survive. Sterling, in *Amanac of the Dead*, is banished and suffers that greatest of losses, the loss of community and family. Yet this community includes not simply human beings, or even the wider community, but the earth itself.[18] The original English definition of the word "landscape" designated a painting—something looked upon from the outside, excluding the viewer. For Silko, however, this sense of objectivity makes the term misleading. To Silko, "viewers are as much a part of the landscape as the boulders they stand on. There is no high mesa edge or mountain peak where one can stand and not immediately be part of all that surrounds. Human identity is linked with all the elements of creation through the clan."[19] According to Lucy Jones:

> "Ancient Pueblos took the modest view that the thing itself [the landscape] could not be improved upon," Silko writes, "The ancients did not presume to tamper with what had already been created." The created thing, the squash blossom, grasshopper, or rabbit was understood as the thing it was. It could not be created by human hand. Because of this, realism in art was eschewed. Relatedness in life continues into death as the dust of the once-living is taken in and recycled by the earth and by other living creatures. "The dead become dust, and in this becoming they are once more joined with the Mother. The ancient Pueblo people called the earth the Mother Creator of all things in this world. Her sister, the Corn Mother, occasionally merges with her because succulent green life rises out of the depths of the earth." In this [attitude], all life cycles are linked together in a chain that always includes the earth.[20]

In *Almanac*, a geologist is stricken for violating Mother Earth. Her short fiction "Storyteller," in the book of the same name, "demonstrates that nature's patience is wearing thin and humankind is threatened"; [t]he prophetic tone of the story is ominous, [suggesting] that mankind will not be able to rescue itself from its own rapaciousness." The essays in *Yellow Woman and a Beauty of the Spirit* "emphasize the inextricable links between human identity, imagination and Mother Earth," links forged and mediated in story.[21]

In this view of the earth, nuclear power holds a special place in Silko's work. The author grew up in Laguna, "not far from Los Alamos uranium mines and the Trinity Site, where on July 16, 1945, the first atomic bomb was detonated."[22] Men from Laguna worked those mines and died as a result.[23] The final denouement of *Ceremony* takes place near these sites, and there is a sense in which the atomic bomb has made all creation one again: "There was no end to it; it knew no boundaries; and he had arrived at the point of convergence where the fate of all living things, and even the earth had been laid." In *Almanac*, the old ones warned against uranium mining because " all the people would pay, and pay terribly, for this desecration, this crime against all living things." In *Sacred Water*, her paean to the sacrality of water for all life, Silko relates the effects of fallout from the Chernobyl disaster on her home in Ketchican. It decreased the toad population and caused a strange red algae to grow in a rain pool behind her house. Rather than destroy the pond, she transplanted water hyacinths into it. She writes:

> The water in the pool began to clear and smell cleaner because water hyacinths digest the worst sorts of wastes and contamination: decomposing rodents and dead toads—nothing is too vile for the water hyacinth. Water hyacinths even remove lead and cadmium from contaminated water. I write in appreciation of the lowly water hyacinth, purifyer of defiled water.
>
> Only the night-blooming datura, jimson weed, sacred plant of the Pueblo priests, mighty hallucinogen and deadly poison, only the datura has the power to purify plutonium contamination. Datura not only thrives in soil contaminated by plutonium, the datura actually removes the plutonium from the soil so that the soil is purified and only the datura itself is radioactive. The datura metabolizes "heavy water," contaminated with plutonium, because, for the datura, all water is sacred.
>
> Across the West, uranium mine wastes and contamination from underground nuclear tests in Nevada ruin the dwindling supplies of fresh water. Chemical pollutants and heavy metals from abandoned mines leak mercury and lead into aquifers and rivers. But human beings desecrate only themselves; the Mother Earth is invioable [*sic*]. Whatever may come of us human beings, the Earth will bloom with hyacinth purple and the white blossoms of the datura.[24]

In all her writings, Silko uses her skills of subversion to defend Native peoples and community, decrying "hundreds of years of exploitation of the Native American people here."[25] Her characters are not merely surviving but resisting. Even the crimes, such as drug dealing and bank robbery, in which the characters engage in *Almanac* are viewed as resistance. The war for Native lands and sovereignty has never ended. As she writes in that volume, "there were hundreds of years of blame that needed to be taken by somebody."

Notes

1. Dexter Fisher, ed., *The Third Woman: Minority Women Writers of the United States* (New York: Houghton Mifflin, 1980), p. 19.

2. Kenneth Rosen, ed., *The Man to Send Rain Clouds* (New York: Random House, 1975), p. 176.

3. David Murray, *Forked Tongues: Speech, Writing and Representation in North American Indian Texts* (Bloomington: Indiana University Press, 1991), p. 80.

4. Arnold Krupat may be correct when he writes in 1989, "Momaday is not only the best known and celebrated contemporary Native American writer, recipient of a Pulitzer Prize for fiction (1969), but for Silko's work to date, the presumptive groundbreaker or forefather." He goes too far, however, when he declares, "Her *Ceremony* (1977), it is said (with some justice), is heavily dependent upon his *House Made of Dawn* (1968); her *Storyteller* (1981) perhaps no more than a rerun of his *The Names* (1976)." *The Voice in the Margin: Native American Literature and the Canon* (Berkeley: University of California Press, 1989), p. 177.

5. Joseph Bruchac, ed., *The Next World: Poems by Third World Americans* (Trumansburg, N.Y.: Crossing Press, 1978), p. 1730, quoted in Louis Owens, *Other Destinies: Understanding the American Indian Novel* (Norman: University of Oklahoma Press, 1992), p. 167.

6. Laura Coltelli, *Winged Words: American Indian Writers Speak* (Lincoln: University of Nebraska Press, 1990); *Man to Send Rain Clouds*, p. 135; Rosen pp. 3–8.

7. Leslie Marmon Silko, *Laguna Woman* (Greenfield Center, N.Y.: Greenfield Review, 1974).

8. Coltelli, *Winged Words*, p. 147.

9. Ibid., pp. 147–48.

10. Ibid., p. 147.

11. Leslie Marmon Silko, *Ceremony* (New York: Viking, 1977). Non-Native writer Barry Lopez captures some of this flavor in his children's book *Crow and Weasel*, written in a supposed Native idiom. In it, Badger tells the protagonists, "The stories people tell have a way of taking care of them. If stories come to you, care for them. And learn to give them away where they are needed. Sometimes a person needs a story more than food to stay alive. That is why we put these stories in each other's memory. This is how people care for themselves. One day you will be good storytellers. Never forget these obligations." Barry Lopez, *Crow and Weasel* (San Francisco: North Point Press, 1990), p. 48. Similarly, Lester Standiford writes, "Properly cared for, preserved intact, a story has the power to sustain an entire culture." "Worlds Made of Dawn: Characteristic Image and Incident in Native American Imaginative Literature," in Wolodymyr T. Zyla and Wendell M. Aycock, eds., *Ethnic literatures since 1776: The Many Voices of America* (Lubbock: Texas Tech Press, 1978). p. 341.

12. Richard Sax, "Laguna Values in Anglo Classrooms: The Delicacy and Strength of the Writings of Leslie Silko," in Thomas E. Shirer and Susan M. Branster, eds., *Native American Values: Survival and Renewal* (Sault Ste. Marie, Mich.: Lake Superior State University Press 1993), p. 139. The story is, as Lincoln observes, itself a ceremony, in which the reader becomes a participant through the reading, reenacting it anew each time. *Native American Renaissance* (Berkeley: University of California Press, 1983).

13. Murray, *Forked Tongues*, p. 87.

14. See Coltelli, *Winged Words,* pp. 143, 149.

15. Leslie Marmon Silko, *Storyteller* (New York: Arcade Publishing, 1981), p. 227.

16. Leslie Marmon Silko, *Almanac of the Dead* (New York: Simon & Schuster, 1991).

17. Thomas King, interview with author, January 27, 1992.

18. I am indebted in many of these remarks to the insights of one of my students, Lucy Jones, who prior to returning for graduate education had a background in botanical work. Lucy Jones, "The Land and Spirit" (unpublished paper, Union Theological Seminary, January 22, 1996). See also Richard F. Fleck, "Sacred Land in the Writings of Momaday, Welch, and Silko," in Thomas E. Shirer, ed., *Entering the 90s: The North American Experience* (Sault Ste. Marie, Mich.: Lake Superior State University Press, 1991), pp. 125–133.

19. Lucy Jones, "The Land," p. 8; Leslie Marmon Silko, "Landscape History and the Pueblo Imagination," in John Elder and Hertha D. Wong, eds., *Family of Earth and Sky* (Boston: Beacon Press, 1994), p. 249.

20. Lucy Jones, "The Land," p. 19; Silko, "Landscape," pp. 247–49.

21. Herb Barrett, "The 'Storyteller' of Leslie Marmon Silko: a Commentary" (unpublished paper, Yale University, December 18, 1996), pp. 17–18; Leslie Marmon Silko, *Yellow Woman and a Beauty of the Spirit* (New York: Simon & Schuster, 1996); *"Yellow Woman and a beauty of the Spirit," Publishers Weekly,* January 22, 1996, p. 54.

22. Coltelli, *Winged Words,* p. 135.

23. See Peter H. Eichstaedt, *If You Poison Us: Uranium and Native Americans* (Santa Fe, N.M.: Red Crane Books, 1994).

24. Leslie Marmon Silko, *Sacred Water* (Tucson, Ariz.: Flood Plain Press, 1993), pp. 72–76.

25. Coltelli, *Winged Words,* p. 152.

Silko's Arroyos as Mainstream

Processes and Implications of Canonical Identity

KENNETH M. ROEMER

♦ ♦ ♦

A T THE 1996 MLA CONVENTION in a provocative paper entitled "When Contemporary Literature Isn't," Molly Hite indicated that she had taken an informal survey of American literature professors, asking them which contemporary American novels they considered most important. Four titles dominated the responses: Toni Morrison's *Beloved*, Ralph Ellison's *Invisible Man*, Thomas Pynchon's *Gravity's Rainbow*, and Leslie Marmon Silko's *Ceremony*. I was delighted to hear that *Ceremony* was included in this select group, but not totally surprised. In the January 1986 issue of *ASAIL [Association for the Study of American Indian Literatures] Notes*, Andrew Wiget announced the results of another informal survey: "[b]y far the most frequently taught novel (over 50%) was *Ceremony*" (4). More recently in March 1993, when I guest lectured at Connecticut College, *Ceremony* was being taught in four programs: women's studies, American literature, religion, and anthropology. In 1992, 1994, 1996, and 1998, the book most often mentioned by the several hundred inquirers and applicants to my American Indian literatures NEH Summer Seminar for high school teachers was *Ceremony*. Silko is still the only Native American author included in the popular Twayne introductions to authors (Salyer). *Ceremony* was the only novel by a Native American author to be ranked in the top twenty-five "most significant twentieth-century books of fiction" (it was eleventh) in the Spring

1999 *Heath Anthology of American Literature Newsletter* survey of several hundred professors (Lauter, "Top 100" 1). On the crossword puzzle cover of the 1999 American Literature "Video & CD Rom" catalog of Films for the Humanities and Sciences, "SILKO" is the only name by a "minority" author. To date, Silko is the only American Indian author to be featured on the NPR "Talk of the Nation" "Book Club of the Air" program. And most recently—just try typing the key words "Silko, Leslie" into the Internet to verify the virtual popularity of *Ceremony* (Dinome 223–24). In one article I certainly cannot pretend to explain why *Ceremony* is so widely recognized by specialists in American Indian literatures and by many other literature and nonliterature teachers in universities and high schools. I can at least touch upon several important forces contributing to its current stature and point to some significant literary, cultural, and political implications of *Ceremony*'s canonization.

Before I begin my "touching upon" and "pointing to," I should state three important qualifications. First, much of this essay, indeed most canon formation studies, could be labeled as speculative Monday-morning quarterbacking—a process of reading current evidence backward to reach self-evident conclusions. Americanists already know that *Ceremony* has won its literary place (at least "for now," to borrow a Silko refrain); and they know that it is much easier to explain *Ceremony*'s canonization than to try to determine which of the many new novels by young Native American authors will be respected. Second, analyses of the developed or developing reputations of several other Native American authors—N. Scott Momaday, Louise Erdrich, and Sherman Alexie, for instance—could offer fascinating case studies in the journeys from the margins to the mainstream(s). Third, many of my arguments about *Ceremony*'s reputation stress cultural, historical, institutional, publication, marketing, and reception contexts. This approach may seem to denigrate the aesthetic and didactic strengths of the novel. Certainly, this is not my intent. In the second section of this essay I emphasize the compelling literary qualities of *Ceremony* that were crucial to its canonization. Nevertheless, I've placed contexts in the first section of this essay because their examination will help us to understand why *Ceremony* has become a privileged "minority" text, why certain "Native American" texts have been recognized, what this acceptance implies about canon formation in America, and how teachers and scholars should respond to a process that can be both liberating and stifling.

WE NEED NOT DWELL on the obvious, but it is crucial to mention that during the 1960s and 1970s, the Civil Rights and ethnic awareness movements within and outside the academy established a strong interest among non-Indian readers and publishers in translations of Native oral literatures and in works written by Indians about Indians. Taken in a negative light, this interest was but another historical demonstration of the power of the forces that dictate when and what kind of books by Native Americans get published. David Murray sums up this situation by noting that the publication of a book by an Indian author "was likely to reflect the taste of a white audience, and conform to a large extent to what at least some of them thought it was appropriate for an Indian to write. Indian *writers* are mainly going to materialize, therefore, only when what they say meets a white need" (Murray's emphasis); (57). A more positive view of the impact of the Civil Rights and ethnic studies movements would be to evoke Mary Louise Pratt's concept of the "contact zone," by stressing how Native American authors of Silko's generation, most of whom were educated in traditional university settings, became adept at using Euro-American genres to articulate Native causes and worldviews.

During the 1960s and 1970s, two other general forces played particularly important roles in establishing interest in a contemporary Native American woman who wrote novels: the women's movement and attitudes about genre hierarchies. In the popular (and much of the academic) mid-twentieth-century imagination, Indian identity was typically a masculine identity, with the obvious exceptions of the squaw and princess stereotypes, and the specific "simulations" (to borrow Gerald Vizenor's use of the term) of Pocahontas and Sakajawea, both celebrated for serving non-Indian males. "Where are the women?" demanded literature teachers and scholars. Silko's *Ceremony* was an exciting answer to this question, one that was enhanced by the incorrect assumption voiced by some scholars that *Ceremony* was the first novel written by a Native American woman.[1]

Both Momaday and Welch had published powerful poems before writing their novels. But as Susan Harris Smith has argued in "Generic Hegemony," genre hierarchies strongly influence the study and promotion of literature in America. To become commercial/critical successes, American authors need to publish a "serious" novel. In the *N. Scott Momaday* film produced by Films for the Humanities & Sciences in 1995, Momaday emphasizes this fact of literary life: "We have a lot of people, young Indian people writing poetry, many more than are writing novels. . . . But it is the novelist who attracts the attention of the public." Typically, to attract this attention, the novel must be different enough to be distinctive but familiar enough to be recognizable. Certainly, a male protagonist on a mythic quest was a familiar narrative pattern. Furthermore, nineteenth- and twentieth-century American fiction writers had established as "familiar enough" a specific focus on the alienated returning veteran, and that helped to make Tayo's story recognizable to literary critics and teachers. Recognizable but not redundant. The distinctive New Mexico landscapes; the Laguna and Navajo concepts of storytelling, place, ritual, and community; the striking and accessible mixed (oral-derived, Euro-American written) narrative form; and the "fact" of female, Native American authorship certainly made *Ceremony* "different enough."

Before the publication of *Ceremony* (even before parts of the novel appeared in *The Journal of Ethic Studies* and *New America* in 1975 and 1976), there were developments in Silko's early fiction writing and publishing career that demonstrate the key roles of academic and publishing connections in canon formation. Though commendable, it is not unusual for talented college writers to publish in student publications and regional journals, as Silko did when attending the University of New Mexico. What was unusual and fortuitous in this case is that one of Silko's classmates, Kenneth Rosen, would, during the early 1970s, be searching for talented Native American writers to contribute to fiction and poetry anthologies to be published by a major commercial publisher, Viking. It is not surprising that Rosen turned to someone he knew, especially in the fiction collection. He used one of Silko's University of New Mexico stories as the title of the anthology, *The Man to Send Rain Clouds* (1974), and Silko's stories dominated the book. Seven out of the nineteen stories are Silko's, including one of her best-known stories," Yellow Woman," which in 1993, became the focus of Melody Graulich's casebook. True, there had been good collections of contemporary Native American fiction before Rosen's, including John R. Milton's *South Dakota Review* anthologies *The American Indian Speaks* (1969) and *American Indian II* (1971). But Rosen's Silko-dominated anthology was the first published by a major commercial press with the advertising and distribution power to alert many teachers to Silko's talents and to supply private and university bookstores with sufficient numbers of copies— and to attract the attention of three influential readers, Martha Foley, Frank MacShane, and Richard Seaver. Foley included Silko's "Lullaby," which did not appear in Rosen's collection, in *The Best Short Stories of 1975* and "Yellow Woman" in *Two Hundred Years of Great American Short Stories* (1976). MacShane specifically mentioned *The Man to Send Rain Clouds* in his rave review of *Ceremony*, which appeared in the *New York Times Book Review* (see later discussion). Richard Seaver was impressed enough to take a chance on this young poet and short-story writer by accepting the manuscript of *Ceremony* as one of the Richard Seaver Books of Viking. The fact that *Man to Send Rain Clouds* was published by Viking gave Silko, if not an "insider" status, at least a "known entity" identity with Viking.

Before commenting on the important roles played by early influential reviews and scholarship, I'd like briefly to draw attention to two influences on the early reception that are often ignored in discussions of canonization—performance skills and photographic images. As anyone who attended a Silko reading during the decade after the publication of *Ceremony* can attest, she can be a fine performer. Her eyes flash, her hands accentuate and punctuate, and her voice combines warmth, excitement, and humor, though when reading excerpts such as the Gallup episode in *Ceremony*, it can also express dark censure and bitterness.

Although the size of the audience that could witness Silko's performance persona of the 1970s was enlarged by filmed interviews (*Running on the Edge of the Rainbow*, 1978, and *Leslie M. Silko*, 1995), Silko's live performance and film images have been seen primarily by academic audiences. A much broader audience saw the promotional black-and-white photograph (taken by Deny Carr) on the back cover of the first edition of *Ceremony* (see page 2).[2] Silko looks attractive, appropriately "Indian," and young. The photograph is not stereotypical, however. The buckskin, beads, and braids that play such a prominent part in the image of Mourning Dove in the frontispiece of *Co-ge-we-a* (1927) are absent in Silko's photo.[3] Still, we do see the youth, the long straight black hair and dark eyes (the black-and-white medium made both appear darker than they are, especially the eyes), and the expected Southwestern landscape.

A smile cannot win canonization. Nonetheless, the natural, relaxed, smiling image of Silko is significant. (This is a recurring characteristic of most of her promotional photographs, including the one used frequently in the widely distributed brochures in the Films for the Humanities & Sciences Native American series, which typically features vertical head-shot line-ups—literary marketing totem poles—of Silko, Momaday, Welch, and Vizenor.) The smile counters the visual stereotypes of the "wooden," "brooding," "dumb" Indian, or beast of burden "squaw" images. It may even relieve some of the anxieties of non-Indians who would like to learn about Native literatures and cultures but are hesitant because of their ignorance or because of ambivalences arising from complicated mixtures of prejudice and guilt. Silko's relaxed smile can be reassuring to such readers, signifying a friendly invitation to begin *Ceremony*.

Silko's image was framed by crucial reviews in widely distributed publications that appeared before many readers saw Silko's photograph and by important scholarship published soon after many readers had made acquaintance with Silko's novel.

The reviews were not always accurate, perceptive, or uniformly favorable. But all of them, carried in publications designed to reach large audiences and/or large numbers of librarians, offered strong words of praise for *Ceremony* and specifically celebrated Silko's ability to bridge the gap between Native experiences and non-Indian readers. The most influential review reflected these emphases. In Frank MacShane's *New York Times Book Review* rave he proclaimed Silko "without question . . . the most accomplished Indian writer of her generation" (15). Although he supported his pronouncement in several ways, his primary emphasis was on Silko's cross-cultural and mediating achievements. He linked her successful narrative to "the way she has woven together the European tradition of the novel with American Indian storytelling" (15). His concluding paragraph—an enthusiastic announcement of a new candidate for canonization—stressed the ways that Silko's background and artistic skills enabled her to bridge the boundaries of culture and gender:

> Leslie Silko is herself part-white, part-Indian. Her dual sensibility has given her the strength to blend two forms of narrative into a single work of art. It may also have given her the perspective, as a woman, to write so movingly about her male characters. Her novel is one of the most realized works of fiction devoted to Indian life that has been written in this country, and it is a splendid achievement. (15)

Literary scholars obviously found *Ceremony* accessible (and "splendid"). It would be difficult to find an author, male or female, who was taken in more quickly by the specialists overseeing a particular type of literature. Again timing was important. As some of the important initial reviews were appearing, the National Endowment for the Humanities and the Modern Language Association sponsored a summer seminar on American Indian literatures in Flagstaff, Arizona. *Ceremony* was a central text, and Silko was the star guest speaker. She gave a dynamic reading and stayed to talk informally with many of the staff and participants. Thus, only a few months after its publication and just as Native American literature was beginning to gain acceptance in English departments, *Ceremony* became a key text for an important core group of scholars.

Again timing was important. Less than a year after *Ceremony*'s publication, the first book-length study of fiction by Native Americans appeared, Charles A. Larson's *American Indian Fiction* (1978). Since at that time Silko was the only female American Indian novelist with a reputation that extended beyond a relatively small circle of specialists, it is not surprising that Larson devoted a section of his book to *Ceremony* (150–61). The assumption that *Ceremony* was a "must" inclusion in the discussion of fiction by Indians was reinforced the next year by the appearance of a special issue (5, no. 1) of *American Indian Quarterly* devoted to *Ceremony*. Within less than two years of its publication, interested scholars and teachers had a convenient guide to numerous "backgrounds" and "sources" for *Ceremony*. Thus, one of the primary barriers to teaching and writing about Native American literature— an ignorance of tribal cultures and literatures—was quickly, conveniently, and convincingly diminished.

Less than six years after *Ceremony*'s publication, its canonical place in the scholarship was firmly established by chapter-length studies in both Alan R. Velie's *Four American Indian Literary Masters* (1982; Silko was the only woman "master," 105–22) and Kenneth Lincoln's highly influential *Native American Renaissance* (1983, 222–50). The special issue and these three initial book-length studies set a precedent that made unthinkable (or at least academically suspect) a book-length study of fiction or a special Native American literature journal issue that did not include discussion of *Ceremony*.

A striking feature of the critical response—as recently documented in William Dinome's extensive annotated Silko bibliography (207–80)— has been its almost consistent laudatory tone. With the notable exceptions of one of Paula Gunn Allen's articles,[4] some ambivalence in Elizabeth Cook-Lynn essays, and especially in Shamoon Zamir's "Literature in a 'National Sacrifice Area,'" *Ceremony* continues to receive enthusiastic praise. This consistency, combined with the assumption that *Ceremony* will be a major topic in any discussion of Native American fiction and the recognition and authority that came with prestigious awards (notably, Silko's inclusion in the first group of MacArthur fellowship recipients in 1981), sends a clear message to university and high school teachers looking for an "Indian" novel to include in their scholarship or courses: *Ceremony* is "safe" and "essential." It has been verified by a strong consensus and is an expected inclusion in the critical discourse of American literary interpretive communities.

THE ENTHUSIASTIC CRITICAL RESPONSE clearly suggests that the canonization story of *Ceremony* should not be reduced to narratives of the quirks of timing and connections, the smiles of promo photos, the needs of powerful magazine and book publishers, or even the grand forces of culture and history. These forces certainly enhance many readers' abilities to perceive specific characteristics and qualities in a text and influence shared discourse about that text. But without particular and recognizable qualities—especially characteristics that make *Ceremony* accessible to many readers—*Ceremony* could not have "benefited" from the complex intersections of culture, reader, and text that generate literary canons.

As indicated earlier, the landscape, re-creations of oral literatures, the Laguna and Navajo concepts of the generative and negative powers of storytelling and ceremony, and the gender and culture and racial background of the author, rendered *Ceremony* "different enough" to be perceived as a distinct and "authentic" Native American text. *Ceremony* is also complex enough in familiar enough ways to justify and facilitate the roles of professional teachers and critics. As William Dinome's survey of the criticism reveals, these and other complex combinations of the familiar and unfair have invited an impressive variety of critical approaches. *Ceremony* obviously creates ample opportunities for many types of critics to display their professional skills.

Still, despite its complexities, *Ceremony* is easier to follow—especially for high school students, non-English majors, and non-English professors—than several of the other highly acclaimed novels by Native American authors, for example, N. Scott Momaday's *House Made of Dawn* (1968), Louise Erdrich's *Love Medicine* (1984, 1993) and *Tracks* (1998), and many of Gerald Vizenor's trickster narratives. *Ceremony* is also accessible to many readers because Silko's omniscient narrator frequently explains, either explicitly or contextually, unfamiliar elements of the narrative. Furthermore, several of the most powerful scenes can be grasped and admired, even if the reader is not a "competent" purveyor of Laguna and Navajo intertextualities, though as Allen's criticism of Larson's *American Indian Fiction* indicates, readers who lack knowledge of tribal beliefs are certainly capable of distorted readings ("Introduction" 1).

The openings of *Ceremony* and *House Made of Dawn* make an interesting case study in comparative accessibility. The first word of the text in each novel would be foreign to almost all readers: *Ts'its'tsi'nako* (*Ceremony* 1) and *Dypaloh* (*House* 1). As Momaday suggested in an interview with Floyd C. Watkins, the opening (and closing) Jemez Pueblo words "appeal" because they are "authentic" (156). The same could be said for Silko's opening. But Silko's storyteller follows her opening Laguna word immediately with "Thought-Woman," and later in the poem identifies the only two other non-English words—*Nau'ts'ity'i, I'tcts'ity'i*—as the "sisters" of Thought-Woman (1). To discover the meaning of *Dypaloh*, a reader would either have to consult with someone familiar with Jamez storytelling conventions or read Watkins' explanation that links the word to traditional Jamez opening formulas (156).

In a 1977 interview with Dexter Fisher, Silko indicated that occasionally "explanations" are necessary: "Maybe if there are words like *arroyo* that aren't clear, those could be explained" (21). She also suggested that too many unfamiliar words can be annoying for readers ("I used to get irritated with T. S. Eliot and all his Greek.") and that she did not believe that readers should have to have abundant specialized knowledge to understand her works (21). *Ceremony* demonstrates her point. Often the novel's narrative, thematic, or psychological contexts provide sufficient backgrounding for readers ignorant of Laguna and Navajo worldviews, though, as she indicated to the Flagstaff participants, explaining everything for uninformed readers would have swelled the novel with hundreds of extra pages (Roemer, "Retrospective" 19–20). Silko's network of explanations, implications, and withholdings reflect her attempts to "answer" the anticipated responses of a readership in between the extraordinary competent Laguna reader and the hopelesssly ignorant non-Indian reader. The canonization of *Ceremony* suggests that her negotiations were successful.

Successful especially because crucial episodes in *Ceremony* can be "understood" and "appreciated" whether the reader is a "competent" reader—in the sense that he or she either already knows or is willing to look up implied reference to Laguna and other tribal literatures—or "competent" in the sense that he or she can perceive and then assemble networks of textual invitations that give powerful meanings to the text even without an awareness of specific cultural overtones. The Night Swan episode (81–106) is a striking example of a textual site that invites either or both competencies. A reader who is familiar with the Southwest or who has read Robert M. Nelson's *Place and Vision* (1993) would know that the trajectory of Night Swan's geographical history traces a pattern of movement toward Mt. Taylor, which is sacred to both Laguna and Navajo (Nelson 16–17); and readers familiar with Laguna mythology or with critical studies, such as Paula Gunn Allen's "Feminine Landscape" or Kathleen Manley's "Silko's Use of Color," would know about the connections between the color coding of whites and especially blues that link Night Swan to Mt. Taylor. But a reader need not be an expert in Southwestern geography or Laguna color symbolism to heed the numerous invitations to perceive the mythical overtones to this realistic character. In her first real appearance (after she's first alluded to as Josiah's "Mexican girl friend," a cause of gossip that disturbs Auntie [32]), Silko combines Faulknerian, Melvillian, and Laguna conventions to mystify Night Swan's entrance. With no apparent transition Silko opens a paragraph with a "She" who has watched Josiah—"I've seen you before many times" (82). This pose of watching is repeated twice on the next page and appears again as Night Swan introduces herself to Tayo: "She had watched him all summer"; " 'I've been watching you a long time'" (99). A reader does not have to be acquainted with the mystifying powers of the Faulknerian third-person pronoun entrance, or the variation on "Call me Ishmael" ("They call me the Night Swan" [84]), or the Laguna tradition of deities watching and waiting for humans to sense the mysterious overtones of Night Swan's entrance. The entrance is followed by numerous invitations to perceive a realistic character—full of wrinkles and life, loneliness and passion—as a manifestation of powerful generative forces: the story of the young love that liberated, terrified, and literally crushed a hypocritical lover (84–86), the networks of negative and positive rattling and crushing sounds, the defining of Mt. Taylor as "*Tse-pi'na* the woman veiled in clouds" (87); the explicit connections with Mt. Taylor (" 'I saw the mountain, and liked the view from here'" (87); the implicit links with Spider Woman and storytelling (94–95) on the pages immediately preceding the encounter with Tayo (96); the ingenious craft with which she weaves her blues and whites, and more blues in Night Swan's little room—all these patterns invite readers, whether they are or are not aware of Laguna (or Faulknerian and Melvillian) traditions, to transform Night Swan from a cause of gossip (Auntie's view) into a powerful source of physical and psychic healing.

Another crucial element of the text fostered canonization—the ending. As David B. Espey, William Bevis, and other critics have argued, the endings of novel by Native Americans are often read (or misread or over-read) as signifiers of the past, present, and future of Indian peoples. There is variety, ingenuity, and power in the conclusions of the best-known novels: the mysterious hope in Abel's tortuous (re)run in *House Made of Dawn* (1968), the high and low tragic comedy of the funeral in *Winter in the Blood* (1974), the bear-trickster visions of *Bearheart* (1979, 1990), the coming home of Lipsha (and his dead mother) in *Love Medicine* (1984, 1993), the braiding imagery and rooftop communion between priests and "Aunt" in *Yellow Raft in Blue Water* (1987), and the humor, honesty, and sadness of the father–son relationship in "Witnesses, Secret and Not" in *Lone Ranger and Tonto Fist Fight in Heaven* (1993). It would be foolish to say that the ending of *Ceremony* is "better" or "simpler" than any of these. But in terms of accessibility to many readers, the conclusion of *Ceremony* has a less ambiguous and more hopeful finish than many other novels by Native Americans. It is certainly *not* a one-dimensional "happy" or "final" ending. The memory of Harley's torture is still fresh in the reader's mind. Emo is still alive. A uranium mine is still operating. And the "witchery" is dead only "for now" (261). It can and will return. Silko's concept of evil has little to do with ultimate victories or defeats and everything to do with cycles of balance and imbalance. Furthermore, there are compelling examples of complex positive endings offered by other Native American writers, for example, Linda Hogan's conclusion to *Solar Storms* (1995) and Greg Sarris's "The Watering Place" ending to his "novel in stories" *Grand Avenue* (1994). Nevertheless, Tayo's remarkable healing is less ambiguous and more hopeful than the healings in many other well-known novels by American Indians. The clarity and optimism is reflected in Tayo's progress from a state of inarticulateness and severe imbalance to a confidence that enables him to tell a narrative valued by the elders in the kiva and to establish a natural order to his life. Certainly, this type of ending would be a great relief to many readers. It relieves the dramatic tensions of the protagonist's narrative and reassures the readers that, despite societal oppression and family tragedies, there are traditional forces of regeneration that can still help Indians to survive and survive beautifully.

THE VARIETY OF AESTHETIC QUALITIES and cultural, historical, and publishing forces that shaped and promoted *Ceremony* suggest the complexities of literary canonization, particularly for "minority" authors. And there is much to celebrate in this canonization. The negative implications are also significant. The popularity and impact of *Ceremony* perpetuate the privileging of contemporary novels as the most influential form of written expression by Indians, especially for literary scholars and critics, but also for many publishers. The importance of educational experiences and contacts suggests that Indian writers outside university networks will have great difficulty finding mentors, linking up with important publishers, getting reviewed in the *New York Times Book Review*, and crafting a voice that can reach many audiences. The early use of words such as "masters" and "renaissance" and the early establishment of an "essential" Native American reading list—which besides Silko, included Momaday, Welch, sometimes Vizenor, and Erdrich and now Alexie—certainly helped to elevate Native American literature in ways that could be clearly defined and integrated in manageable ways into nonspecialized courses and general literary histories. This early internal canonization can also work to keep new authors or even subsequent works by the "masters" out of Indian and American canons. There are many possible literary, ideological, and practical (e.g., length) "explanations" for the different receptions to *Ceremony* and to Silko's second novel *Almanac of the Dead* (1991). Two possibilities are that admiring readers of *Ceremony* wanted Silko to write another *Ceremony* (instead, she offered a very different and sometimes frightening reading experience) and that scholars and teachers had decided that they already had their Silko novel. Overworked specialists in Indian literatures, Americanists, and generalists may thus rationalize that they have filled their quota of Indian "greats" and do not have space in their syllabi, articles, days, or minds for new entries.

Then there is the controversial issue of the narrative and identity paradigms established by the canonization of *Ceremony*: the significance of "homing," of cyclical time, and of myth and ritual for mixed-blood protagonists in need of healing. As complex as this paradigm is, it can invite readers whose knowledge of Indian literature and Indians is limited to assume that The Indian Issue, or at least the central Indian narrative, is the drama of the mixed-blood hero finding his way home. As Elizabeth Cook-Lynn and Robert Warrior argue, this limited view (which Silko would not advocate) can divert attention away from narratives of tribal sovereignty and other crucial paradigms of Indian experience.

In an ideal world, there would be an easy solution to the problems caused by canonizing *Ceremony*, and by implication, by the process of canonizing Indian literatures in general. Simply provide two-year sabbaticals to all teachers, critics, and scholars who would like to teach or write about *Ceremony*, so that they could visit authors, reservations, and Indian urban centers and become acquainted with many of the texts discussed in A. La Vonne Ruoff's *American Indian Literatures* (1990), my *Native American Writers of the United States* (1997), and Daniel Littlefield and James Parins's biobibliographies and their Native American Press Archives at the University of Arkansas, Little Rock.

In the real world, we will have to settle for more modest proposals. For teachers and critics two modest pedagogical and scholarly proposals are particularly relevant. Especially if *Ceremony* is the only text by an Indian presented in a literature, history, anthropology, or religion class, the instructor should, as part of the presentation, stress that the novel grew out of very particular geographical, cultural, familial, educational, literary, marketing, and reception circumstances. Certainly, there are many significant generalitites about novels by Native Americans and Indian worldviews and issues that can be drawn from *Ceremony*. Still, the arid Southwestern landscape, the complex centuries-old multiculturalism of Laguna, the specific Laguna and Navajo images, and *Ceremony*'s particular combinations and juxtapositions of oral and written conventions and experiments should not be used as a paradigm on which to construct generic models of Indian texts and Indian experience. Indeed, Silko even warns against representing her views as Laguna views. "It's my point of view, coming from a certain kind of background and place" (Fisher 21).

The other modest proposal is to use the story of *Ceremony's* canonization as a touchstone for discussions of the processes and implications of canonization. As Gerald Graff has argued on a general level, for instance, in "Teach the Debate" and *Professing Literature* (1987), and Evers, Krupat, Littlefield, and I have argued in reference to Native literatures,[5] foregrounding the narrative of how and why particular texts have been included or excluded from canons raises the types of fundamental questions about literary criteria, the cultural work of texts, and power structures that we should be asking all the time but often do not. The study of *Ceremony's* canonization is a fascinating case study. The case can be approached in terms of Silko's own canon—how *Ceremony's* popularity has influenced the reception of her poetry and short fiction, *Almanac,* and *Gardens in the Dunes* (1999). Or the case can be approached from a comparative angle. There are enough striking parallels between *Ceremony's* canonization and the canonization of other works by Native Americans, as well as by African American authors, or even by Hawthorne and Melville, as reconstructed by Jane Tompkins and Paul Lauter, to allow general speculation about the historical circumstances that create needs for particular types of authors and texts and about relevant networks of educational, production, distribution, and interpretive communities. And there are enough striking differences to encourage questions about how particular forces, as broad as gender and racial attitudes and as specific as visual images, determine the which, the when, and the how of reading canonical texts.

The case of *Ceremony's* canonization raises essential questions especially relevant to differing paradigms of the dynamics of culture formation in a diversified nation emerging from a series of inter- and intranational colonial experiences. What does Professor Hite's MLA convention announcement of *Ceremony's* privileged position signify? An astounding and welcome transition from voicelessness to elite voice? A dramatic "opening up" of the American canon signifying increased diversity and multiculturalism? A triumph of "contact zone" writing representing an appropriation and exploitation of Euro-American conventions for Native American goals? Evidence of a discouraging displacement of Western aesthetics and values? A transitory reoccurrence in the cycles of Indian fads? The repackaging and selling-out of communal Indian narratives and knowledge to gain a large readership and individual fame? Another chapter in the colonialization and exploitation of Native American properties?

I suppose my concluding remarks have deconstructed much of my argument by offering yet another reason why *Ceremony* is "essential" reading. There are, however, different sorts of "must" reading experiences. The reading that leads to premature closures by inviting genre hierarchies, rigid identity paradigms, generic models, and formidable entry barriers for new works should certainly come under attack as what Gerald Vizenor calls "terminal endings." A more liberating and constructive reading is one that enthusiastically acknowledges the literary qualities of a text, while maintaining an awareness of the cultural, historical, and publication forces that promote literary reputations. My hope is that *Ceremony*'s addition to the canon will invite liberating, not terminal readings.[6]

Notes

1. See, for example, Blicksilver's "Leslie Marmon Silko." Dinome repeats this misinformation (207).

2. This photo had appeared earlier with Silko's *Sun Tracks* interview conducted by Evers and Carr (33). I would Like to thank *Sun Tracks* for permission to reproduce this photograph.

3. In an early headshot, not used for *Ceremony* or *Storyteller*, Silko is wearing a headband. See Roemer, *Native American Writers* (276).

4. Most of Allen's published commentary is laudatory. One of the exceptions is "Special Problems in Teaching," in which she questions Silko's use of traditional oral narratives (see this volume).

5. See Evers, "Cycles"; Krupat, *Voice* (96–131) and "Scholarship and Native American Studies"; Littlefield, "American Indians"; and Roemer, "Contemporary American Indian Literature" and "The Nightway."

6. This essay is a condensed and updated version of "Silko's Arroyos as Mainstream: Processes and Implications of Canonical Identity," *Modern Fiction Studies* 45.1 (1999): 10–37. An early version of this essay was presented at the "Native American Literature: Ethnicity and the Problem of Multicultural Identity" Conference in Eugene, Oregon on 15 May 1997. I would especially like to thank Jim Ruppert, Kari Winter, and Helen Jaskoski for their comments on the paper and Nancy J. Peterson for her comments on the *MFS* version. I would also like to thank Robert Nelson and Phillipa Kafka, for suggesting revisions to early versions of the essay, and Linda Jackson, for alerting me to relevant sections of Silko's interviews.

Work Cited

Allen, Paula Gunn. "The Feminine Landscape of Leslie Marmon Silko's *Ceremony*." Allen. *The Sacred Hoop: Recovering the Feminine in American Indian Traditions*. Boston: Beacon, 1986. 118–26.

————. "Introduction." *Studies in American Indian Literature: Critical Essays and Course Designs*. Ed. Allen. New York: MLA, 1983. vii–xiv.

————. "Special Problems in Teaching Leslie Marmon Silko's *Ceremony*." *American Indian Quarterly* 14 (1990): 379–86.

Blicksilver, Edith. "Leslie Marmon Silko." *American Women Writers: A Critical Reference Guide from Colonial Times to the Present*. Vol. 4. Ed. Lina Mainiero. New York: Ungar, 1982. 81–82.

Cook-Lynn, Elizabeth. "The American Indian Fiction Writer." *Wicazo Sa* 9.2 (1993): 26–36

Dinome, William. "Laguna Woman: An Annotated Leslie Silko Bibliography." *American Indian Culture and Research Journal* 21.1 (1997): 207–80.

Espey, David B. "Ending in Contemporary American Indian Fiction." *Western American Literature* 13 (1978): 1333–39.

Evers, Larry. "Cycles of Appreciation." *Studies in American Indian Literature: Critical Essays and Course Designs*. Ed. Paula Gunn Allen. New York: MLA, 1983. 23–32.

Fisher, Dexter, ed. *The Third Woman: Minority Women Writers of the United States*. Boston: Houghton, 1980.

Foley, Martha, ed. *The Best Short Strories of 1975*. Boston: Houghton, 1975.

————. *Two Hundred Years of Great American Short Stories*. Boston: Houghton, 1975.

Graff, Gerald. *Professing Literature: An Institutional History*. Chicago: University of Chicago Press, 1987.

————. "Teach the Debate about What Books Are In and Out." *Christian Science Monitor* 22 Apr. 1988: B6–B7.

Graulich, Melody, ed. *Leslie Marmon Silko, "Yellow Woman."* New Brunswick: Rutgers University Press, 1993.

Hite, Molly. "When Contemporary Literature Isn't." American Literature Section. MLA Convention. Washington, D.C., 28 December 1996.

Krupat, Arnold. "Scholarship and Native American Studies: A Response to Daniel Littlefield, Jr." *American Studies* 34.2 (1993): 81–100.

————. *The Voice in the Margin: Native American Literature and the Canon*. Berkeley: University of California Press, 1989.

Larson, Charles R. *American Indian Fiction*. Albuquerque: University of New Mexico Press, 1978.

Lauter, Paul. "The Heath Top 100." *Heath Anthology of American Literature Newsletter* no. 19 (1999): 1–5.

————. "Melville Climbs the Canon." *American Literature* 66 (1994): 1–24

Leslie M. Silko. Videocassette. Dir Matteo Bellinelli. Prod. Matteo Bellinelli and TSI Swisse Television, Lugano. Native American Novelists series 3. Princeton: Films for the Humanities & Sciences. 1995. 45 min.

Lincoln, Kenneth. *Native American Renaissance.* Berkeley: University of California Press, 1983.

Littlefield, Daniel F., Jr. "American Indians, American Scholars and the American Literary Canon." *American Studies* 33.2 (1992): 95–111.

Littlefield, Daniel F., Jr., James w. Parins, eds. *A Biobibliography of Native American Writers, 1772–1924.* Metuchen: Scarecrow, 1981.

————, eds. *A Biobibliography of Native American Writers, 1772–1924: A Supplement.* Metuchen: Scarecrow, 1985.

MacShane, Frank. "American Indians, Peruvian Jews." Rev. of *Ceremony.* by Leslie Marmon Silko. *New York Times Book Review* 12 June 1977: 15.

Manley, Kathleen. "Leslie Marmon Silko's Use of Color in *Ceremony.*" *Southern Folklore* 46 (1981): 133–46.

Milton, John R., ed. *The American Indian Speaks.* Vermillion: University of South Dakota Press, 1969.

————, ed. *American Indian II.* Vermillion: University of South Dakota Press, 1971.

Momaday, N. Scott. *House Made of Dawn.* New York: Harper & Row, 1968.

Murray, David. *Forked Tongues: Speech, Writing and Representation in North American Indian Texts.* Bloomington: Indiana University Press, 1991.

N. Scott Momaday. Videocassette. Dir. Matteo Bellinelli. Prod. Matteo Bellinelli and TSI Swisse Television, Lugano. Native American Novelists series 3. Princeton: Films for the Humanities & Sciences. 1995. 45 min.

Nelson, Robert M. *Place and Vision: The Function of Landscape in Native American Fiction.* New York: Peter Lang, 1993.

Roemer, Kenneth M. "Contemporary American Indian Literature: The Centrality of Canons on the Margins." *American Literary History* 6 (1994): 583–99.

————. "The Nightway Questions American Literature." *American Literature* 66 (1994): 817–29.

————. "A Retrospective Prospective: Audience, Oral Literatures, and Ignorance." *Studies in American Indian Literatures* 9.3 (1997): 17–24.

————, ed. *Native American Writers of the United States,* Dictionary of Literary Biography 175. Detroit: Bruccoli Clark Layman/Gale Research, 1997.

Rosen, Kenneth, ed. *The Man to Send Rain Clouds: Contemporary Stories by American Indians.* New York: Viking, 1974.

Running on the Edge of the Rainbow. Videocassette. Dir. Dennis W. Carr. Prod. Lawrence Evers. Tucson, Div. of Media and Instructional Services. Dist. Norman Ross. 1978. 28 min.

Ruoff, A. LaVonne Brown. *American Indian Literatures: An Introduction, Bibliographic Review, and Selected Bibliography.* New York: MLA, 1990.

Sands, Kathleen M., ed. *Leslie Marmon Silko's Ceremony.* Special issue of *American Indian Quarterly* 5.1 (1979): 1–75.

Silko, Leslie Marmon. *Almanac of the Dead.* New York: Simon & Schuster, 1991.

———. *Ceremony.* New York: Seaver/Viking, 1977.

———. "A Conversation with Leslie Marmon Silko." With Larry Evers and Denny Carr. *Sun Tracks* 3.1 (1976): 28–33.

———. "from a novel not yet titled." *Journal of Ethnic Studies* 3.1 (1975): 72–87.

———. "Gallup, New Mexico—Indian Capital of the World." *New America: A Review* 3.2 (1976): 30–32.

———. "A Leslie Marmon Silko Interview." With Kim Barnes. *Journal of Ethnic Studies* 13.4 (1986): 83–105.

———. "The Man to Send Rainclouds." *New Mexico Quarterly* 38.4–39.1 (1969): 33–36.

———. *Storyteller.* New York: Seaver/Viking, 1981.

———. "Tony's Story." *Thunderbird* [student magazine; University of New Mexico] (1969): 2–4.

Smith, Susan Harris. "Generic Hegemony: American Drama and the Canon." *American Quarterly* 41 (1989): 112–22.

Tompkins, Jane. "Masterpiece Theater: The Politics of Hawthorne's Literary Reputation." *Sensational Designs: The Cultural Work of American Fiction, 1790–1860.* New York: Oxford University Press, 1985. 3–39.

Velie, Alan R. *Four American Indian Literary Masters.* Norman: University of Oklahoma Press, 1982.

Warrior, Robert Allen. *Tribal Secrets: Recovering American Indian Intellectual Traditions.* Minneapolis: University of Minnesota Press, 1995.

Wiget, Andrew. "Identity and Direction: Reflections on the *ASAIL Notes* Survey." *ASAIL Notes* 3.1 (1986): 4.

Zamir, Shamoon. "Literature in a 'National Sacrifice Area.'" *New Voices in Native American Literary Criticism.* Ed. Arnold Krupat. Studies in Native American Literatures 1. Washington, D.C.: Smithsonian Institution Press, 1993. 396–415.

Leslie Marmon Silko

LAURA COLTELLI

◆　◆　◆

Laura Coltelli (LC): In *Ceremony*, Thought-Woman thinks and creates a story; you are only the teller of that story. Oral tradition, then: a tribal story-teller, past and present, no linear time but circular time. Would you comment on that?

Silko: The way I experienced storytelling as a young child, I sensed that people—the person you know or loved, your grandma or uncle or neighbor—as they were telling you the story, you could watch them, and you could see that they were concentrating very intently on something. What I thought they were concentrating on was they were trying to put themselves in that place and dramatize it. So I guess as I wrote those words, Ts'its'nako, Thought-Woman, and then Spider, I did not exactly mean in the sense of the Muse, at least as I understand the Muse with a capital "M." What was happening was I had lived, grown up around, people who would never say they knew exactly, or could imagine exactly, because that's an extremely prideful assertion; they knew what they felt, but you could try those words and all that follows about Thought-Woman, the Spider, as being a storyteller's most valiant—and probably falling short at the same time—attempt to imagine what a character in a story would be like, and what she would see, and how in the logic of that old belief system, then, things would come into creation.

LC: As is said of some archaic societies, there is a revolt against historical time? What about the concept of time?

Silko: I just grew up with people who followed, or whose world vision was based on a different way of organizing human experience, natural cycles. But I didn't know it, because when you grow up in it, that's just how it is, and then you have to move away and learn. I think that one of the things that most intrigued me in *Ceremony* was time. I was trying to reconcile Western European ideas of linear time—you know, someone's here right now, but when she's gone, she's gone forever, she's vaporized—and the older belief which Aunt Susie talked about, and the old folks talked about, which is: there is a place, a space-time for the older folks. I started to read about space-time in physics and some of the post-Einsteinian works. I've just read these things lately, I should tell you, because in Indian school, in elementary school, I got a very poor background in mathematics and science. So it has only been recently that I've ventured, because I'm so curious. And why am I interested suddenly in the hard, hard cold, cold (something I thought I would never be) so-called sciences? Because I am most intrigued with how, in many ways, there are many similarities in the effect of the so-called post-Einsteinian view of time and space and the way the old people looked at energy and being and space-time. So now I am doing reading and what I am finding is that if the particular person, the scientist, is a good writer—can write in an expository manner clearly—then I'm finding if I read along doggedly, reading it as you would poetry, not trying to worry if you're following every single line, I'm starting to have a wonderful time reading about different theories of space and distance and time. To me physics and mathematics read like poetry, and I'm learning what I try to tell people from the sciences: you know, don't get upset, don't demand to follow it in a logical step-by-step [fashion]. Just keep reading it. Relax. And that's what I did. I just went with it. I would get little glimmers of wonderful, wonderful points that were being made. I got so excited. I told somebody: "I'm only understanding a fifth of it, because I never had very good mathematics or physics or anything. But, you know, I really like to keep on learning." That's what I'm doing right now. In some ways you would say what I'm reading and thinking about and working on is many light-years away from the old folks I grew up with, and how they looked at time. But not really. Really what I'm doing now is just getting other ideas about it. Although you might not notice it from the books you would see around, I am working on just that right now. And of course this new book I'm working on is also about time, so it's very important to me.

LC: *Ceremony* has a male protagonist, but it is a story created by a woman, told by a woman [but a story] already known by another woman, Tayo's grandmother, whose words conclude the novel. Does it stress women's role and importance in the Pueblo society?

Silko: Certainly, that's part of it, just because women hold such an important position in temporal matters—the land-title, the house, the lineage of the children; the children belong to the mother's line first, and secondarily of course to the father. There is not any of this peculiar Christian, Puritan segregation of the sexes. So there is very much wholeness there. Women remembering listening, hearing the things that are said and done. There's no prohibition against a woman repeating a funny story that's basically about the copulation of say, two coyotes, any more than a man. There's no difference, but you do find that in different cultures. Therefore, a girl has as much of a chance, as she grows up, to be a teller, to be a storyteller, as a boy-child. And as we always like to say, the women are tougher and rougher and live longer, so chances are we'll live to tell our version last, because of course we all know that there are different versions. I can say I will outlive so-and-so and then tell that story one time when she cannot be around, or later whisper it to somebody. But the viewpoint in the novel wasn't intentional; I mean, I didn't sit down and say, "This is what I'm going to do." About two-thirds of the way through I was pleased for what I knew then; I was pleased with those characters. I'm not really pleased with some of them now, especially the women. I think I understand why they're not as fully realized as the men.

LC: There are three women who play a very important role in the novel: Night Swan, Ts'eh, Betonie's grandmother; all associated with the color blue, the color, by the way, which is associated also with the West, yet their relationship with each other is somehow mysterious, even if Night Swan seems to be an anticipation of Ts'eh. Is that correct?

Silko: I am interested in certain convergences and configurations, where many times the real focal point is the time. I'm interested in these things that aren't all linked together in some kind of easy system. For example, the Ute woman, Helen-Jean, appears very briefly. She's in the bar when Rocky's friends, the drunks he hangs around with, Harley and Emo, are there. She is telling herself, "pretty soon I'm going to go home" and she does try to send money back to this poor, poor reservation. She's just there, and she goes. In one way, if you were judging her by more conventional structural elements of a novel, she just sort of comes and goes. But I would rather have you look at her, and get a feeling for her, so that when we make a brief reference to Tayo's mother, the one who dies early and is disgraced and so on, then I don't have to tell you that story. I'm trying to say that basically what happened to Tayo's mother is what happened to Helen-Jean, is what happened to—on and on down the line. These things try to foreshadow, or resonate *on* each other.

LC: Actually, the Gallup story and the Helen-Jean story at first seem to be separate stories within the main plot. Do you relate them to the story-within-a-story technique of the old storytellers?

Silko: When I was writing *Ceremony*, I just had this compulsion to do Helen-Jean. But the other part, about Gallup, is the only surviving part of what I call stillborn novels; and the Gallup section is from one of the still-borns. And you remember that when I was writing *Ceremony* I was twenty-three, maybe twenty-four, years old; I really didn't expect anything to happen. So I figured nothing's going to happen with this anyway, and I really like the Gallup section, and in a strict sense it sort of hangs off like feathers or something. It's tied to it, and it belongs there, but its relationship is different. I put that in for exactly the same reason, vis-à-vis structure, as I did the Helen-Jean part. Again, it was important to see a woman caught somewhere—I wouldn't even say between two cultures—she was just caught in hell, that would be the woman who was Tayo's mother, or the woman who is Helen-Jean, or the woman who was down in the arroyo with the narrator of the Gallup section. And the reason I did this—which in a way only storytellers can get away with, narratives within narratives within narratives—is that [the stories] are in the ultimate control of the narrator. But for me there was something necessary about taking a perspective which pulled me and the listener-reader back always. It's tough to write about humans living under inhuman conditions; it's extremely difficult just to report it; one gets caught up in one's own values, and politics, and so forth. And I think I fear too much a kind of uncontrolled emotion. And so it had to be done like that. But it's the old theme, which the old lady at the end articulates: "Seems like I've heard these stories before."

One of the things that I was taught to do from the time I was a little child was to listen to the story about you personally right now. To take all of that in for what it means right now, and for what it means for the future. But at the same time to appreciate how it fits in with what you did yesterday, last week, maybe ironically, you know, drastically different. And then ultimately I think we make a judgment almost as soon as we store knowledge. A judgment that somehow says, "I've heard stories like that" or "I would tend to judge her harshly except I remember now . . . " All of this happens simultaneously. When I was working on *Ceremony*, these were deliberate breaks with point of view. And I agonized over them, because after all I knew that those kinds of shifts are disturbing. But ultimately the whole novel is a bundle of stories.

LC: In a story there are many stories.

Silko: Right. You can get away with it. I was aware of that. What caused those first two attempts at the novel to be stillborn was that I had a narrator who was a young woman, about my own age. And it just did not work. It just becomes yourself. And then you have to look at how limited you are, and so the only way you can break out of your personal limitations is to deal with a fictional character. Fictional characters are very wonderful. They are parts of ourselves, but then you get to fix up the parts that don't work so well for you in your mind.

LC: A young man named Tayo is the main character of a legend transcribed by Franz Boas. Is it still a Laguna or Pueblo name?

Silko: I don't know for sure, but I think it probably is. The sound of it was on my mind. I guess in Spanish, Tayo Dolores is like Theodore, or something, but I didn't even think of that. I just liked the sound of it.

LC: It's a familiar name.

Silko: It's a familiar sound. When I say I liked the way it sounded, I mean comfortable, intimate, the person you're going to travel with. As a writer you're going to have to follow this character. You'd better really feel comfortable with him.

LC: In "Storyteller" there is an intriguing association concerning the red and the white colors. The color yellow is very often associated with something connected with the whites: "yellow machines"; "yellow stains melted in the snow where men had urinated"; "the yellow stuffing that held off the coat"; "the yellow flame of the oil stove." What's the meaning of all that?

Silko: First of all, of course, yellow in the Pueblo culture is an important color. It's a color connected with the East, and corn, and corn pollen, and dawn, and Yellow Woman [the heroine of the abduction myths]. So I don't think we can go too far in a traditional direction, with what yellow means. It's one of my favorite stories, because it's outside of the Southwest. And it's taking myself as a writer, and working with stories, and making radical changes. To tell you the truth, in that particular arctic landscape I suppose to hunters, anywhere except in the town, yellow could be a sign that a herd that freshly been by. In other words, I guess what I'm trying to say is maybe in this particular piece it's fairly insular; how the color works isn't so easily tied to any particular belief system. But certainly up there, just an endless field of white, and that cold pure yellow is kind of an extreme, and when it appears, it's intrusive.

LC: That's the word.

Silko: And it stops things. The rising of the moon, and the way the stars look up there is wonderful, part of that is the color. And certain colors which you can find in the sky, for example, with the aurora, mean more. The key figure I guess is the field of white, if you want to talk about the field of white like a painter, the blank or whatever. Generally yellow, on that field of white, is, in the winter, abnormal—it's just within that story that yellow works like that. It's very much the context of the northern landscape.

LC: How does the oral tradition go on?

Silko: By that you mean at Laguna or any given place?

LC: Among Indian people.

Silko: That's a very difficult question really. One day it dawned on me. I had this sudden recognition that already there were things that I had seen and done, and people that I had been with at home, who had taught me things, that had been gone a long time. What I see is astonishing, on one hand, very exhilarating, and on the other hand very frightening, the rapid change. I was born in 1948; I'm talking about things I saw in 1954 done on the reservation, vis-à-vis the Pueblo people, or maybe some of the Navajo, or even some of the white people that lived on ranches nearby. That part of America, the small rancher, the Pueblo people, the Navajos and the Spanish-speaking land-grant people. It's been such a change, that I would have to be a terrible, pompous liar to sit here and tell you that it's just in my area that I see it. The change in outlook and how the people live in these very distinct racial and cultural communities in New Mexico, and in America, since the middle fifties, is just amazing. It makes me want to laugh at some of the older ethnologists and ethnographers. I would say that most of the material—not most; now I'm starting to use words that are a little too far-spreading—but I think that many of the models that were constructed in the late fifties and early sixties by so-called social scientists, ethnologists, ethnographers, about acculturation, social changes, how humans learn language, how language affects the way you think, and so on, were so incomplete that those models have to be overturned. Not just for Indian people in New Mexico or Arizona, but African tribal people, all of the people who have gone through this period of colonialism. That is, in a sense, what I am concerned with writing about, what I'm working with right now. It goes on.

LC: You said once that we should make English speak for us.

Silko: At that time it hadn't really occurred to me that people who are born English speakers are trying to make English speak for them too. What

I was saying was a little naive. The great struggle is to make whatever language you have really to speak for you. But I won't back down from it, in the sense that I like to take something that is a given, a given medium or a given mode, and then treat it as if it were a fantastical contest or trick. Here are the givens; you only have this and this; this is what you are trying to describe; these are the persons you are trying to describe this to; we don't want them to just see it and hear it; we want them to be it and know it. This is language and you deal in it. That's the most intriguing thing of all. And of course all artists to one degree or another, whether it's with sculpture or music or whatever, are working with that. And I stand by that. And there are certain things, for example, when you talk about space-time, and all kinds of little insoluble puzzles about time-space, and how it is that we can use language to define language. We have to use language in order to define language. I'm getting more and more humbled, to the point where I think it's a wonder we can express the most simple desire in our given tongue, clearly. And sometimes I wonder if we can even hope for that.

LC: What's the process by which you move from the oral tradition to the written page? How does it work?

Silko: It just happens. From the time I could hear and understand language, I have been hearing all these stories, and actually I have been involved in this whole way of seeing what happened—it's some kind of story. But when it finally happened, I wasn't conscious about mixing the two. I was exposed [to stories] before school, and then I went to school and read what you read in America for literature and history and geography and so on. And then at the age of nineteen, I was at the University of New Mexico. And I had just had a baby—Robert, who's now nineteen—and Robert's father, my first husband, said how would you like to take a class where you could get an easy A? And I said, well, I would like that, you know, because having this baby and all, it would be nice to bring up my grade-point average. So I took a creative-writing class. The professor gave us little exercises. Then he said one day, "We want a character sketch," even a character, and I thought, oh no! I had thousands. And so I did it. And then he said, "We want a story," I thought, Is he serious? Is this all it is? I just cashed in on all those things I'd heard.

But a more important, fundamental thing happened, probably in the very beginning, which was in the first grade. I learned to love reading, and love books, and the printed page and therefore was motivated to learn to write. The best thing, I learned, the best thing you can have in life is to have someone tell you a story; they are physically with you, but in lieu of that, since at age five or six you get separated from all of those people who hold you and talk to you, I learned at an early age to find comfort in a book, that a book would talk to me when no one else would. Or a book would say things that would soothe in a way that no person could.

So the fifth grade is when I really started actually writing secretly; but it wasn't until I was nineteen and got to the university, that the two things just fell into place, which was all of my early attitudes and things I'd heard; plus, I'd read Faulkner, I'd read Flannery O'Connor, Henry James, Kate Chopin, Isak Dinesen. And then this guy says, "Write a story." A lot of people were saying, "I don't know what I'm going to write about." And I thought, I don't know what I'm going to start writing about first. And so the two things just kind of crashed together. What I learned from all the years of reading Thomas Hardy and reading *Julius Caesar* were little mundane things, because Shakespeare has all these clowns and these little underlings who have funny little squabbles but have their little moment when they pipe up and say something that makes the bigger story roll around. That experience from reading helped me realize what a rich storehouse I had. And then, I like to get A's, and I like to have people pat me on the head. So I could just do it. But that's how come I could, because I'd had a rich oral tradition for quite a long time; I mean even now if I go home I can hear all these wild stories about what my family's done, and my cousins and stuff. But also I was encouraged to read. I loved books. And when things were rough, when I was in a bad situation, I could read a book. It wasn't conscious, but it just happened in my life.

LC: Do you feel that as in the oral tradition, the relationship between the storyteller and his and her audience, must be a dynamic one?

Silko: It would be easier on me, in what I have to do in order to satisfy these urges, if there were a place. I really think that it was wonderful during the time when the storyteller could practice her or his art. I went to China for three weeks; the Chinese Writers Association invited a group of American writers. They showed us this teahouse, and there were these two seats, with little wooden chairs with nice little pillows, and they said every night of the week, except Friday and Sunday or something, storytellers come. People buy their tea from us [the writers] and they sit in there, and these two storytellers sit across from them—sometimes it's two old men and sometimes it's two old women—and the teahouse people. This was in Sh'eie, near where all the terracotta warriors were dug up. Anyway, they showed us this room because one of our interpreters said, "Hey look, this is what still goes on in China." And all these people are sitting there listening and drinking their tea. And there's another storyteller there so you can say, "Well, isn't that what you think?" Or you can do routines like, "Oh, you always tell it like that!" I really think that that's wonderful, interacting directly like that, even having another storyteller there who might be trying to catch you on something, which of course means you get to catch them, if you can, with the people there. A wonderful kind of positive energy is generated which you can partake in, and you can get more; I'm not saying I don't get any when I write, or I wouldn't be sitting here a lot. I really think that to me the real, the ultimate moment, is when you have a couple of storytellers and a really engaged, respectful audience. So that I guess in a strange sort of way I'm saying that in Western European culture, the theater, drama, and/or what we have in the United States, mostly it's kind of declined now. The stand-up comedians, someone like Lenny Bruce, that play an older kind of role of the traveling teller or the troubadour, are the storytelling experience.

LC: How do you try to achieve it in your works?

Silko: I'm very aware of a physical audience, whether I'm reading at some distant place, or whether I'm sitting with people. I'm so aware of it, that when I sit down at the typewriter, there's only me. I feel the distance dramatically. Do you see what I mean? At Laguna I have an uncle who's very young; he's only ten years older, he's just like a brother, and his wife and his sisters are very brilliant. They've traveled and gone places to school. They've all come back. The have funny ways of saying things; they like to laugh and tell horrifying stories, but the way they tell them is really funny, and you're laughing. But when I'm writing I have to go into that room, I have to go in there alone, and I'm the one who makes me go in there, day after day. And I'm the one that has to put up with the days when it looks really bad—the words that I write. Then in that area I am just doing what I do, and I have no thought of anyone ever reading it, because I can only relate to someone who's sitting there. I really don't consciously think that much about an audience. I'm telling the story, I'm trying to tell it the best way I can, in writing, but I'm not thinking, Maybe we better have him do this, or Maybe we better not have her do that. I don't think that way.

LC: Humor is one of the main features of modern American Indian literature, central to the real meaning of the story itself. Is there a difference between the use of humor in the old Indian stories and in the contemporary ones?

Silko: You know I haven't really thought about whether there's a difference. I'm so attuned to seeing the many similarities. Same thing, referring to the same incident, especially areas in justice, loss of land, discrimination, racism, and so on, that there's a way of saying it so people can kind of laugh or smile. I mean, I'm really aware of the ways of saying things so you don't offend somebody, so you can keep their interest, so you can keep talking to them. Oftentimes these things are told in a humorous way. Even punning—you know, the people at Laguna have such a delight with language, going back to how the Korean people loved language and words. So that in English they like to make puns, and they know a little Spanish, or a little Navajo, or a little anything. So their sheer delight in such things, that goes on and always has—that's an area where I can't see that there's been any big shift.

LC: In an interview in 1976 with Per Seyersted about the American Indian Movement, you said, "It is more effective to write a story like 'Lullaby' than to rant and rave."

Silko: Certainly for me the most effective political statement I could make is in my art work. I believe in subversion rather than straight-out confrontation. I believe in the sands of time, so to speak. Especially in America, when you confront the so-called mainstream, it's very inefficient, and in every way possible destroys you and disarms you. I'm still a believer in subversion. I don't think we're numerous enough, whoever "we" are, to take them by storm.

LC: So is it a matter of how to awaken public opinion to Indian problems, or is it just a matter concerning the very nature of the American Indian Movement?

Silko: No, I think it's more a question of how. You know, I understand the tactics, every step of the way. In a way I'm not even critical of anything particularly that the American Indian Movement has done. I'm just saying that with the givens that I have, with what I do best, and sort of where I found myself, that that isn't where I can do the best work. I certainly understand and a lot of times share the anger and bitterness, and the confusion over certain kinds of policies and attitudes. America is strange; it's very strange for Americans to have to confront whatever color you are. You can be a black American, a Native American, or an Asian American. If you're very upper-middle class and extremely comfortable, you can drive through any city or town home from your job, and if you have a brain that half-way works at all, just driving home you will see things. We can drive from where I drove today up here, and you can see where the distribution method is pretty much unfair toward people with lesser opportunities, and so on. If you're a very sensitive person, it can be real disturbing, just to be around at any time. I understand it, though I also understand, maybe in a more practical way, the conservatism, and the kind of respect yet for order and law that Americans have. And I don't care what color they are. It's kind of heartbreaking, in South Africa, some of the interviews with

South African blacks and colored people, these old folks who are in their sixties. My heart breaks. I think about them like the old folks that were around at Wounded Knee, and when that stuff was going on. That isn't the kind of world they saw. And some of their children, and almost all their grandchildren are doing things, saying things, and having things done to them, and I would say that is not a unique or peculiar experience to those little old people in South Africa. You could have gone to Belfast ten years ago; I mean, fill in the blanks. And that moves me, that moves me. Therefore, I was born in the in-between. I understand why the old folks cry, and don't understand why they have to keep burying. You know, I'm in a strange place. And I don't condemn one or the other. I do understand where I am most effective, if you want to call yourself a tool, which I don't really call myself. I'm better off doing what I do. As a terrorist or militant I'd be good for like one suicide raid, and then that'd be the end of me. Now, you know, if you want to use me like that—and I'm not a good spy.

LC: Could you describe your creative process?

Silko: Well, when I was younger, I figured it was just that certain things that I heard I didn't forget. And then I would have a professor or somebody tell me I had an assignment. So I would just go and I would pull it out, and what I would pull out, of course I would always work on. And sometimes I would just take bits and pieces and make it up, because even when I was a little girl I had sort of a wild imagination. Now I'm beginning to realize that almost everything that happens to me is interesting, and I make notes but I don't really have to make notes. I started just recently though to keep notes and little scribbles here and there, and I do it to laugh at what I thought was important, and what I thought I should remember writing, and then how I feel about it six or eight months later. And what's really, really going to be an important image or theme or character trait stays with me.

And I can remember what some of the old folks said. Years ago these [recording] machines were new, and dad believed in technology. And he'd go to the old-timers and say, "just go ahead and tell it, and that way if all these kids around here don't remember . . ." And you know, he'd count himself in, "I never listen, better tell it to a machine; you can't trust all of us, we might not remember." And some of the old folks agreed, and did it, archival stuff. But a lot said, "If what I have to say, if my story is really important and has"—they wouldn't say relevance, but that's what it is— "relevance to people, then they'll remember it, and they will say it again, and if it doesn't then it's gone, and it dies out." That's a very harsh point of view, but the older I get, the more I come around to it. And in writing I've discovered that that's how my brain works.

What happened with this novel [*Almanac of the Dead*] now around about September 1980, I just started feeling parts and places and characters; it was as if you had shattered a two-hour movie. Some of it didn't have dialogue. Like if you took two hours of a feature film and tore it or chopped it up and mixed it all up. These things started coming to me. I began making notes, and I did other things. I finished *The Arrow Boy and the Witches* movie, and still these things came, and they came and they came. I would do extended work on sections, and finally in the summer of 1983, I figured I'd better start. I'd be with people. We'd be at a restaurant, nice people, people I basically liked, or [I'd be] talking to someone and having a fine conversation, and then I would think of something, and I'd have to start saying, "Oh, excuse me," and then I would scribble a note. And so I knew it was there. It was as if I would see things. I have many, many boxes of newspaper clippings, especially about Central America, Nicaragua, politically the right-wing shift in America. It was as if somewhere else something was going on, and every now and then some would float up to the top. And I'd have to write it down. Then I knew I had to start. By then I even had characters; I didn't have all of them, and I didn't know everything. But, it's a very big book and it has very many characters. It literally just imposes itself upon me. I find that it's predictable—predictably, there's certain interest and areas. It has a lot to do with where Tucson is, because the U.S. military is very nervous about instability in Central America, and of course Mexico. The day of the earthquake, the bankers who were so glad to lend them money, the serious American bankers who wanted to make money off those people, found out that the International Monetary Fund said no to Mexico, and then the earthquake came. Anyway there's a bunch of military generals all along this border, who full-well believe that the economic situation in Central America and Mexico can only get worse, that it will be destabilized; there will be basically a kind of movement to try to shift around. Whether we can dare call it a revolution, I don't want to say. This is the first place and the only place I've lived in six years—but the CIA base for helicopters and training is right over there. That is a part of right now and my life and what's happening right now. And also I find very much has blossomed out in this novel. But my process is mostly, not totally, subconscious, not conscious. The reason I write is to find out what I mean. I know some of the things I mean, I couldn't tell you the best things I know. And I can't know the best thing I know until I write.

LC: Could you speak a little bit more of your new novel [*Almanac of the Dead*], still in progress?

Silko: Well, you know it's about time, and what's called history, and story, and who makes the story, and who remembers. And it's about the Southwest. But this time I have purposely, deliberately, taken Indian characters, one in particular, and I've dumped him off the reservation early. He's an older man, too; he's a man and he retired. He spent years working on the railroad in California; he was away from the reservation. But many people of my grandfather's and even of my father's generation, when the time comes, they're going to retire back home. Well, he does. And he's quite a lady's man and a little bit of a show-off. He gets into some trouble, and he's told he has to leave. And he intends to go to Phoenix, but he accidentally ends up in Tucson. And who he meets up with are Mexican Indians, some of whom are Yaquis from the mountains. But others are remnants of other entire cultures and tribes that were destroyed, early on, after the Europeans came in. And it [the novel] is ambitious because it's saying, "Well, suppose we get rid of the reservation; let's even get you from any of that when you're seven, let's do that." And different groups: "Let's tear you from Yaqui history, and let's form something more indefinite, you now, and let's add this guy who got kicked out. So then, should we say these people aren't living on the reservation, or never had a reservation, or were there but never really believed?" So what does that mean? And to watch them as characters, and see how they behave, and that's where we pick up. So that's what it's about. So it's really ambitious. It goes back in time.

It's called *Almanac of the Dead*, which is a reference to the Mayan almanacs which are not only used for planting, not just for auspicious planting, but it would also tell you about famine and death, revolution and conquest. They are fragmentary manuscripts, and of course what have I done? I have created a character who has a fragment that nobody else has. So I get to say what it is. So there's only four Mayan codexes. There's the Madrid, the Paris, the Mexico City, and the Dresden copies of Mayan almanacs. And they're just fragments. They're written in Latin or Spanish by Indians, Mayans, full-bloods. They are the first generation of young children, Indian children, young boys that the priests put in schools. And they could read and write. When they went home, the elders saw that the oral tradition could not be maintained, where you have genocide on this scale. We have no guarantee in this new world of the European conquest, we have no guarantee that the three of us [my two sons and I] will still live.

The old folks thought about it, had people explain to them what writing was. It dawned on them; it's a tool. It's a tool. So in my novel, they call in a person who is trained in the omens. and the old people, men and women, sit down and say, this is how we see it: we've got to start writing.

In fact, they theorize something similar to what actually happened, except that my characters have a fragment that no one else has.

Another thing that happens is, I have caretakers of these few pages. At different times they've had to change them around, so they won't be found. Because you do know that the priests would destroy those materials. Some of the keepers have been well-meaning, but they have encoded, they have made a narrative that isn't really the entire narrative. They made a narrative that's a code narrative. And so it makes it extremely strange. What the characters end up with in the contemporary times is a strange bundle, a few fragments of which are originals, but many have traveled and been hidden and stolen and lost. In the novel, there's not that many pages where you actually get to see much of that. But that's in there too.

So I can do anything I want in pre-Columbian times. I'm not even going to call it Mayan. And then because the people believe that these almanacs projected into the future, I can write about a dream I had, which is that the helicopters come from Mexico en route to Tucson, full of American soldiers; that a great battle in this hemisphere will come down. But I connect it to hundreds of years of exploitation of the Native American people here. And I see Marxism as being here, but no better than Christianity. Certainly there are some Marxists, as there are some Catholic nuns and priests, who do some very good things. And I even have a character who actually assassinates—I haven't done it yet—but he's going to assassinate a sort of intellectual Marxist. He's an Indian, and he's very primitive, sort of wonderful, because he just says, "These guys don't want to listen to those guys." Back to the old thing, which is very simple-minded in a way, that it's "our land." And of course, he's a politician; his name is the Ugly One. He says, "We're not interested in any fucking ideology that these outsiders have, we're interested in love." And I don't know about the rest of it, but I'm working hard.

I definitely identify much more with that older generation—so maybe I am a leftover. In terms of the evolution of an ideology, if you want to look at political ideology, I have an awful lot of the old folks' point of view left in me. And I find that in my attraction for the stories, and places, and things I read. There's a lot I don't know. But as a writer and as a person, I like to think of myself in a more old-fashioned sense, the way the old folks felt, which was, first of all, you're a human being; secondly, you originate from somewhere, and from a family, and a culture. But first of all, human beings. And in order to realize the wonder and power of what we share, we must understand how different we are too, how different things are. I'm really intrigued with finding out similarities in conditions, and yet divergences in responses, of human beings. I'm really interested in that. Without forgetting that first of all, before we can ever appreciate what's the same, we have really to love and respect and be able to internalize freedom of expression.

Of Apricots, Orchids, and Wovoka

An Interview with
Leslie Marmon Silko

ROBIN COHEN

◆ ◆ ◆

W**HEN LESLIE MARMON SILKO** visited Southwest Texas State
University on October 21–22, 1998, I discovered that one does not so
much interview her as try to keep up with her in conversation, her lively
intelligence and imagination bounding like an antelope. She was generous
with her thoughts, open, and funny. I have tried to maintain her voice and
her spontaneity in editing her remarks.

Participants in this interview/conversation, in addition to Ms. Silko,
were Robin Cohen (RC), Paul Cohen (PC), and René LeBlanc (RL). Although much of this interview, originally published in *Southwestern American
Literature* (April 1999), covered *Gardens in the Dunes* (in press at the time), the
wide-ranging discussion also included her other works. Those portions of
the interview pertaining to *Ceremony* are excerpted below.

RL: How do you think living in Alaska affected *Ceremony?* That novel is just
so beautiful in its evocation of place.

Silko: Exactly, it was key, because I was on an island. Most of the island
was precipitous and steep; it was the most alien thing, and I went from
thirteen inches of rain when I was living in Chinle before I went up there
to 180 inches of rain. There was ocean, fog, tall trees; I felt sort of claustro-
phobic. I suffered. Now they understand that there can be depressions trig-

gered by lack of sunshine. I had a terrible kind of depression like that, and that was before I really got started writing. I finally wrote this short story; it's never been published. It is not very good, but I remember writing that and it got me out of this terrible kind of depression. So I literally wrote *Ceremony* to save my life. That is why it is called *Ceremony*, because I know that I could not have made it if I had not been writing *Ceremony* for those two years. I was so homesick for that Southwestern landscape that that's why I completely remade it. While I was writing the novel, I was not in Ketchikan and the rain anymore; I was back in the Southwest. That is why every description, the rocks, the land—I was literally putting myself in the act of writing.

I was leaving where I was because that is something that I learned when I was an unhappy child in the fifth grade. I could leave behind all of my limitations, and wherever I was, I could transcend and escape. In *Ceremony* the distances perhaps are not accurate, but I literally remade that whole area, and it is accurate. You can go there and travel around and can find all those sites.

RC: I remember that in one of your essays you said that traditional stories can almost be used as road maps.

Silko: Actually, that is exactly what I did in *Ceremony*, and I did it because I was homesick and alienated, and of course my then-husband, his family weren't very nice to me, so there was a real social isolation, although my two sisters followed me up there. The marriage was really falling apart. I remember literally thinking, boy if I did not have this little kid, I would be out of this marriage. So the marriage was in awful shape, and so when I started *Ceremony*, I was as sick as Tayo was. I was having nausea and all kinds of weird symptoms and stuff and then as he starts to get better, of course, I was starting, so there is this parallel.

I was really isolated, no other writers, and I had never taken the course called "The Novel," so I worked alone, and when I finally finished it, I sent it to my friend Mei-Mei Berssenbrugge, and I sent it to my editor. Mei-Mei, who is a wonderful poet, called right away after she finished it and she said, "Oh it's wonderful, it's just wonderful, and I really like the way that you did not put it into chapters." And I went "Ahhh no! I knew there was something I forgot." How could I have forgotten that novels are supposed to be in chapters? But you see, there is this one part of me that wants to conform, write the sell-out novel, sell out as an artist, but then fortunately there is the other part of me that just doesn't. Because I knew very well, I had been reading novels since I was in the fifth grade, and of course novels are in chapters. So when I got off the phone I thought, my God, there is still time to put it into chapters and tell Richard Seaver that it can be fixed and please do not decline this novel. And then I sat down and started trying to put it into chapters and realized that it did not want to be in chapters. And of course Richard Seaver is the one who brought Samuel Beckett in translation into this country, so it did not bother him at all. I did not really know if it was a novel. I sort of had not taken that course called "The Novel," but you see, I have enough of a conformist in me that I sort of have to trick myself or some part of me tricks myself.

PC: I was recently teaching Naguib Mahfouz, the Egyptian novelist; he *did* take the course in the novel. He specialized at Cairo University in the European novel, and then he wins a Nobel prize and all these westerners say, oh, finally, a great Egyptian writer, a great writer from the Arab world. It seems to me that this is because what they are really saying is, oh, here is someone who writes what we expect him to write. I wonder, in the great flowering of Native American literature in the last two or three decades, to what extent this has to do with Native American writers starting to use forms that are more accessible to their Anglo readers as with Mahfouz.

Silko: Well you know I worry about *Gardens in the Dunes*; maybe at some level I was trying to. . . . In terms of structure I don't think it is as wild as either *Almanac* or *Ceremony*. I just do what I do, and that is a concern, and there is this tendency, I mean even as we sit and speak, with the way publishing is becoming, of real narrowing. So that if someone really tries to break out and be innovative, you worry about not being accepted or recognized, especially now. I do think there is something to that, and I suppose I kind of worry that the structure of *Gardens in the Dunes* isn't daring enough, and I wonder if I have succumbed, knuckled under, or tried to do more of what they call a traditional novel—although there is no such thing. The genre to me is the most wonderful, the novel, that genre is so wide open. But I just decided, you know, I just do what I want to do and you can't worry about what people say, but I recognize that that is a factor.

Some of the reviewers, in terms of structure in *Almanac*, they really wanted to see something that fit more of their traditional ideas, so I've run into that. I kind of did what I could with *Gardens in the Dunes*, but it is probably the most traditionally structured.

RC: Maybe this will be the one that will win the Pulitzer.

Silko: I don't know; I have too many enemies and don't need to win any other prizes, even though I am careful about my translators so I can have a shot at the Nobel. The MacArthur Fellowship means more to me than anything else.

RC: It gave you freedom.

Silko: Oh, yes. And the first group was really amazing people, too. I was really proud to be in the first group. Elaine Pagels sent me that book [*The Gnostic Gospels*] after we met at the first reunion. I was in the middle of *Almanac*, so I did not have a chance to read it. Then I started on this book, and I wrote to her that I read it and said, "Sixteen years ago you sent me your book, thank you," and she wrote back. She was in the group; so it did matter who was in that first group. Derek Walcott was in our group. And some really famous particle physicists that I did not know their names.

RL: Tell me, does *Garden in the Dunes* incorporate, I want to say poetry, or passages similar to the parts of *Ceremony* that you have said should simply be though of as spoken word and not poetry in that sense?

Silko: It seems to me that *Gardens in the Dunes* is pretty literary in that way. The person in the class this morning thought that she could hear, in what I was reading the other night, that this was coming out of strorytelling. I think that is always true with my work, but in this case it is pretty subtle. It's not as obvious as in *Ceremony* and *Almanac*.

RC: What are your thoughts on the genre of Native American literature and the certain amount of sniping about who is and who isn't and what is it and who writes it?

Silko: I think that the time has come to get rid of those designations. I especially thought about that down at San Antonio at the book fair this year, reading with Wendy Rose, Linda Hogan, Joe Bruchac, and Jesse [Bruchac]—that there is such a huge variety and difference and each writer is so distinctive so as to make grouping us together and calling us Native American—I think that it is divisive. I always make very clear that I have Mexican and white ancestors, and I am very close to the old ancestor spirits in Germany and the Celts. I love that I have connections with Mexico, and I love Spanish, and I identify with the Chicanos, and that is really different from, say, Joe Bruchac, who is so specifically so Abenaki. It really bothers me, and it really started to bother me more and more because it is a kind of ghetto—they did that to Jewish writers in the 50s. Gradually, that has sort of broken down so they do not say Saul Bellow, Jewish writer, gets this award or something like that. If I could break down for Jewish writers, it can be broken down for others.

Writers don't feel that way. James Wright did not correspond with me, or Richard Hugo [didn't correspond with me], as a Native American— their response to my work wasn't on that level. The most primary level is literature. It bothers me, and yet scholars and teachers are saying that there is not room for you because you will not be studied. There is American literature, which means white male, maybe a few females. When the book fair people called me and said, we are having sort of this Native American focus, I almost started to say I am not going to go, I am sick of this. Then I thought, well, I love and respect the writers that would be there, but I was really torn. I was really getting tired of it, and MLA perpetuates it with their little subcommittees; I don't know. I understand why they do it, but I am not really at peace with it at all.

PC: And of course it has that same kind of insidious political subtext that you keep talking about. I am teaching world literature right now and I am talking about a particular Nigerian writer, and my students talk to me about African writers, and then the same students talk to me about—I see this actual phrase in their essays—the African government. It is one place over there, and if they can treat Native America as just this unitary thing that can be set apart like that, it brings real problems.

RC: Yet, as a teacher, I have taught Native American lit. courses—

Silko: Oh, I have, too; I teach them all the time.

RC: ————and I kind of feel that way, too, toward women's lit. classes—same thing. On the one hand you think, am I perpetuating this generalization by doing it? And yet if I don't do it, the material won't get taught.

Silko: Exactly; it is something that continues to cry out.

RC: I took an American lit. class at Texas A&M from Dr. Larry Oliver, and he does teach Faulkner and Hemingway, but he also teaches you and Louise Erdrich and Sandra Cisneros. . . .

Silko: That is how it is supposed to be. There should just be American literature. As much as I have against calendar time, maybe if you need to break it, break it in terms of time, even though that is skewed, because some people are really far ahead of their time. But if you have to make it manageable, maybe use some criterion like that. Maybe it should just be "World Literature." I always wanted to do a class where you could read *Things Fall Apart, The Ambassador* by Henry James—for me it is just literature.

RC: You mentioned Faulkner and reading *The Sound and the Fury.* Did he have a big impact on your development as a writer?

Silko: He did, because I could tell that he had come out of a storytelling [tradition]—*Absalom, Absalom*—I intuitively could tell. I knew that the South had this heavy storytelling tradition when I was just a high school kid without anybody telling me. I could intuit that through reading him—his connection with place and animals. I really responded very much to the Southern Fugitives. John Crowe Ransom, the Agrarian Movement—I responded to that. And of course I loved Flannery O'Connor. I always mourned that she could not live longer. So Faulkner was important, Steinbeck was important, Norman Mailer was important. Flannery O'Connor was a special love of mine. I love Virginia Woolf; I found her early on. She just blew my mind.

RC: You mentioned too that you liked Gertrude Stein the other night.

Silko: Ohhh. I love Gertrude Stein; she is the most neglected, misunderstood, defamed, attacked person, and she is so important to world writing, not just American writing. Maybe some day the philistines will see that and begin to recognize that. She is so brilliant. I love some of her stuff—*Black Sparrow*—some years ago I came across a whole cache of Gertrude Stein pieces that you hardly ever see. Something about the atomic bomb meditations. I love so many of her pieces. I stay away from universities so I will never have this chance, and I would also love to teach Shakespeare, but I would love to do a class where I could do Stein and Achebe, just all kinds of potpourri. I don't see why you couldn't, and if you need the historical cultural contexts, you just have the students read about a lot of different places just like you do for Shakespeare. You have to read the Trevelyan and those little dudes.

RC: I know you read mostly nonfiction; are there any contemporary novelists that you like to read?

Silko: I do mostly read nonfiction. Let's see; that is a tough one. Toni Morrison, of course, I read Toni; Ishmael Reed. . . . Surely, I'm forgetting people that I will feel bad for not mentioning. Oh, Terry McMillan— she was in Tucson for awhile and I read her; I liked her earlier novels. Oh. Maxine Hong Kingston—her manuscript burned up in the Oakland fire. I love her work, but you know, she lost work in progress, just like what happened to Ralph Ellison.

RC: You quoted Said earlier—do you read any other post-colonial theory or other kinds of social theorists?

Silko: You know, occasionally I read Said, and I do like to read Mahfouz. I try to get outside the United States, but not too much theory. I had fun for a while with Wittgenstein because someone told me that people couldn't read the *Tractatus,* that people had difficulty with it, and so I thought OK, here's a challenge. Then I discovered that if you read Wittgenstein like it's poetry, it really works. So my favorite book of Wittgenstein is his last book, which I think is called *The Theory of Color*, and it's sheer poetry. Then I've heard that philosophers say, that man is a poet. But the poetry—actually my friend Mei-Mei Berssenbrugge, Barbara Guest, some of the really way out, really tripping, far-out poets, are really difficult for a lot of people—I don't know how it works, but I get inspired from reading poetry or reading Wittgenstein in some weird way. I read particle physics like I read poetry, since I have no background in math or science. I just decided, just as I had to do with *Tractatus*, don't fret; you don't need to know in a kind of linear 1-2-3—things don't always have to add up immediately. Read and read and something will come through. So I do that with pieces on particle physics and stuff like that. An so that kind of stuff is exciting for me.

RC: What comes next?

Silko: When I finish a book, I don't know if I'll ever have another book to write again. I don't just start up a new project immediately. My publishers hate it. Each book is such a commitment of energy and time. Every novel costs a relationship. I can't just crank it out again.

So I'm waiting to see what will happen. Now I'm reading about dreams, books on communications with the dead from early 1900s. And I'm interested in the Anglo-European occult. So maybe something will come of all that.

Selected Bibliography

◆　◆　◆

Selected Primary Sources

Novels

Almanac of the Dead. New York: Simon & Schuster, 1991.
Ceremony. New York: Viking, 1977.
Gardens in the Dunes. New York: Simon & Schuster, 1999.

Other Book-Length Works

The Delicacy and Strength of Lace: Letters between Leslie Marmon Silko and James Wright. Ed. Anne Wright. St. Paul, MN: Graywolf Press, 1986.
Laguna Woman: Poems by Leslie Silko. Greenfield Center, NY: Greenfield Review Press, 1974.
Rain. [With Lee Marmon]. New York: Library Fellows of the Whitney Museum of American Art, 1996.
Sacred Water. Tucson: Flood Plain Press, 1993.
Storyteller. New York: Arcade, 1981.
Yellow Woman and a Beauty of the Spirit: Essays on Native American Life Today. New York: Simon & Schuster, 1996.

Interviews

Arnold, Ellen L., ed. *Conversations with Leslie Marmon Silko*. Jackson: University Press of Mississippi, 2000.

Cohen Robin. "Of Apricots, Orchids, and Wovoka: An Interview with Leslie Marmon Silko." *Southwestern American Literature* 24.2 (1999): 55–71.

Perry, Donna. "Leslie Marmon Silko." *Backtalk: Women Writers Speak Out*. New Brunswick, N.J.: Rutgers University Press, 1993. 313–40.

Selected Secondary Sources

Aithal, S. Krishnamoorthy. "American Ethnic Fiction in the Universal Human Context." *American Studies International* 21.5 (1983): 61–66.

Aldama, Arturo J. "Tayo's Journey Home: Crossblood Agency, Resistance, and Transformation in *Ceremony* by Leslie Marmon Silko." *Cross-Addressing: Resistance Literature and Cultural Borders*. Ed. John C. Hawley. Albany, NY: SUNY Press, 1996. 157–80.

Allen, Paula Gunn. "The Feminine Landscape of Leslie Marmon Silko's *Ceremony*." *Studies in American Indian Literature: Critical Essays and Course Designs*. New York: MLA, 1983. 127–33. Rpt. in *Critical Perspectives on Native American Fiction*. Ed. Richard F. Fleck. Washington, DC: Three Continents, 1993. 233–39.

———. "The Psychological Landscape of *Ceremony*." *American Indian Quarterly* 5.1 (1979): 7–12.

———. "Special Problems in Teaching Leslie Marmon Silko's *Ceremony*." *American Indian Quarterly* 14.4 (1990): 379–86.

Antell, Judith A. "Momaday, Welch, and Silko: Expressing the Feminine Principle through Male Alienation." *American Indian Quarterly* 12.3 (1988): 213–20.

Arnold, Ellen L. "An Ear for the Story, An Eye for the Pattern: Rereading *Ceremony*." *Modern Fiction Studies* 45.1 (1999): 69–92.

Beidler, Peter G. "Animals and Theme in *Ceremony*." *American Indian Quarterly* 5.1 (1979): 13–18.

Bell, Robert C. "Circular Design in *Ceremony*." *American Indian Quarterly* 5.1 (1979): 47–62.

Benediktsson, Thomas E. "The Reawakening of the Gods: Realism and the Supernatural in Silko and Hulme." *Critique* 33.2 (1992): 121–31.

Bennani, Benjamin, and Catherine Warner Bennani. "No Ceremony for Men in the Sun: Sexuality, Personhood, and Nationhood in Ghassan Kanafani's *Men in the Sun* and Leslie Marmon Silko's *Ceremony*." *Critical Perspectives on Native American Fiction*. Ed. Richard F. Fleck. Washington, DC: Three Continents, 1993. 246–55.

Berner, Robert L. "Trying to Be Round: Three American Indian Novels." *World Literature Today: A Literary Quarterly of the University of Oklahoma* 58.3 (1984): 341–44.

Bird, Gloria. "Towards a Decolonization of Mind and Text I: Leslie Marmon Silko's *Ceremony*." *Wicazo Sa Review* 9.2 (1993): 1–8.

Blaeser, Kimberly. "Pagans Rewriting the Bible: Heterodoxy and the Representation of Spirituality in Native American Literature." *Ariel* 25.1 (1994): 12–31.

Blair, Barbara. "Textual Expressions of the Search for Cultural Identity." *American Studies in Scandinavia* 27.1 (1995): 48–63.

Blair, Ruth. "Leslie Marmon Silko's *Ceremony* in the Context of a Course Entitled 'Language, Literature, and Environment'" *Isle* 3.2 (1996): 169–70.

Blumenthal, Susan. "Spotted Cattle and Deer: Spirit Guides and Symbols of Endurance and Healing in *Ceremony*." *American Indian Quarterly* 14.4 (1990): 367–77.

Brice, Jennifer. "Earth as Mother, Earth as Other in Novels by Silko and Hogan." *Critique* 39.2 (1998): 127–38.

Caton, Lou. "Western Eyes and Indian Visions." *North Dakota Quarterly* 65.2 (1998): 110–29.

Cederstrom, Lorelei. "Myth and Ceremony in Contemporary North American Native Fiction." *Canadian Journal of Native Studies* 2.2 (1982): 285–301.

Cohen, Robin. "Reintegration and Regeneration through Ritual in Silko's *Ceremony*." *Southwestern American Literature* 22.2 (1997): 49–62.

Coltelli, Laura. "Re-enacting Myths and Stories: Tradition and Renewal in *Ceremony*." *Native American Literatures: Forum* 1 (1989): 173–83.

Comer, Krista. "Sidestepping Environmental Justice: 'Natural' Landscapes and the Wilderness Plot." *Breaking Boundaries: New Perspectives on Women's Regional Writing.* Ed. Sherrie A. Inness and Diana Royer. Iowa City: University of Iowa Press, 1997. 216–36.

Copeland, Marion W. "*Black Elk Speaks* and Leslie Silko's *Ceremony*: Two Visions of Horses." *Critique* 24.3 (1983): 158–72.

Couser, G. Thomas. "Oppression and Repression: Personal and Collective Memory in Paule Marshall's *Praisesong for the Widow* and Leslie Marmon Silko's *Ceremony*." *Memory and Cultural Politics: New Approaches to American Ethnic Literatures.* Ed. Amritjit Singh, Joseph T. Skerrett, Jr., Robert E. Hogan. Boston: Northeastern University Press, 1996. 106–20.

Cousineau, Diane. "Leslie Silko's *Ceremony*: The Spiderweb as Text." *Revue Francaise d'Etudes Américaines* 15.43 (1990): 19–31.

Cummings, Kate. "Reclaiming the Mother(s) Tongue: *Beloved*, *Ceremony*, *Mothers and Shadows*." *College English* 52.5 (1990): 552–69.

Dasenbrock, Reed Way. "Forms of Biculturalism in Southwestern Literature: The Work of Rudolfo Anaya and Leslie Marmon Silko." *Genre* 21.3 (1988): 307–19.

Dollar, J. Gerard. "Reading the Land, Telling the Story: Desert Landscapes and Narrative Form in *Death Comes for the Archbishop* and *Ceremony*." *Approaches to Narrative Fiction*. Ed. Jon Buscall and Outi Pickering. Turku, Finland: University of Turku Press, 1999. 20–37.

Dunsmore, Roger. "No Boundaries, on Silko's *Ceremony*." *Earth's Mind: Essays in Native Literature*. Albuquerque: University of New Mexico Press, 1997. 15–32.

Erben, David. "The Sacred Ghost: The Role of the Elder(ly) in Native American Literature." *Aging and Identity*. Ed. Saramunson Deats and Tallent Lagretta Lenker. Westport, CT: Praeger, 1999. 129–38.

Evasdaughter, Elizabeth N. "Leslie Marmon Silko's *Ceremony*: Healing Ethnic Hatred by Mixed Breed Laughter." *MELUS* 15.1 (1988): 83–95.

Farrer, Claire R. "Reprise of Swan's Song and Farrer's Chorus." *American Indian Quarterly* 14.2 (1990): 167–71.

———. "The Sun's in Its Heaven, All's *Not* Right with the World: Rejoinder to Swan." *American Indian Quarterly* 14.2 (1990): 155–59.

Flores, Toni. "Claiming and Making: Ethnicity, Gender, and the Common Sense in Leslie Marmon Silko's *Ceremony* and Zora Neale Hurston's *Their Eyes Were Watching God*." *Frontiers* 10.3 (1989): 52–58.

Franks, Bruce. "Consciousness of Landscape in Leslie Marmon Silko's *Ceremony*." *The Image of Nature in Literature, the Media and Society*. Ed. Will Wright and Steven Kaplan. Pueblo: University of Southern Colorado Press, 1993. 337–45.

Freese, Peter. "Marmon Silko's *Ceremony*: Universality versus Ethnocentrism." *Amerikastudien/American Studies* 37.4 (1992): 613–45.

Garcia, Reyes. "Senses of Place in *Ceremony*." *MELUS* 10.4 (1983): 37–48.

Getz, John. "Healing the Soldier in White: *Ceremony* as War Novel." *War, Literature, & the Arts*. 9.1 (1997): 123–40.

Gilderhaus, Nancy. "The Art of Storytelling in Leslie Silko's *Ceremony*." *English Journal* 83.2 (1994): 70–72.

Gross, Konrad. "Survival or Orality in a Literate Culture: Leslie Silko's Novel *Ceremony*." *Modes of Narrative: Approaches to American, Canadian, and British Fiction*. Ed. Reingard M. Nischik and Barbara Korte. Würzburg: Königshausen and Neumann, 1990. 88–99.

Hailey, David E., Jr. "The Visual Elegance of Ts'its'tsi'nako and the Other Invisible Characters in *Ceremony*." *Wicazo Sa Review* 6.2 (1990): 1–6.

Harvey, Valerie. "Navajo Sandpainting in *Ceremony*." *Critical Perspectives on Native American Fiction*. Ed. Richard F. Fleck. Washington, DC: Three Continents, 1993. 256–59.

Herzog, Kristin. "Thinking Woman and Feeling Man: Gender in Silko's *Ceremony*." *MELUS* 12.1 (1985): 25–36.

Hiatt, Shannon T. "The Oral Tradition as a Nativization Technique in Three Novels." *Journal of Indian Writing in English* 14.1 (1986): 10–21.

Hobbs, Michael. "Living In-Between: Tayo as Radical Reader in Leslie Marmon Silko's *Ceremony*." *Western American Literature* 28.4 (1994): 301–12.

Hochbruck, Wolfgang. "'I Have Spoken': Fictional 'Orality' in Indigenous Fiction." *College Literature* 23.2 (1996): 132–42.

Hoilman, Dennis. "'A World Made of Stories': An Interpretation of Leslie Silko's *Ceremony*." *South Dakota Review* 17.4 (1979): 54–66.

Hokanson, Robert O'Brien. "Crossing Cultural Boundaries with Leslie Marmon Silko's *Ceremony*." *Rethinking American Literature*. Ed. Lil Brannon and Brenda M. Greene. Urbana, IL: National Council of Teachers of English, 1997. 115–27.

Hunt, Daniel P. "Women Writing Men: Leslie Marmon Silko's *Ceremony* and Isabel Allende's *El Plan Infinito*." *Selecta: Journal of the Pacific Northwest Council on Foreign Languages*. 14 (1993): 16–19.

Jahner, Elaine. "An Act of Attention: Event Structure in *Ceremony*." *American Indian Quarterly* 5.1 (1979): 37–46.

———. "Leslie Marmon Silko." *Dictionary of Native American Literature*. Ed. Andrew Wiget. New York and London: Garland, 1994. 499–511.

Jaskoski, Helen, and G. Lynn Nelson. "Thinking Woman's Children and the Bomb." *Explorations in Ethnic Studies* 13.2 (1990): 1–24.

Kang, Ja Mo. "A Postcolonialist Reading of Leslie Marmon Silko's *Ceremony*." *The Journal of English Language & Literature* 43.3 (1997): 609–27.

Keyes, Claire. "Tradition and Narrative Form in Leslie Marmon Silko's *Ceremony*." *Journal of Literary Studies/Tydskrif vir Literaturwetenskap* 15.1–2 (1999): 119–31.

Larson, Charles R. "Survivors of the Relocation." *American Indian Fiction*. Albuquerque: University of New Mexico Press, 1978. 133–64.

Larson, Sidner. "Pragmatism and American Indian Thought." *Studies in American Indian Literatures* 9.2 (1997): 1–10.

Lincoln, Kenneth. "Grandmother Storyteller: Leslie Silko." *Native American Renaissance*. Berkeley: University of California Press, 1983. 222–50.

Lynch, Tom. "What Josiah Said: Uncle Josiah's Role in *Ceremony*." *North Dakota Quarterly* 63.2 (1996): 138–52.

Mahala, Daniel, and Jody Swilky. "Constructing the Multicultural Subject: Colonization, Persuasion, and Difference in the Classroom." *Pre-Text* 15.3–4 (1994): 182–216.

Manley, Kathleen. "Decreasing the Distance: Contemporary Native American Texts, Hypertext, and the Concept of Audience." *Southern Folklore* 51.2 (1994): 121–35.

———. "Leslie Marmon Silko's Use of Color in *Ceremony*." *Southern Folklore* 46.2 (1989): 133–46.

Meese, Elizabeth A. "Crossing Cultures: Narratives of Exclusion and Leslie Silko's *Ceremony.*" *(Ex)tensions: Re-Figuring Feminist Criticism.* Urbana: University of Illinois Press, 1990, 29–49.

Mitchell, Carol. "*Ceremony* as Ritual." *American Indian Quarterly* 5.1 (1979): 27–35.

Moore, David L. "Myth, History, and Identity in Silko and Young Bear: Post-Colonial Praxis." *New Voices in Native American Literary Criticism.* Ed. Arnold Krupat. Washington, DC: Smithsonian Institution Press, 1995. 370–93.

Nelson, Robert M. "The Function of the Landscape of *Ceremony.*" *Place and Vision: The Function of Landscape in Native American Fiction.* American Indian Studies 1. New York: Peter Lang, 1993. 11–39.

——. "The Kaupata Motif in Silko's *Ceremony*: A Study of Literary Homology." *Studies in American Indian Literatures* 11.3 (1999): 2–21.

——. "Place and Vision: The Function of Landscape in *Ceremony.*" *Journal of the Southwest* 30.3 (1988): 281–316.

Norden, Christopher. "Ecological Restoration as Post-Colonial Ritual of Community in Three Native American Novels." *Studies in American Indian Literatures* 6.4 (1994): 94–106.

Oandasan, William. "A Familiar Love Component of Love in *Ceremony.*" *Critical Perspectives on Native American Fiction.* Ed. Richard F. Fleck. Washington, DC: Three Continents, 1993. 240–45.

Orr, Lisa. "Theorizing the Earth: Feminist Approaches to Nature and Leslie Marmon Silko's *Ceremony.*" *American Indian Culture and Research Journal* 18.2 (1994): 145–57.

Owens, Louis. "'The Very Essence of Our Lives': Leslie Silko's Webs of Identity." *Other Destinies: Understanding the American Indian Novel.* Norman: University of Oklahoma Press, 1992. 167–91.

Pace, Stephanie. "Lungfish, or Acts of Survival in Contemporary Female Writing [in Tillie Olsen's 'I Stand Here Ironing,' Gloria Naylor's *Women of Brewster Place*, Leslie Marmon Silko's *Ceremony*, and Louise Erdrich's *Love Medicine*]." *Frontiers* 10.1 (1988): 29–33.

Parker, Michael. "Searching for the Center: Tayo's Quest in Leslie Silko's *Ceremony.*" *Mount Olive Review* 7 (1993–94): 23–29.

Pasquaretta, Paul. "Sacred Chance: Gambling and the Contemporary Native American Indian Novel." *MELUS* 21.2 (1996): 21–33.

Peacock, John. "Un-Writing Empire by Writing Oral Tradition: Leslie Marmon Silko." *Un-Writing Empire.* Ed. Theo D'haen. Amsterdam: Rodopi, 1998. 295–308.

Pérez Castillo, Susan. "The Construction of Gender and Ethnicity in the Texts of Leslie Silko and Louise Erdrich." *Yearbook of English Studies* 24 (1994): 228–36.

————. "A Map for Survival: The Community of Laguna Pueblo in Leslie Marmon Silko's *Ceremony*." *Chiba Review* 12 (1990): 41–51.

Piper, Karen. "Police Zones: Territory and Identity in Leslie Marmon Silko's *Ceremony*." *American Indian Quarterly* 21.3 (1997): 483–97.

Purdy, John. "The Transformation: Tayo's Genealogy in *Ceremony*." *Studies in American Indian Literatures* 10.3 (1986): 121–33.

Rabinowitz, Paula. "Naming, Magic, and Documentary: The Subversion of the Narrative in *Song of Solomon, Ceremony,* and *China Men*." *Feminist Re-Visions: What Has Been and Might Be*. Ed. Vivian Patraka and Louise A. Tilly. Ann Arbor: University of Michigan Press, 1983. 26–42.

Rainwater, Catherine. *Dreams of Fiery Stars: The Transformations of Native American Fiction*. Philadelphia: University of Pennsylvania Press, 1999.

————. "The Semiotics of Dwelling in Leslie Marmon Silko's *Ceremony*." *American Journal of Semiotics* 9.2–3 (1992): 219–40.

Rand, Naomi. "Surviving What Haunts You: The Art of Invisibility in *Ceremony, The Ghost Writer,* and *Beloved*." *MELUS* 20.3 (1995): 21–32.

Riley, Patricia. "The Mixed Blood Writer as Interpreter and Mythmaker." *Understanding Others: Cultural and Cross-Cultural Studies and the Teaching of Literature*. Ed. Joseph Trimmer and Tilly Warnock. Urbana, IL: National Council of Teachers of English, 1992. 230–42.

Roberts, Jill. "Between Two 'Darknesses': The Adoptive Condition in *Ceremony* and *Jasmine*." *Modern Language Studies* 25.3 (1995): 77–97.

Roemer, Kenneth M. "Silko's Arroyos as Mainstream: Processes and Implications of Canonical Identity." *Modern Fiction Studies* 45.1 (1999): 10–37.

Ronnow, Gretchen. "Tayo, Death, and Desire: A Lacanian Reading of *Ceremony*." *Narrative Chance: Postmodern Discourse on Native American Indian Literatures*. Ed. Gerald Vizenor. Albuquerque: University of New Mexico Press, 1989. 69–90.

Rubenstein, Roberta. "Boundaries of the Cosmos: Leslie Silko." *Boundaries of the Self*. Urbana: University of Illinois Press, 1987. 190–208.

Ruppert, James. "Dialogism and Mediation in Leslie Marmon Silko's *Ceremony*." *Explicator* 51.2 (1993): 219–34.

————. "No Boundaries, Only Transitions: *Ceremony*." *Mediation in Contemporary Native American Fiction*. Norman: University of Oklahoma Press, 1995. 74–91.

————. "The Reader's Lessons in *Ceremony*." *Arizona Quarterly* 44.1 (1988): 78–85.

St. Andrews, B.A. "Healing the Witchery: Medicine in Silko's *Ceremony*." *Arizona Quarterly* 44.1 (1988): 86–94.

Salyer, Gregory. *Leslie Marmon Silko*. New York: Twayne, 1997.

————. "Myth, Magic and Dread: Reading Culture Religiously." *Literature and Theology* 9.3 (1995): 261–77.

Samantaray, Rabi Narayana. "The American Mosaic: A Study through Bernard Malamud's *The Tenants* and Leslie Marmon Silko's *Ceremony*." *Indian Journal of American Studies* 24.2 (1994): 80–82.

Sanders, Scott P. "Southwestern Gothic." *Weber Studies* 4.2 (1987): 36–53.

Sands, Kathleen Mullen. "Preface: A Symposium Issue." *American Indian Quarterly* 5.1 (1979): 1–5.

Sands, Kathleen M., and A. LaVonne Ruoff, eds. "A Discussion of *Ceremony*." *American Indian Quarterly* 5.1 (1979): 63–70.

Scarberry, Susan J. "Memory as Medicine: The Power of Recollection in *Ceremony*." *American Indian Quarterly* 5.1 (1979): 19–26.

Schein, Marie. "Identity in Leslie Marmon Silko's *Ceremony* and N. Scott Momaday's *Ancient Child*." *Southwestern American Literature* 18.2 (1993): 228–36.

Schweninger, Lee. "A Skin of Lakeweed: An Ecofeminist Approach to Erdrich and Silko." *Multicultural Literatures through Feminist/Poststructuralist Lenses*. Ed. Barbara Frey Waxman. Knoxville: University of Tennessee Press, 1993. 37–56.

———. "Writing Nature: Silko and Native Americans as Nature Writers." *MELUS* 18.2 (1993): 47–60.

Sequoya-Magdaleno, Jana. "Telling the Difference: Representations of Identity in the Discourse of Indianness." *The Ethnic Canon: Histories, Institutions, and Interventions*. Ed. David Palumbo-Liu. Minneapolis: University of Minnesota Press, 1995. 88–116.

Seyersted, Per. *Leslie Marmon Silko*. Western Writers Series 45. Boise, ID: Boise State University Press, 1980.

Shaddock, Jennifer. "Mixed-Blood Women: The Dynamic of Women's Relations in the Novels of Louise Erdrich and Leslie Silko." *Feminist Nightmares: Women at Odds: Feminism and the Problem of Sisterhood*. Ed. Susan Ostrov-Weisser and Jennifer Fleischner. New York: New York University Press, 1994. 106–21.

Sheldon, Mary F. "Reaching for a Universal Audience: The Artistry of Leslie Marmon Silko and James Welch." *Entering the 90s: The North American Experience: Proceedings from the Native American Studies Conference at Lake Superior State University, October 27–28, 1989*. Ed. Thomas E. Schirer. Saulte Ste. Marie, MI: Lake Superior University Press, 1991. 114–24.

Siebert, Gayle Ruth. "Frontiering Tayo's Interior Landscapes: A Vizenorian Exploration of the Fragmented Self." *The Image of the Frontier in Literature, the Media and Society*. Ed. Will Wright and Steven Kaplan. Pueblo: University of Southern Colorado Press, 1997. 198–204.

Slowik, Mary. "Henry James, Meet Spider Woman: A Study of Narrative Form in Leslie Silko's *Ceremony*." *North Dakota Quarterly* 57.2 (1989): 104–20.

Smith, Patricia Clark, with Paula Gunn Allen. "Earthy Relations, Carnal Knowledge: Southwestern American Indian Women Writers and Landscape." *The*

Desert Is No Lady: Southwestern Landscapes in Women's Writing and Art. Ed. Vera Norwood and Janice Monk. New Haven: Yale University Press, 1987. 174–96. Rpt. in *"Yellow Woman"/Leslie Marmon Silko*. Ed. Melody Graulich. New Brunswick, NJ: Rutgers University Press, 1993. 115–50.

Stein, Rachel. "Contested Ground: Nature, Narrative, and Native American Identity in Leslie Marmon Silko's *Ceremony* and *Almanac of the Dead*." *Shifting the Ground: American Women Writers' Revisions of Nature, Gender, and Race*. Charlottesville: University Press of Virginia, 1997. 114–44.

Stonestreet, Linda. "Tayo's Ceremonial Quest." *The Bulletin of the West Virginia Association of College English Teachers* 16 (1994): 26-31.

Swan, Edith. "Answer to Farrer: All Is Right with the World as Laguna Notions Speak for Themselves." *American Indian Quarterly* 14.2 (1990): 161–66.

———. "Feminine Perspectives at Laguna Pueblo: Silko's *Ceremony*." *Tulsa Studies in Women's Literature* 11.2 (1992): 309–27.

———. "Healing via the Sunwise Cycle in Silko's *Ceremony*." *American Indian Quarterly* 12.4 (1988): 313–28.

———. "Laguna Prototypes of Manhood in *Ceremony*." *MELUS* 17.1 (1991–92): 39–61.

———. "Laguna Symbolic Geography and Silko's *Ceremony*." *American Indian Quarterly* 12.3 (1988): 229–49.

Taylor, Paul Beekman. "Repetition as Cure in Native American Story: Silko's *Ceremony* and Momaday's *Ancient Child*." *Repetition*. Ed. Andreas Fischer. Tubingen: Narr, 1994. 221–42.

Todd, Jude. "Knotted Bellies and Fragile Webs: Untangling and Re-spinning in Tayo's Healing Journey." *American Indian Quarterly* 19 (1995): 155–70.

Truesdale, C. W. "Tradition and *Ceremony*: Leslie Marmon Silko as an American Novelist." *North Dakota Quarterly* 59.4 (1991): 200–28.

Turner, Frederick. "Voice Out of the Land: Leslie Marmon Silko's *Ceremony*." *Spirit of Place: The Making of an American Literary Landscape*. San Francisco: Sierra Club Books, 1989. 323–60.

TuSmith, Bonnie. "Storytelling as Communal Survival: Leslie Marmon Silko's *Ceremony*." *All My Relatives: Community in Contemporary Ethnic American Literatures*. Ann Arbor: University of Michigan Press, 1993. 119–29.

Van Dyke, Annette. "Curing Ceremonies: The Novels of Leslie Marmon Silko and Paula Gunn Allen." *The Search for a Woman-Centered Spirituality*. New York: New York University Press, 1992.12–40.

Velie, Alan R. "Leslie Silko's *Ceremony*: A Laguna Grail Story." *Four American Indian Literary Masters: N. Scott Momaday, James Welch, Leslie Marmon Silko, and Gerald Vizenor*. Norman: University of Oklahoma Press, 1982. 104–21.

Von Rosk, Nancy. "Returning and Remembering: The Recovery of the

Maternal in Leslie Silko's *Ceremony*." *Southwestern American Literature* 22.2 (1997): 33–48.

Wald, Allen. "The Culture of 'Internal Colonialism': A Marxist Perspective." *MELUS* 8.3 (1981): 18–27.

Wallace, Karen L. "Liminality and Myth in Native American Fiction: *Ceremony* and *The Ancient Child*." *American Indian Culture and Research Journal* 20.4 (1996): 91–119.

Warner, Nicholas O. "Images of Drinking in 'Woman Singing,' *Ceremony*, and *House Made of Dawn*." *MELUS* 11.4 (1984): 15–30.

Wilson, Norma C. "From Alienation to Reciprocity. (Leslie Marmon Silko)." *Teaching American Ethnic Literatures: Nineteen Essays*. Ed. John R. Maitino and David R. Peck. Albuquerque: University of New Mexico Press, 1996. 69–82.

———. "Outlook for Survival." *Denver Quarterly* 14.4 (1980): 22–30.

Winsbro, Bonnie. "Calling Tayo Back, Unravelling Coyote's Skin: Individuation in Leslie Marmon Silko's *Ceremony*." *Supernatural Forces: Belief, Difference, and Power in Contemporary Works by Ethnic Women*. Amherst: University of Massachusetts Press, 1993. 82–108.

Zamir, Shamoon. "Literature in a 'National Sacrifice Area'." *New Voices in Native American Literary Criticism*. Ed. Arnold Krupat. Washington, DC: Smithsonian Institution Press, 1993. 396–415.